THE A~~LEXAND~~

General Editor
R.B. Kennedy

Edited by S.M. Farrow ad R.B. Kennedy

HENRY V

William Shakcspcarc

COLLINS
CLASSICS

Harper Press
An imprint of HarperCollins*Publishers*
77–85 Fulham Palace Road
Hammersmith
London W6 8JB

This Harper Press paperback edition published 2011

A catalogue record for this book is available from the British Library

ISBN-13: 978-0-00-790232-3

Printed and bound in Great Britain by Clays Ltd, St Ives plc

MIX
Paper from
responsible sources
FSC™ C007454

FSC™ is a non-profit international organisation established to promote
the responsible management of the world's forests. Products carrying the
FSC label are independently certified to assure consumers that they come
from forests that are managed to meet the social, economic and
ecological needs of present and future generations,
and other controlled sources.

Find out more about HarperCollins and the environment at
www.harpercollins.co.uk/green

Life & Times section © Gerard Cheshire
Introduction by Donald MacKenzie
Shakespeare: Words and Phrases adapted from
Collins English Dictionary
Typesetting in Kalix by Palimpsest Book Production Limited,
Falkirk, Stirlingshire

10 9 8 7 6 5 4 3 2 1

Prefatory Note

This Shakespeare play uses the full Alexander text. By keeping in mind the fact that the language has changed considerably in four hundred years, as have customs, jokes, and stage conventions, the editors have aimed at helping the modern reader – whether English is their mother tongue or not – to grasp the full significance of the play. The Notes, intended primarily for examination candidates, are presented in a simple, direct style. The needs of those unfamiliar with British culture have been specially considered.

Since quiet study of the printed word is unlikely to bring fully to life plays that were written directly for the public theatre, attention has been drawn to dramatic effects which are important in performance. The editors see Shakespeare's plays as living works of art which can be enjoyed today on stage, film and television in many parts of the world.

CONTENTS

The Theatre in Shakespeare's Day vii

Shakespeare: A Timeline xiii

Life & Times xvii

Money in Shakespeare's Day xx

Introduction 1

List of Characters 5

Text 8

Summing Up 255

Theme Index 267

Further Reading 269

Shakespeare: Words and Phrases 271

An Elizabethan playhouse. Note the apron stage protruding into the auditorium, the space below it, the inner room at the rear of the stage, the gallery above the inner stage, the canopy over the main stage, and the absence of a roof over the audience. ~

The Theatre in Shakespeare's Day

On the face of it, the conditions in the Elizabethan theatre were not such as to encourage great writers. The public playhouse itself was not very different from an ordinary inn-yard; it was open to the weather; among the spectators were often louts, pickpockets and prostitutes; some of the actors played up to the rowdy elements in the audience by inserting their own jokes into the authors' lines, while others spoke their words loudly but unfeelingly; the presentation was often rough and noisy, with fireworks to represent storms and battles, and a table and a few chairs to represent a tavern; there were no actresses, so boys took the parts of women, even such subtle and mature ones as Cleopatra and Lady Macbeth; there was rarely any scenery at all in the modern sense. In fact, a quick inspection of the English theatre in the reign of Elizabeth I by a time-traveller from the twentieth century might well produce only one positive reaction: the costumes were often elaborate and beautiful.

Shakespeare himself makes frequent comments in his plays about the limitations of the playhouse and the actors of his time, often apologizing for them. At the beginning of *Henry V* the Prologue refers to the stage as 'this unworthy scaffold' and to the theatre building (the Globe, probably) as 'this wooden O', and emphasizes the urgent need for imagination in making up for all the deficiencies of presentation. In introducing Act IV the Chorus goes so far as to say:

> . . . we shall much disgrace
> With four or five most vile and ragged foils,
> Right ill-dispos'd in brawl ridiculous,
> The name of Agincourt, (lines 49–52)

In *A Midsummer Night's Dream* (Act V, Scene i) he seems to dismiss actors with the words:

The best in this kind are but shadows.

Yet Elizabeth's theatre, with all its faults, stimulated dramatists to a variety of achievement that has never been equalled and, in Shakespeare, produced one of the greatest writers in history. In spite of all his grumbles he seems to have been fascinated by the challenge that it presented him with. It is necessary to re-examine his theatre carefully in order to understand how he was able to achieve so much with the materials he chose to use. What sort of place was the Elizabethan playhouse in reality? What sort of people were these criticized actors? And what sort of audiences gave them their living?

The Development of the Theatre up to Shakespeare's Time

For centuries in England noblemen had employed groups of skilled people to entertain them when required. Under Tudor rule, as England became more secure and united, actors such as these were given more freedom, and they often performed in public, while still acknowledging their 'overlords' (in the 1570s, for example, when Shakespeare was still a schoolboy at Stratford, one famous company was called 'Lord Leicester's Men'). London was rapidly becoming larger and more important in the second half of the sixteenth century, and many of the companies of actors took the opportunities offered to establish themselves at inns on the main roads leading to the City (for example, the Boar's Head in Whitechapel and the Tabard in South-wark) or in the City itself. These groups of actors would come to an agreement with the inn-keeper which would give them the use of the yard for their performances after people had eaten and drunk well in the middle of the day. Before long, some inns were taken over completely by companies of players and thus became the first public theatres. In 1574 the officials of the City of London issued an order which shows clearly that these theatres were both popular and also offensive to some respectable people, because the order complains about 'the inordinate haunting of great multitudes of people, specially youth, to plays interludes and shows; namely occasion of frays and quarrels, evil practices of incontinency in great inns . . .' There is evidence that, on public holidays, the theatres on the banks of the Thames were crowded with noisy apprentices and tradesmen, but it would be wrong to think that audiences were always undiscriminating and loudmouthed. In spite of the disapproval of Puritans and the more staid members of society, by the 1590s, when Shakespeare's plays were beginning to be performed, audiences consisted of a good cross-section of English society, nobility as well as workers, intellectuals as well as simple people out for a laugh; also (and in this respect English theatres were unique in Europe), it was quite normal for respectable women to attend plays. So Shakespeare had to write plays which would appeal to people of widely different kinds. He had to provide 'something for everyone' but at the same time to take care to unify the material so that it would not seem to fall into separate pieces as they watched it. A speech like that of the drunken porter in *Macbeth* could provide the 'groundlings' with a belly-laugh, but also held a deeper significance for those who could appreciate it. The audience he wrote for was one of a number of apparent drawbacks which Shakespeare was able to turn to his and our advantage.

Shakespeare's Actors

Nor were all the actors of the time mere 'rogues, vagabonds and sturdy beggars' as some were described in a Statute of 1572. It is true that many of them had a hard life and earned very little money, but leading actors could become partners in the ownership of the theatres in which they acted: Shakespeare was a shareholder in the Globe and the Blackfriars theatres when he was an actor as well as a playwright. In any case, the attacks made on Elizabethan actors were usually directed at their morals and not at their acting ability; it is clear that many of them must have been good at their trade if they were able to interpret complex works like the great tragedies in such a way as to attract enthusiastic audiences. Undoubtedly some of the boys took the women's parts with skill and confidence, since a man called Coryate, visiting Venice in 1611, expressed surprise that women could act as well as they: 'I saw women act, a thing that I never saw before . . . and they performed it with as good a grace, action, gesture . . . as ever I saw any masculine actor.' The quality of most of the actors who first presented Shakespeare's plays is probably accurately summed up by Fynes Moryson, who wrote, '. . . as there be, in my opinion, more plays in London than in all the parts of the world I have seen, so do these players or comedians excel all other in the world.'

The Structure of the Public Theatre

Although the 'purpose-built' theatres were based on the inn-yards which had been used for play-acting, most of them were circular. The walls contained galleries on three storeys from which the wealthier patrons watched, they must have been something like the 'boxes' in a modern theatre, except that they held much larger numbers – as many as 1500. The 'groundlings' stood on the floor of the building, facing a raised stage which projected from the 'stage-wall', the main features of which were:

1 a small room opening on to the back of the main stage and on the same level as it (rear stage),
2 a gallery above this inner stage (upper stage),
3 canopy projecting from above the gallery over the main stage, to protect the actors from the weather (the 700 or 800 members of the audience who occupied the yard, or 'pit' as we call it today, had the sky above them).

In addition to these features there were dressing-rooms behind the stage and a space underneath it from which entrances could be made through trap-doors. All the acting areas – main stage, rear stage, upper stage and under stage – could be entered by actors directly from their dressing rooms, and all of them were used in productions of Shakespeare's plays. For example, the inner stage, an almost cavelike structure, would have been where Ferdinand and Miranda are 'discovered' playing chess in the last act of *The Tempest*, while the upper stage was certainly the balcony from which Romeo climbs down in Act III of *Romeo and Juliet*.

It can be seen that such a building, simple but adaptable, was not really unsuited to the presentation of plays like Shakespeare's. On the contrary, its simplicity guaranteed the minimum of distraction, while its shape and construction must have produced a sense of involvement on the part of the audience that modern producers would envy.

Other Resources of the Elizabethan Theatre

Although there were few attempts at scenery in the public theatre (painted backcloths were occasionally used in court performances), Shakespeare and his fellow playwrights were able to make use of a fair variety of 'properties', lists of such articles have survived: they include beds, tables, thrones, and also trees, walls, a gallows, a Trojan horse and a 'Mouth of Hell'; in a list of properties belonging to the manager, Philip Henslowe, the curious item 'two mossy banks' appears. Possibly one of them was used for the

> bank whereon the wild thyme blows,
> Where oxlips and the nodding violet grows

in *A Midsummer Night's Dream* (Act II, Scene i). Once again, imagination must have been required of the audience.

Costumes were the one aspect of stage production in which

trouble and expense were hardly ever spared to obtain a magnificent effect. Only occasionally did they attempt any historical accuracy (almost all Elizabethan productions were what we should call 'modern-dress' ones), but they were appropriate to the characters who wore them: kings were seen to be kings and beggars were similarly unmistakable. It is an odd fact that there was usually no attempt at illusion in the costuming: if a costume looked fine and rich it probably was. Indeed, some of the costumes were almost unbelievably expensive. Henslowe lent his company £19 to buy a cloak, and the Alleyn brothers, well-known actors, gave £20 for a 'black velvet cloak, with sleeves embroidered all with silver and gold, lined with black satin striped with gold'.

With the one exception of the costumes, the 'machinery' of the playhouse was economical and uncomplicated rather than crude and rough, as we can see from this second and more leisurely look at it. This meant that playwrights were stimulated to produce the imaginative effects that they wanted from the language that they used. In the case of a really great writer like Shakespeare, when he had learned his trade in the theatre as an actor, it seems that he received quite enough assistance of a mechanical and structural kind without having irksome restrictions and conventions imposed on him; it is interesting to try to guess what he would have done with the highly complex apparatus of a modern television studio. We can see when we look back to his time that he used his instrument, the Elizabethan theatre, to the full, but placed his ultimate reliance on the communication between his imagination and that of his audience through the medium of words. It is, above all, his rich and wonderful use of language that must have made play-going at that time a memorable experience for people of widely different kinds. Fortunately, the deep satisfaction of appreciating and enjoying Shakespeare's work can be ours also, if we are willing to overcome the language difficulty produced by the passing of time.

Shakespeare: A Timeline

Very little indeed is known about Shakespeare's private life; the facts included here are almost the only indisputable ones. The dates of Shakespeare's plays are those on which they were first produced.

1558   Queen Elizabeth crowned.

1561   Francis Bacon born.

1564   Christopher Marlowe born.   William Shakespeare born, April 23rd, baptized April 26th.

1566   Shakespeare's brother, Gilbert, born.

1567   Mary, Queen of Scots, deposed.
       James VI (later James I of England) crowned King of Scotland.

1572   Ben Jonson born.
       Lord Leicester's Company (of players) licensed; later called Lord Strange's, then the Lord Chamberlain's and finally (under James) the King's Men.

1573   John Donne born.

1574   The Common Council of London directs that all plays and playhouses in London must be licensed.

1576   James Burbage builds the first public playhouse, The Theatre, at Shoreditch, outside the walls of the City.

1577   Francis Drake begins his voyage round the world (completed 1580).
       Holinshed's Chronicles of England, Scotland and Ireland published (which

Shakespeare later used extensively).

1582		Shakespeare married to Anne Hathaway.
1583	The Queen's Company founded by royal warrant.	Shakespeare's daughter, Susanna, born.
1585		Shakespeare's twins, Hamnet and Judith, born.
1586	Sir Philip Sidney, the Elizabethan ideal 'Christian knight', poet, patron, soldier, killed at Zutphen in the Low Countries.	
1587	Mary, Queen of Scots, beheaded. Marlowe's *Tamburlaine (Part I)* first staged.	
1588	Defeat of the Spanish Armada. Marlowe's *Tamburlaine (Part II)* first staged.	
1589	Marlowe's *Jew of Malta* and Kyd's *Spanish Tragedy* (a 'revenge tragedy' and one of the most popular plays of Elizabethan times).	
1590	Spenser's *Faerie Queene* (Books I–III) published.	
1592	Marlowe's *Doctor Faustus* and *Edward II* first staged. Witchcraft trials in Scotland. Robert Greene, a rival playwright, refers to Shakespeare as 'an upstart crow' and 'the only Shake-scene in a country'.	*Titus Andronicus* *Henry VI, Parts I, II and III* *Richard III*
1593	London theatres closed by the plague. Christopher Marlowe killed in a Deptford tavern.	*Two Gentlemen of Verona* *Comedy of Errors* *The Taming of the Shrew* *Love's Labour's Lost*
1594	Shakespeare's company becomes The Lord Chamberlain's Men.	*Romeo and Juliet*

1595	Raleigh's first expedition to Guiana. Last expedition of Drake and Hawkins (both died).	*Richard II* *A Midsummer Night's Dream*
1596	Spenser's *Faerie Queene* (Books IV–VI) published. James Burbage buys rooms at Blackfriars and begins to convert them into a theatre.	*King John* *The Merchant of Venice* Shakespeare's son Hamnet dies. Shakespeare's father is granted a coat of arms.
1597	James Burbage dies, his son Richard, a famous actor, turns the Blackfriars Theatre into a private playhouse.	*Henry IV (Part I)* Shakespeare buys and redecorates New Place at Stratford.
1598	Death of Philip II of Spain	*Henry IV (Part II)* *Much Ado About Nothing*
1599	Death of Edmund Spenser. The Globe Theatre completed at Bankside by Richard and Cuthbert Burbage.	*Henry V* *Julius Caesar* *As You Like It*
1600	Fortune Theatre built at Cripplegate. East India Company founded for the extension of English trade and influence in the East. The Children of the Chapel begin to use the hall at Blackfriars.	*Merry Wives of Windsor* *Troilus and Cressida*
1601		*Hamlet*
1602	Sir Thomas Bodley's library opened at Oxford.	*Twelfth Night*
1603	Death of Queen Elizabeth. James I comes to the throne. Shakespeare's company becomes The King's Men. Raleigh tried, condemned and sent to the Tower	
1604	Treaty of peace with Spain	*Measure for Measure* *Othello* *All's Well that Ends Well*
1605	The Gunpowder Plot: an attempt by a group of Catholics to blow up the Houses of Parliament.	

1606	Guy Fawkes and other plotters executed.	*Macbeth* *King Lear*
1607	Virginia, in America, colonized. A great frost in England.	*Antony and Cleopatra* *Timon of Athens* *Coriolanus* Shakespeare's daughter, Susanna, married to Dr. John Hall.
1608	The company of the Children of the Chapel Royal (who had performed at Blackfriars for ten years) is disbanded. John Milton born. Notorious pirates executed in London.	Richard Burbage leases the Blackfriars Theatre to six of his fellow actors, including Shakespeare. *Pericles, Prince of Tyre*
1609		Shakespeare's Sonnets published.
1610	A great drought in England	*Cymbeline*
1611	Chapman completes his great translation of the *Iliad*, the story of Troy. Authorized Version of the Bible published.	*A Winter's Tale* *The Tempest*
1612	Webster's *The White Devil* first staged.	Shakespeare's brother, Gilbert, dies.
1613	Globe theatre burnt down during a performance of *Henry VIII* (the firing of small cannon set fire to the thatched roof). Webster's *Duchess of Malfi* first staged.	*Henry VIII* *Two Noble Kinsmen* Shakespeare buys a house at Blackfriars.
1614	Globe Theatre rebuilt in 'far finer manner than before'.	
1616	Ben Jonson publishes his plays in one volume. Raleigh released from the Tower in order to prepare an expedition to the gold mines of Guiana.	Shakespeare's daughter, Judith, marries Thomas Quiney. Death of Shakespeare on his birthday, April 23rd.
1618	Raleigh returns to England and is executed on the charge for which he was imprisoned in 1603.	
1623	Publication of the Folio edition of Shakespeare's plays	Death of Anne Shakespeare (née Hathaway).

Life & Times

William Shakespeare the Playwright

There exists a curious paradox when it comes to the life of William Shakespeare. He easily has more words written about him than any other famous English writer, yet we know the least about him. This inevitably means that most of what is written about him is either fabrication or speculation. The reason why so little is known about Shakespeare is that he wasn't a novelist or a historian or a man of letters. He was a playwright, and playwrights were considered fairly low on the social pecking order in Elizabethan society. Writing plays was about providing entertainment for the masses – the great unwashed. It was the equivalent to being a journalist for a tabloid newspaper.

In fact, we only know of Shakespeare's work because two of his friends had the foresight to collect his plays together following his death and have them printed. The only reason they did so was apparently because they rated his talent and thought it would be a shame if his words were lost.

Consequently his body of work has ever since been assessed and reassessed as the greatest contribution to English literature. That is despite the fact that we know that different printers took it upon themselves to heavily edit the material they worked from. We also know that Elizabethan plays were worked and reworked frequently, so that they evolved over time until they were honed to perfection, which means that many different hands played their part in the active writing process. It would therefore be fair to say that any play attributed to Shakespeare is unlikely to contain a great deal of original input. Even the plots were based on well known historical events, so it would be hard to know what fragments of any Shakespeare play came from that single mind.

One might draw a comparison with the Christian bible, which remains such a compelling read because it came from the collaboration of many contributors and translators over centuries, who each adjusted the stories until they could no longer be improved. As virtually nothing is known of Shakespeare's life and even less about his method of working, we shall never know the truth about his plays. They certainly contain some very elegant phrasing, clever plot devices and plenty of words never before seen in print, but as to whether Shakespeare invented them from a unique imagination or whether he simply took them from others around him is anyone's guess.

The best bet seems to be that Shakespeare probably took the lead role in devising the original drafts of the plays, but was open to collaboration from any source when it came to developing them into workable scripts for effective performances. He would have had to work closely with his fellow actors in rehearsals, thereby finding out where to edit, abridge, alter, reword and so on.

In turn, similar adjustments would have occurred in his absence, so that definitive versions of his plays never really existed. In effect Shakespeare was only responsible for providing the framework of plays, upon which others took liberties over time. This wasn't helped by the fact that the English language itself was not definitive at that time either. The consequence was that people took it upon themselves to spell words however they pleased or to completely change words and phrasing to suit their own preferences.

It is easy to see then, that Shakespeare's plays were always going to have lives of their own, mutating and distorting in detail like Chinese whispers. The culture of creative preservation was simply not established in Elizabethan England. Creative ownership of Shakespeare's plays was lost to him as soon as he released them into the consciousness of others. They saw nothing wrong with taking his ideas and running with them, because no one had ever suggested that one shouldn't, and Shakespeare probably regarded his work in the same way. His plays weren't sacrosanct works of art, they were templates for theatre folk to make their livings from, so they had every right to mould them into productions that drew in the crowds as effectively as possible. Shakespeare was like the helmsman of a sailing ship, steering the vessel but wholly reliant on the team work of his crew to arrive at the desired destination.

It seems that Shakespeare certainly had a natural gift, but the genius of his plays may be attributable to the collective efforts of Shakespeare and others. It is a rather satisfying notion to think that *his* plays might actually be the creative outpourings of the Elizabethan milieu in which Shakespeare immersed himself. That makes them important social documents as well as seminal works of the English language.

Money in Shakespeare's Day

It is extremely difficult, if not impossible, to relate the value of money in our time to its value in another age and to compare prices of commodities today and in the past. Many items *are* simply not comparable on grounds of quality or serviceability.

There was a bewildering variety of coins in use in Elizabethan England. As nearly all English and European coins were gold or silver, they had intrinsic value apart from their official value. This meant that foreign coins circulated freely in England and were officially recognized, for example the French crown (écu) worth about 30p (72 cents), and the Spanish ducat worth about 33p (79 cents). The following table shows some of the coins mentioned by Shakespeare and their relation to one another.

GOLD	British	American	SILVER	British	American
sovereign (heavy type)	£1.50	$3.60	shilling	10p	24c
sovereign (light type)	66p–£1	$1.58–$2.40	groat	1.5p	4c
angel					
royal	33p–50p	79c–$1.20			
noble	50p	$1.20			
crown	25p	60c			

A comparison of the following prices in Shakespeare's time with the prices of the same items today will give some idea of the change in the value of money.

ITEM	PRICE British	American	ITEM	PRICE British	American
beef, per lb.	0.5p	1c	cherries (lb.)	1p	2c
mutton, leg	7.5p	18c	7 oranges	1p	2c
rabbit	3.5p	9c	1 lemon	1p	2c
chicken	3p	8c	cream (quart)	2.5p	6c
potatoes (lb)	10p	24c	sugar (lb.)	£1	$2.40
carrots (bunch)	1p	2c	sack (wine) (gallon)	14p	34c
8 artichokes	4p	9c	tobacco (oz.)	25p	60c
1 cucumber	1p	2c	biscuits (lb.)	12.5p	30c

INTRODUCTION

We have little regard these days for hereditary qualifications. If a man inherits money, or position, or power, or a title, by the accident of birth, we feel he has not earned it and is unlikely to prove worthy of it. We almost expect such men to be incompetent weaklings, enfeebled by inbreeding and mollycoddling, so that it is a pleasant surprise to find one who is intellectually and physically vigorous and adequately endowed with the qualities of leadership which his position requires.

King Henry V, as Shakespeare has presented him to us, is more than adequately endowed with such qualities: youthful directness and honesty combined with mature wisdom and a commanding presence, vigour in action together with a superb ability to use language. We shall discuss him more fully in the summing-up after the play, but it is worth emphasizing here the sheer competence of everything he does: he is the sort of man a failing firm would like to bring in as managing director to put it back on its feet. We may disagree with his methods, we may not like him as a person, but his success commands admiration.

The historical figure was in fact idolized by Shakespeare's contemporaries, who looked back nearly two hundred years to see in him one of their greatest national heroes, the inspiration of English patriotism. He was born in 1387, during the reign of Richard II, and his father was the Bolingbroke who in 1399 usurped the throne to become Henry IV. As Prince of Wales, the young Henry was engaged while he was only a teenager in fighting and successfully containing the Welsh rebellion of Glendower, and in helping to control the many disorders which beset his father's reign. In between times he seems to have enjoyed a low life in London which would be more appropriate to a sailor on leave than to a royal prince in his capital city, and at one stage it was even rumoured that he intended to do away with his father so that he could become king himself. However, when his father died in 1413 he succeeded legally, and at once displayed a religious devotion, a passion for justice, and a sense of responsibility that made his earlier exploits seem a strangely deliberate preparation. His brilliant personality, his fighting experience, his knowledge and understanding of his fellow-men and of the ways of the world all now contributed to his leadership. Within two years he had won nation-wide support for his expedition to France, and achieved a tremendous victory over the French at Agincourt; within seven years he had captured Normandy and other parts of France, concluded a treaty which made him heir to the throne of France, and firmly established himself as king of an England which was united at home and respected abroad.

Thus, in spite of his early death, the young King Harry lived on as a national hero, the *mirror of all Christian kings*, providing Shakespeare with a perfect subject for a play expressing some of the ideals of his own age. In the play Henry displays all the qualities associated with a Renaissance prince: he has charm, wit, elegance of both speech and behaviour; he is athletic, virile, an accomplished general and politician, and a brave leader; and while he is always conscious of his unique responsibilities as a man in control of his own and his country's destiny, at the same time he looks to God for blessing on his campaigns and gives to God all credit for his triumphs. This conception of the man helps us to see the point of some of the tedious exposition in the early part of the play: Canterbury's speech about the Salic Law, for example, is necessary to establish the Divine Right of Henry's claim to the French throne.

Another Elizabethan ideal which permeates the play is the sense of order, the belief that the orderly movements of the stars and planets reflected the order which

God maintained in heaven and intended, but for the fall of Adam, to establish and maintain on earth. Man, it was felt, must strive to recreate what Adam had destroyed, by subordinating his passions to his will and obediently fulfilling the tasks appointed by his ruler, who must in his turn govern wisely, firmly and justly. Shakespeare must have felt that Henry V came nearer to this ideal than any other English monarch, except perhaps his own Elizabeth.

We are not, of course, likely to find as much human or dramatic interest in such a man as we are in, say, a Hamlet, who though endowed with equally brilliant gifts is not quite self-confident enough to control his destiny. There is a contrast between the tentative fatalism of Hamlet's

There's a divinity that shapes our ends,
Rough-hew them how we will.

and the determined aggressiveness of Henry's

Now are we well resolved . . .
France being ours, we'll bend it to our awe,
Or break it all to pieces.

(Act I, Scene ii, lines 222–5)

A failure such as Hamlet's gives the writer more scope for psychological analysis and investigation of the human predicament than a success story like *Henry V*. The task Shakespeare set himself here was quite different, namely to chronicle a splendid period in our history and to express the ideals and patriotic fervour of his own age.

But although *Henry V* lacks the subtle poetry of the later plays, it does contain a wonderfully rich variety of language, from the exuberant lyricism of the Prologues to the absurdities of the low characters, from the strength of Henry's great battle speeches to his sensitive contemplation of the isolation of leadership. The experiences of war, its glamour and its horror, its heroism and its comradeship, are magnificently verbalized; and while, in our modern way, we may find the unashamed bias of the patriotism distinctly unfair, we can still enjoy the humour and spirit of the invective.

The contrasting attitudes of the English and the French prepare us for the David-and-Goliath outcome at Agincourt. Certainly there is something satisfying about a giant-killer story, but Shakespeare is saying more than that: he seems to be demonstrating that mortal men, organized in such a nation and inspired by such a leader, can achieve almost anything.

LIST OF CHARACTERS

Chorus

King Henry the Fifth

Duke of Gloucester
Duke of Bedford } brother to the King

Duke of Exeter   uncle to the King

Duke of York   cousin to the King

Earl of Salisbury

Earl of Westmoreland

Earl of Warwick

Archbishop of Canterbury

Bishop of Ely

Earl of Cambridge
Lord Scroop } conspirators against the King
Sir Thomas Grey

Sir Thomas Erpingham
Gower
Fluellen } officers in the King's army
Macmorris
Jamy

Bates
Court
Williams
Nym } soldiers in the King's army
Bardolph
Pistol

Boy

A Herald

Charles the Sixth   King of France

Lewis, the Dauphin

Duke of Burgundy

Duke of Orleans

Duke of Britaine

Duke of Bourbon
The Constable of France
Rambures
Grandpre } French Lords
Governor of Harfleur
Montjoy   a French herald
Ambassadors to the King of England
Isabel   Queen of France
Katherine   daughter to Charles and Isabel
Alice   a lady attending her
Hostess of the Boar's Head, Eastcheap; formerly Mrs Quickly, now married to *Pistol*
Lords, Ladies, Officers, Soldiers, Messengers, Attendants

The Scene: England and France

ACT ONE

PROLOGUE

Today a chorus is usually a group of singers or dancers. But the word originally meant the band of singers in ancient Greek plays who used to comment on the action of the play and interpret the moral issues involved. In Shakespeare's day, however, it usually consisted of one actor only; he wore a long, black, velvet cloak, spoke directly to the audience, and took no part in the action. He was not often needed, but he might come on to introduce the play or explain a dumbshow (gestures without speech).

In this particular play, Shakespeare adapted the Chorus idea to a different purpose, and made fuller use of it than was usual, either with him or with other writers. This Chorus has a Prologue to speak before every Act and an Epilogue at the end of the play. He seems to have four jobs to do:

(i) to stimulate the audience to imaginative co-operation, so that they will see, in the mind's eye, the great castles and battlefields and the majestic armies of England and France – even though they are in fact looking at a mere handful of actors on a miserably inadequate stage;

(ii) to rouse patriotic feelings about England in general and King Henry in particular;

(iii) to create an exciting atmosphere (e.g. bustling activity in the Prologue to Act II, quiet suspense in the Prologue to Act IV);

(iv) to bridge big jumps of time and distance by preparing the audience for the following scenes and narrating some of the events that have occurred in between.

In this first Prologue, the emphasis is on the first of the four functions: the Chorus longs for *A kingdom for a stage, princes to act*, apologizes for the inadequate substitutes to be presented, and begs the audience to help out by using their imagination.

1–2. *O for a Muse of fire . . . invention:* 'O for the kind of inspiration that would make our words brilliantly creative.' A *Muse*, in ancient Greek myth, was a goddess who inspired poets, and *fire* suggests ardour and heroism. It was the lightest of the four elements of which it used to be thought everything was made (earth, air, water, and fire), and was therefore the most likely to *ascend The brightest heaven*.

4. *swelling:* majestic.

5. *Harry:* colloquial for Henry. *like himself:* like the real king in history.

6. *Assume the port of Mars:* 'take on the bearing of Mars', the Roman god of war.

7. *Leash'd in like hounds:* tied together on one strap. The three killers, famine, sword, and fire, are likened to three menacing hunting dogs crouching at the king's heels, waiting to be set loose. Note that *Leash'd* is pronounced as one syllable, in the normal modern way, whereas *Leashed*, without the apostrophe, would be two syllables. Compare *unraised* in line 9, in which the *-ed* has to be pronounced as a separate syllable to give the line its rhythmical ten syllables.

PROLOGUE

[Enter CHORUS*]*

Chorus
    O for a Muse of fire, that would ascend
    The brightest heaven of invention,
    A kingdom for a stage, princes to act,
    And monarchs to behold the swelling scene!
    Then should the warlike Harry, like himself,   5
    Assume the port of Mars; and at his heels,
    Leash'd in like hounds, should famine, sword, and fire,

8. *gentles:* gentlefolk.

9. *flat unraised spirits:* dull, uninspired performers (i.e. in comparison with the original personalities whom they represent). *spirits . . . hath* sounds ungrammatical to us, but the use of a singular verb with a plural subject is common in Shakespeare's English.

10. *scaffold:* stage.

11. *cockpit:* tiny arena (referring to the theatre). Setting cocks to fight each other and betting on the result was a favourite pastime until it was made illegal on the grounds of cruelty. The birds fought in a small pit in the ground known as the cockpit.

8–14. Note how the words emphasize the contrast between the presentation Shakespeare would like to give and what is in fact to be given: instead of the *kingdom for a stage* that he would like he has an *unworthy scaffold*, a mere *cockpit*, a *wooden O*; instead of *princes to act* he has only *flat unraised spirits*. Later (from line 19 onwards) the language resumes the grandeur of lines 1–8, stimulating our imagination to see *two mighty monarchies* etc.

12. *vasty:* vast.

12–14. *Or may we cram . . . Agincourt?* 'We cannot bring into the theatre the actual helmets (i.e. the actual soldiers) . . .' An appropriate figure of speech as the plumed and visored helmets would be frightening.

13. *wooden O.* The theatre, which was more or less circular (see the illustration on page 8). *casques:* helmets.

15–18. *O, pardon! . . . work:* 'Forgive us. And although we are nothing in ourselves, imagine that we stand for something great, just as a row of noughts can stand for a million.' Both *a crooked figure* and *ciphers* are noughts, which can *attest in little place a million* (i.e. represent in a small space a vast quantity like a million. *accompt:* account, in the sense of (1) sum and (2) story.

18. *imaginary forces:* your imaginations.

19. *Suppose:* imagine that.

21. *high upreared and abutting fronts:* referring to the cliffs of England and France, which face each other across the narrow English Channel.

23. 'Make up for our deficiencies by using your imagination.'

25. *puissance:* armies.

28. *deck:* equip. He is asking the audience to provide, in imagination, such equipment as horses, which must carry the kings about and jump, not only in space, but in time too (the play covers the years 1414 to 1420).

30–1. *Turning th'accomplishment . . . hour-glass:* 'passing through the events of many years in an hour only.' An hourglass is an instrument for measuring time; two bulbs of glass joined by a narrow passage through which sand or mercury runs in just an hour.

30. *th':* the, pronounced as one syllable with the *acc-* of *accomplishment* to improve the rhythm.

31. *for the which supply:* 'to help to accomplish this.'

Crouch for employment. But pardon, gentles all,
The flat unraised spirits that hath dar'd
On this unworthy scaffold to bring forth   10
So great an object. Can this cockpit hold
The vasty fields of France? Or may we cram
Within this wooden O the very casques
That did affright the air at Agincourt?
O, pardon! since a crooked figure may   15
Attest in little place a million;
And let us, ciphers to this great accompt,
On your imaginary forces work.
Suppose within the girdle of these walls
Are now confin'd two mighty monarchies,   20
Whose high upreared and abutting fronts
The perilous narrow ocean parts asunder.
Piece out our imperfections with your thoughts:
Into a thousand parts divide one man,
And make imaginary puissance;   25
Think, when we talk of horses, that you see them
Printing their proud hoofs i' th' receiving earth;
For 'tis your thoughts that now must deck our kings,
Carry them here and there, jumping o'er times,
Turning th' accomplishment of many years   30
Into an hour-glass; for the which supply,
Admit me Chorus to this history;
Who, prologue-like, your humble patience pray
Gently to hear, kindly to judge, our play.

[Exit]

SCENE I

The play itself opens in the middle of a conversation between the Archbishop of Canterbury, who is head of the Church in England (which at this time was Catholic) and one of the king's chief advisers, and another bishop about a proposal to strip the Church of a large part of its wealth and give it to the king. This proposal was part of an anti-Church campaign conducted by a group known as the Lollards, who claimed among other things that the Church was too concerned with material property (it owned a great deal of land) and should confine its interest to spiritual matters. The king, who has to make the final decision, is at present inclined to take the side of the Church, and we see here the Archbishop's plan to make sure of his support. But more important to the play is his vivid account of Henry's 'conversion', and his glowing description of the young king's great qualities – exaggerated, no doubt, but eloquent, and stimulating our interest in the hero-king who is the central figure of the play.

1. *self:* same.

2. *eleventh year:* i.e. 1410.

3–5. *Was like . . . question:* 'would probably have been passed against us if the disturbances in the country at that time had not prevented it.' *scambling:* disorganized, unruly.

7. *It must be thought on:* 'We shall have to work out an answer.'

8. *the better half of our possession:* 'more than half of our property.'

9. *temporal:* the non-ecclesiastical Church estates.

10. *By testament:* in their wills. Devout landowners have often bequeathed property to the Church to provide an income for priests, etc.

11–19. *being valu'd thus . . . year:* 'the property to be taken from the Church and given to the king is as much as would enable him adequately to finance fifteen earls, etc.'

14. *esquires:* young men who attended on knights, hoping to become knights themselves later on.

15. *lazars:* lepers.

15–16. *and weak age . . . toil:* 'and of poor old folk who are too weak to do any work.'

17. *alms-houses . . . supplied:* well-equipped charity-homes.

20. *drink deep:* cut deeply into our possessions.

ACT ONE
SCENE I

London. An ante-chamber in the King's place

[Enter the ARCHBISHOP OF CANTERBURY *and the* BISHOP OF ELY*]*

Canterbury
 My lord, I'll tell you: that self bill is urg'd
 Which in th' eleventh year of the last king's reign
 Was like, and had indeed against us pass'd
 But that the scambling and unquiet time
 Did push it out of farther question.   5
Ely
 But how, my lord, shall we resist it now?
Canterbury
 It must be thought on. If it pass against us,
 We lose the better half of our possession;
 For all the temporal lands which men devout
 By testament have given to the church   10
 Would they strip from us; being valu'd thus—
 As much as would maintain, to the King's honour,
 Full fifteen earls and fifteen hundred knights,
 Six thousand and two hundred good esquires;
 And, to relief of lazars and weak age,   15
 Of indigent faint souls, past corporal toil,
 A hundred alms-houses right well supplied;
 And to the coffers of the King, beside,
 A thousand pounds by th' year: thus runs the bill.
Ely
 This would drink deep.   20
Canterbury
       'Twould drink the cup and all.
Ely
 But what prevention?

22–3. Not really a change of subject, although it leads to one. The two Churchmen are having to rely, for *prevention* (stopping the proposed legislation), on the king's devotion to the *holy Church* – which, ironically, they aim to exploit in a somewhat unholy way.

24. Before he became king, Henry had been a wild young man.

26. *mortified.* The literal meaning is 'killed', but the word refers particularly to the religious practice of mortifying (destroying) the sinful desires of the body by self-denial.

28–37. In describing how suddenly Henry's behaviour improved when his father (King Henry IV) died, Canterbury uses three metaphors: (i) the idea of the *offending Adam*, the sinful part of human nature which we have inherited from the first sinner; this part was driven out of Henry's character in the same way as Adam himself was driven out of the Garden of Eden by God (*Genesis*, ch. 3); (ii) the dirt swept away by a flood of water; (iii) the Hydra of Lerna, a mythical nine-headed monster which, whenever one head was cut off, grew two more in its place, until Hercules solved the problem by cutting off each head and thrusting a burning brand into the bleeding stump before the new heads could appear.

28. *Consideration:* profound contemplation (of himself and his sins in relation to God).

34. *heady currance:* powerful (headlong) current.

36. *seat:* throne, position of supremacy.

38–52. Canterbury speaks enthusiastically of five qualities which the king now exhibits: (i) his understanding of theology (*divinity*); (ii) his grasp of his people's problems (*commonwealth affairs*); (iii) his mastery of military tactics (*discourse of war*); (iv) his solving of political problems (*any cause of policy*); and (v) his gift of words (*his sweet and honey'd sentences*). Shakespeare is preparing us for the appearance of his 'star'.

40. *prelate:* bishop.

42. *all in all his study:* 'the sole preoccupation of his studies.'

43. *List:* listen to.

44. *render'd you in music:* described in a delightfully fluent way.

46. *The Gordian knot.* A very intricate knot about which it was said that whoever untied it would rule over Asia; however, Alexander the Great apparently cheated by cutting it with his sword, and claiming the honour for himself. Nowadays we use the expression metaphorically for any apparently impossible problem, especially if the person who solves it will gain great distinction.

47. *Familiar as his garter.* We might say, 'As easily as he undoes his shoelaces.'

47–50. *that, when he speaks . . . sentences.* Henry discusses all these subjects so masterfully and eloquently that even the air is still when he speaks, and hides in silent rapture in men's ears to make sure of capturing every word.

48. *charter'd libertine:* the air, which in nature is allowed to behave as boisterously as it wills, is charmed into stillness.

51–2. *practic . . . theoric:* his understanding (*theoric*) is of the kind that usually comes only from practical experience (*the art and practic part of life*).

Canterbury
    The King is full of grace and fair regard.
Ely
    And a true lover of the holy Church.
Canterbury
    The courses of his youth promis'd it not.
    The breath no sooner left his father's body   25
    But that his wildness, mortified in him,
    Seem'd to die too; yea, at that very moment,
    Consideration like an angel came
    And whipp'd th' offending Adam out of him,
    Leaving his body as a paradise   30
    T' envelop and contain celestial spirits.
    Never was such a sudden scholar made;
    Never came reformation in a flood,
    With such a heady currance, scouring faults;
    Nor never Hydra-headed wilfulness   35
    So soon did lose his seat, and all at once,
    As in this king.
Ely
                        We are blessed in the change.
Canterbury
    Hear him but reason in divinity,
    And, all-admiring, with an inward wish
    You would desire the King were made a prelate;   40
    Hear him debate of commonwealth affairs,
    You would say it hath been all in all his study;
    List his discourse of war, and you shall hear
    A fearful battle render'd you in music.
    Turn him to any cause of policy,   45
    The Gordian knot of it he will unloose,
    Familiar as his garter; that, when he speaks,
    The air, a charter'd libertine, is still,
    And the mute wonder lurketh in men's ears
    To steal his sweet and honey'd sentences;   50
    So that the art and practic part of life
    Must be the mistress to this theoric;

53. 'It's remarkable that the prince has been able to gain it', (considering how he has spent his life up to this time).

55. companies: friends. **unletter'd:** uneducated. **rude:** coarse.
(One of Henry's former friends was Sir John Falstaff, whose way of life is hinted at in Act II, Scene iii.)

56. riots: wild parties.

58. sequestration: shutting himself away for quiet study.

59. open haunts: places where common people met for the pleasures of wine, women, song, gambling, fighting – not at all suitable for a royal prince.

60–6. Strawberries really do thrive in wild and shady surroundings, but it is difficult to see how Henry's serious-mindedness could have benefited from his wild and shady companions. Ely's parallel seems illogical and unhelpful. The only significant similarity is the surprised delight of finding something useful and beautiful beneath rubbish.

66. crescive in his faculty: having a natural tendency to grow.

68–9. And therefore . . . perfected: 'We have to accept this natural (as opposed to miraculous) explanation of how the change came about.

70. 'How are we going to take the sting out of this bill?'

72. indifferent: taking neither one side nor the other.

74. th' exhibiters against us: our opponents, those who have pushed the bill forward.

75–81. Here we see the Archbishop of Canterbury, not merely as the head of the Church, but also as a prominent political figure, indeed as a crafty manipulator of events. It seems that, in his anxiety to divert the king from the disputed bill, which would ruin the Church, he has himself suggested the renewal of hostilities against France, and even goes as far as to offer a large sum of money from Church funds to help finance it.

76. convocation: a meeting ('synod') of clergy that decided important Church matters.

78. open'd to his Grace at large: explained to the king in general outline.

79. touching: concerning.

81. withal: with.

Which is a wonder how his Grace should glean it,
Since his addiction was to courses vain,
His companies unletter'd, rude, and shallow,
His hours fill'd up with riots, banquets, sports;   55
And never noted in him any study,
Any retirement, any sequestration
From open haunts and popularity.

Ely

The strawberry grows underneath the nettle,
And wholesome berries thrive and ripen best   60
Neighbour'd by fruit of baser quality;
And so the Prince obscur'd his contemplation
Under the veil of wildness; which, no doubt,
Grew like the summer grass, fastest by night,
Unseen, yet crescive in his faculty.   65

Canterbury

It must be so; for miracles are ceas'd;
And therefore we must needs admit the means
How things are perfected.

Ely

               But, my good lord,
How now for mitigation of this bill
Urg'd by the Commons? Doth his Majesty   70
Incline to it, or no?

Canterbury

             He seems indifferent
Or rather swaying more upon our part
Than cherishing th' exhibiters against us;
For I have made an offer to his Majesty—
Upon our spiritual convocation   75
And in regard of causes now in hand,
Which I have open'd to his Grace at large,
As touching France – to give a greater sum
Than ever at one time the clergy yet
Did to his predecessors part withal.   80

Ely

How did this offer seem receiv'd, my lord?

Canterbury

With good acceptance of his Majesty;

86. The details of how the titles should, by obvious and legal lines of succession, have descended to Henry.

89. *Edward:* King Edward III of England, son of Isabella, who as daughter of King Philip IV of France should, according to the English, have inherited the French crown and passed it on to her descendants.

95. *embassy:* message.

96–7. King Henry has already made a claim to the French titles, but the result is entirely predictable: the French can hardly do anything but reject it.

SCENE II

Stage Direction. *The Presence Chamber:* the room in which the king conducted the formal business of his office. Now twenty-seven years old and in the second year of his reign, here in this scene he receives his council of close advisers and later the French Ambassadors. It is a ceremonial state occasion; everyone is dressed appropriately.

2. *in presence:* 'in Your Majesty's presence.'
3. *my liege:* a term of respect for the lord to whom the speaker owes allegiance (loyalty).
4. *we would be resolv'd:* 'I want to make up my mind'. He will not make a hurried decision, nor will he see the Ambassadors until he knows exactly what he is going to say to them, *we:* referring to himself. It was customary for the monarch to use 'we' instead of 'I', 'us' instead of 'me' etc., and is still, on certain formal occasions.

Save that there was not time enough to hear,
As I perceiv'd his Grace would fain have done,
The severals and unhidden passages   85
Of his true titles to some certain dukedoms,
And generally to the crown and seat of France,
Deriv'd from Edward, his great-grandfather.

Ely

What was th' impediment that broke this off?

Canterbury

The French ambassador upon that instant   90
Crav'd audience; and the hour, I think, is come
To give him hearing: is it four o'clock?

Ely

It is.

Canterbury

Then go we in, to know his embassy:
Which I could with a ready guess declare,   95
Before the Frenchman speak a word of it.

Ely

I'll wait upon you, and I long to hear it.

[Exeunt]

Scene II

London. The Presence Chamber in the King's palace

[Enter the KING, GLOUCESTER, BEDFORD, EXETER,
WARWICK, WESTMORELAND *and* ATTENDANTS]

King

Where is my gracious Lord of Canterbury?

Exeter

Not here in presence.

King

Send for him, good uncle.

Westmoreland

Shall we call in th' ambassador, my liege?

King

Not yet, my cousin; we would be resolv'd,   19

5. *some things of weight:* important matters.

6.*That task our thoughts:* 'that weigh upon my mind'.

8. *And make you long become it!* 'and enable you to grace the throne for many years'.

Sure, we thank you. The king's reply to Canterbury's exaggerated opening compliment sounds startled, perhaps slightly amused.

10. *religiously:* with the sort of scrupulous care and honesty one would expect from an Archbishop. Here and later in the speech (lines 13–17) the king seems to be half-expecting Canterbury to be slightly dishonest in his presentation of the facts.

11. *the law Salique.* This law is the crux of the dispute over the French throne, and Canterbury has evidently been called in as the expert on these legal matters. See the explanation of his speech in lines 33–95.

12. *Or should or should not:* either should or should not. *bar:* obstruct, block.

14. *fashion:* shape. *wrest:* twist.

bow: bend, warp.

reading: interpretation.

15–17. *Or nicely charge . . . truth:* 'or commit the sin of deliberately making me think I have a legal right to the throne of France when the strict truth is that I have not.'

nicely: here means cunningly, contrary to popular modern usage.

understanding: 'aware of what is going on'.

miscreate: (miscreated) mistaken.

18–20. 'For God knows the vast amount of good healthy blood that is going to be spilt if I start this war you are urging me to.'

approbation: 'the action of proving something true'. Lives will be lost proving the truth of Canterbury's case.

21. *impawn our person:* commit me to this enterprise. Henry seems to depend on Canterbury's advice: if Canterbury says that the claim is just and worth fighting for, Henry will fight for it. Canterbury is like a man giving an article to a pawnbroker (a type of money-lender) in return for a loan, but in this case the article is the king himself, who does not want to be 'pawned' for nothing.

22. *sleeping.* There had been a truce between England and France for twenty-five years.

24. *contend:* fight.

25–8. *whose guiltless drops . . . mortality:* 'every drop of blood shed by the innocent victims of war is like a howl of bitter, grieving protest against those whose wrongdoings are the cause of such destruction.'

28. *brief mortality:* human life, which is short enough without war cutting it even shorter.

29. *conjuration:* solemn oath (see line 23). Henry is putting Canterbury on oath, like a witness in a court case.

31–2. *wash'd . . . baptism.* Christian baptism (washing or anointing with holy water) symbolizes washing sin from the soul.

33–95. Canterbury's long speech is too tedious for modern audiences and is usually shortened, but Shakespeare probably thought it worth including for its convincing legal justification of Henry's claim to the French throne.

Before we hear him, of some things of weight   5
That task our thoughts, concerning us and France.

[Enter the ARCHBISHOP OF CANTERBURY *and the*
BISHOP OF ELY]

Canterbury
    God and his angels guard your sacred throne,
    And make you long become it!
King
                                    Sure, we thank you.
    My learned lord, we pray you to proceed,
    And justly and religiously unfold   10
    Why the law Salique, that they have in France,
    Or should or should not bar us in our claim;
    And God forbid, my dear and faithful lord,
    That you should fashion, wrest, or bow your
        reading,
    Or nicely charge your understanding soul   15
    With opening titles miscreate whose right
    Suits not in native colours with the truth;
    For God doth know how many, now in health,
    Shall drop their blood in approbation
    Of what your reverence shall incite us to.   20
    Therefore take heed how you impawn our person,
    How you awake our sleeping sword of war—
    We charge you, in the name of God, take heed;
    For never two such kingdoms did contend
    Without much fall of blood; whose guiltless drops 25
    Are every one a woe, a sore complaint,
    'Gainst him whose wrongs gives edge unto the swords
    That makes such waste in brief mortality.
    Under this conjuration speak, my lord;
    For we will hear, note, and believe in heart,   30
    That what you speak is in your conscience wash'd
    As pure as sin with baptism.
Canterbury
    Then hear me, gracious sovereign, and you peers,

He also enjoyed making fun of long-winded politicians, especially fussy old men like Polonius in *Hamlet*.

The quarrel between the French and the English arose in this way: it was normal for a king to be succeeded by his eldest son, or by his daughter if he had no son. However, in 1328 the French nobles rejected Isabella, the apparent heir to the throne after all her brothers had died, in favour of her cousin, son of the former king's younger brother, and therefore junior to her. As Isabella was married to the English king, Edward II, her descendants, besides being kings of England, believed they had a legal claim to be kings of France too. The French replied by quoting an ancient law, the 'Salique law', to the effect that no woman could ever be Queen of France. From this they argued that neither Isabella nor her descendants had any claim. Canterbury demolishes this in two ways: (i) He shows that 'Salique land' is not France itself, as the French claim, but a small area in Germany which the French had colonized in A.D. 805. Moreover, the alleged founder of the Salique law, King Pharamond, had, according to legend, died four centuries before that date and so could hardly have invented the law. (ii) He quotes three examples which show that the French themselves accept the idea of inheriting through a female; indeed the present king himself, he says, is a descendant of the female line.

34. *owe yourselves:* In return for the lands and titles which the king had given them, the peers (nobles) had to serve him and fight for him when required.

35–6. *no bar To make:* no legal objection which can be made.

37. *Pharamond:* a legendary king.

40. *gloze:* explain.

45. *floods:* rivers.

46. *subdu'd:* conquered.

48. *holding in disdain:* despising.

48–51. The French settlers must have found the German women too loose in their morals to be worthy of owning titles or property. *Dishonest* in Shakespeare's day often meant immoral, promiscuous.

51. *inheritrix:* female heir.

58. *defunction:* death.

59. *Idly:* inaccurately.

60. *of our redemption:* after Christ (a.d.).

62. *seat:* settle.

64. *Eight hundred five.* Comparing this with the figures in lines 57 and 61, we see that Canterbury's arithmetic is wrong.

66. *heir general:* any heir, whether through the male or female line.

That owe yourselves, your lives, and services,
To this imperial throne. There is no bar   35
To make against your Highness' claim to France
But this, which they produce from Pharamond:
'In terram Salicam mulieres ne succedant'—
'No woman shall succeed in Salique land';
Which Salique land the French unjustly gloze   40
To be the realm of France, and Pharamond
The founder of this law and female bar.
Yet their own authors faithfully affirm
That the land Salique is in Germany,
Between the floods of Sala and of Elbe;   45
Where Charles the Great, having subdu'd the
    Saxons,
There left behind and settled certain French;
Who, holding in disdain the German women
For some dishonest manners of their life,
Establish'd then this law: to wit, no female   50
Should be inheritrix in Salique land;
Which Salique, as I said, 'twixt Elbe and Sala,
Is at this day in Germany call'd Meisen.
Then doth it well appear the Salique law
Was not devised for the realm of France;   55
Nor did the French possess the Salique land
Until four hundred one and twenty years
After defunction of King Pharamond,
Idly suppos'd the founder of this law;
Who died within the year of our redemption   60
Four hundred twenty-six; and Charles the Great
Subdu'd the Saxons, and did seat the French
Beyond the river Sala, in the year
Eight hundred five. Besides, their writers say,
King Pepin, which deposed Childeric,   65
Did, as heir general, being descended
Of Blithild, which was daughter to King Clothair,
Make claim and title to the crown of France.
Hugh Capet also, who usurp'd the crown
Of Charles the Duke of Lorraine, sole heir male   70

23

72. 'To bolster up his claim with some plausible justification.' This was necessary because he had *usurp'd the crown* (seized it illegally).

74. *Convey'd himself as:* pretended to be.

79. *keep quiet in* . . .: retain any peace of mind.

82. *Was lineal of:* was a direct descendant of.

88. *King Lewis his satisfaction.* Nowadays we should use the simple possessive: 'King Lewis's satisfaction'. The *satisfaction* is the soothing of his conscience referred to in lines 77–83.

88–9. *all appear . . . female.* These three men all justified themselves on the basis of the legal right of women to inherit the crown and pass it on to their descendants.

91. *Howbeit:* although.

93–5. *And rather choose . . . progenitors:* 'the French kings prefer to take cover behind this network of legal quibbles and contradictions rather than admit that, as the law they use against you applies also to themselves, they have in fact usurped the crown from you and your ancestors.'

94. *amply to imbar:* to invalidate completely.

96. *May I . . . claim?* Henry's brief and perhaps impatient question follows a long and involved argument. What he wants is a short straight answer. The archbishop, however, is not so easily stopped!

97. *The sin upon my head:* 'I'll take the punishment if we're committing a sin'.

98–100. In addition to his other arguments, Canterbury now quotes from the Bible as the highest authority of all.

100. And here he begins a passionate appeal to Henry's warlike instincts.

101. *Stand for your own:* stand up and claim what is yours. *unwind your bloody flag:* referring to the banner carried into battle.

102. *Look back into . . . ancestors:* 'Follow the example of your mighty ancestors.' We might say: 'Look to your ancestors for inspiration and example.'

104. *invoke:* summon. He means: 'Summon inspiration from him.' Both Edward III and his son, the Black Prince (probably so-called because of his custom of wearing black armour), were *warlike* (full of spirit and courage).

Of the true line and stock of Charles the Great,
To find his title with some shows of truth—
Though in pure truth it was corrupt and naught—
Convey'd himself as th' heir to th' Lady Lingare,
Daughter to Charlemain, who was the son   75
To Lewis the Emperor, and Lewis the son
Of Charles the Great. Also King Lewis the Tenth,
Who was sole heir to the usurper Capet,
Could not keep quiet in his conscience,
Wearing the crown of France, till satisfied   80
That fair Queen Isabel, his grandmother,
Was lineal of the Lady Ermengare,
Daughter to Charles the foresaid Duke of Lorraine;
By the which marriage the line of Charles the Great
Was re-united to the Crown of France.   85
So that, as clear as is the summer's sun,
King Pepin's title, and Hugh Capet's claim,
King Lewis his satisfaction, all appear
To hold in right and title of the female;
So do the kings of France unto this day,   90
Howbeit they would hold up this Salique law
To bar your Highness claiming from the female;
And rather choose to hide them in a net
Than amply to imbar their crooked titles
Usurp'd from you and your progenitors.   95

King

May I with right and conscience make this claim?

Canterbury

The sin upon my head, dread sovereign!
For in the book of Numbers is it writ,
When the man dies, let the inheritance
Descend unto the daughter. Gracious lord,   100
Stand for your own, unwind your bloody flag,
Look back into your mighty ancestors.
Go, my dread lord, to your great-grandsire's tomb,
From whom you claim; invoke his warlike spirit,
And your great-uncle's, Edward the Black Prince,   105

Who on the French ground play'd a tragedy,
Making defeat on the full power of France,
Whiles his most mighty father on a hill
Stood smiling to behold his lion's whelp
Forage in blood of French nobility. 110
O noble English, that could entertain
With half their forces the full pride of France,
And let another half stand laughing by,
All out of work and cold for action!

Ely

Awake remembrance of these valiant dead, 115
And with your puissant arm renew their feats.
You are their heir; you sit upon their throne;
The blood and courage that renowned them
Runs in your veins; and my thrice-puissant liege
Is in the very May-morn of his youth, 120
Ripe for exploits and mighty enterprises.

Exeter

Your brother kings and monarchs of the earth
Do all expect that you should rouse yourself,
As did the former lions of your blood.

Westmoreland

They know your Grace hath cause and means and
        might— 125
So hath your Highness; never King of England
Had nobles richer and more loyal subjects,
Whose hearts have left their bodies here in England
And lie pavilion'd in the fields of France.

Canterbury

O, let their bodies follow, my dear liege, 130
With blood and sword and fire to win your right!
In aid whereof we of the spiritualty
Will raise your Highness such a mighty sum
As never did the clergy at one time
Bring in to any of your ancestors. 135

King

We must not only arm t' invade the French,

137–9. *But lay down* . . . *advantages:* 'arrange for part of our army to defend our northern border against the Scots, who will use our absence to attack with everything in their favour.'

140. *marches:* the border country between England and Scotland. *They of those marches* are the people who live there.

143–4. *Coursing* was the sport of chasing hares with greyhounds, in which the kill was known as the 'snatch'. *The coursing snatchers* are, metaphorically, the small-time Scottish raiders who cross the border to plunder odd animals and crops. The king is not worried about them; perhaps they can, as Canterbury suggests, be kept in their place by the local people. Instead he fears *the main intendment of the Scot* i.e. a full-scale invasion.

145. *still:* always. (The Scots and the English were old enemies.) *giddy:* unreliable, untrustworthy.

146. *For you shall read:* For the history books will tell you.

148–9. *But that* . . . *pouring:* without the Scots invading his undefended kingdom.

149. *breach:* a gap or break in a sea-wall, through which a flood-tide could burst.

150–4. The idea of flooding – the Scots pouring into England – underlies the words here: *ample and brim fullness of his force* suggests the Scottish army was overflowing with soldiers; and they were *galling* (wearing away) the *gleaned* (defenceless) land with *hot assays* (violent assaults), and like a flood *girdling* (encircling) castles and towns. This is typical of the way a metaphor would become so vivid in Shakespeare's mind that it coloured his choice of words for several lines. Even *shook and trembled* suggests the way the ground and buildings near the sea reverberate to the pounding of heavy waves.

154. *ill neighbourhood:* bad neighbourliness.

155. *She* is England, and *fear'd* in this context means 'frightened': England was more afraid of what the Scots might do than harmed by the little damage they actually did. Is Canterbury's attempt to reassure the king logical and convincing?

156. *For hear her but exampled by herself:* 'you only have to look at her history for an example.'

157. *chivalry:* warriors.

158. England is seen metaphorically as a widow mourning for her nobles – not because they are dead, but because they are away at war.

160. *impounded as a stray.* A very contemptuous way to treat a king. 'To impound' is to put into a 'pound' – an enclosure in which stray animals were kept until their owners claimed them.

161–5. A Scottish king, David II, was in fact captured in 1346, but it seems to have been a false rumour that he was taken to France so that Edward III could show him off as a 'prize prisoner'.

her chronicle means the history of England, which sparkles with such glories, just as the muddy slime under the sea sparkles with the many treasures sunk there.

sumless means countless, priceless.

But lay down our proportions to defend
Against the Scot, who will make road upon us
With all advantages.

Canterbury

They of those marches, gracious sovereign,   140
Shall be a wall sufficient to defend
Our inland from the pilfering borderers.

King

We do not mean the coursing snatchers only,
But fear the main intendment of the Scot,
Who hath been still a giddy neighbour to us;   145
For you shall read that my great-grandfather
Never went with his forces into France
But that the Scot on his unfurnish'd kingdom
Came pouring, like the tide into a breach,
With ample and brim fulness of his force,   150
Galling the gleaned land with hot assays,
Girdling with grievous siege castles and towns;
That England, being empty of defence,
Hath shook and trembled at th' ill neighbourhood.

Canterbury

She hath been then more fear'd than harm'd, my
     liege;   155
For hear her but exampled by herself:
When all her chivalry hath been in France,
And she a mourning widow of her nobles,
She hath herself not only well defended
But taken and impounded as a stray   160
The King of Scots; whom she did send to France,
To fill King Edward's fame with prisoner kings,
And make her chronicle as rich with praise
As is the ooze and bottom of the sea
With sunken wreck and sumless treasuries.   165

Westmoreland

But there's a saying, very old and true:
          'If that you will France win,
          Then with Scotland first begin'.

169. *in prey:* in pursuit of her prey.

170. *weasel:* a long, slender, carnivorous animal of the stoat family that sucks the goodness out of eggs.

170–3. There is an abrupt change of metaphor: first the Scot is a weasel attacking and robbing an eagle's nest, then a mouse playing havoc while the cat is away.

174–83. Exeter jumps on the cat and mouse idea and shows that it is a false analogy, for it suggests that the cat has to stay at home all the time to keep the mice quiet. But there are such things as mouse-traps to take the cat's place; there is an easy answer to the necessity of keeping the cat at home, so it is *crush'd*, i.e. reduced to nothing. He answers metaphor with metaphor: government is like the human body, which has different parts doing different jobs at the same time yet all working together for one common purpose; or like music, in which many parts combine to produce an harmonious whole. In short, it is a simple matter for an English army to go to France and leave behind another army to defend the borders.

177. *pretty:* cunning, artful.

179. *Th'advised head:* the controlling part of the body. *advised* here means 'wise', or as we might say 'well-advised'.

180. *For government, though high, and low, and lower:* the various levels of responsibility in government (like various registers of voices), from the king at the top down through the nobles to ordinary men.

181–3. Government is like music in that the work is *put into parts* (divided up among the singers or instruments) which yet *keep in one consent* (keep time). *Congreeing* seems to be a word formed by combining 'concord' (or 'congrue' or 'consent') with 'agree': we should have to say 'agreeing with each other in pleasant harmony.' A *close* is a cadence, the end of a melody, the final sustained chord in which the instruments or voices are united.

183–7. *Therefore doth heaven divide . . . Obedience:* therefore God has given men different jobs to do, so that they can all carry on working in their own way for the good of everyone. A *butt* was a mark for aiming at in archery practice; in this case the aim is *Obedience*, which means not only doing what you're told but also working for the common good.

187–9. *for so work the honey bees . . . kingdom:* this is the way the bees work, creatures that by pure instinct set an example of sensible organisation to human kingdoms. The point has already been well made, and there seems no need for yet another parallel, but perhaps Shakespeare was absorbed in the fun of working it out, and as he develops the idea there are some delightful links between insect and human, e.g. the soldiers (line 193) that *make boot upon* (plunder) the flowers, and then bring the *pillage* (booty, here the honey) home to their emperor.

197. *busied in his majesty:* busy doing his job of governing.

For once the eagle England being in prey,
To her unguarded nest the weasel Scot 170
Comes sneaking, and so sucks her princely eggs,
Playing the mouse in absence of the cat,
To tear and havoc more than she can eat.

Exeter

It follows, then, the cat must stay at home;
Yet that is but a crush'd necessity, 175
Since we have locks to safeguard necessaries
And pretty traps to catch the petty thieves.
While that the armed hand doth fight abroad,
Th' advised head defends itself at home;
For government, though high, and low, and lower, 180
Put into parts, doth keep in one consent,
Congreeing in a full and natural close,
Like music.

Canterbury

        Therefore doth heaven divide
The state of man in divers functions,
Setting endeavour in continual motion; 185
To which is fixed as an aim or butt
Obedience; for so work the honey bees,
Creatures that by a rule in nature teach
The act of order to a peopled kingdom.
They have a king, and officers of sorts, 190
Where some like magistrates correct at home;
Others like merchants venture trade abroad;
Others like soldiers, armed in their stings,
Make boot upon the summer's velvet buds,
Which pillage they with merry march bring home 195
To the tent-royal of their emperor;
Who, busied in his majesty, surveys
The singing masons building roofs of gold,
The civil citizens kneading up the honey,

200. *mechanic:* to us, someone who looks after machines, but to Shakespeare someone who worked like a machine – i.e. did manual labour.

203. *executors:* executioners. The different types of bee seem to have their human equivalents, but the drone (the male bee which does not make honey) is treated more harshly than a lazy human usually is.

204. *I this infer:* 'I conclude the following.'

204–13. Canterbury is only elaborating what Exeter said in lines 180–4, long-windedly adding further analogies of his own. The *dial* (line 210) is a sun-dial with its many converging lines.

205–6. *having full reference To one consent:* entirely directed to one agreed end.

212–13. *End in one purpose . . . defeat:* 'even though the thousand actions may be all different, they can all proceed efficiently without obstructing each other, and successfully achieve their one common purpose.'

216. *withal:* (with it) even with that quarter. The word had various uses in Shakespeare's English, but it is now obsolete. *Gallia* is an old name for France.

218. *dog:* the Scots.

219–20. *Let us be worried . . . policy:* 'We ought to be gnawed by *the dog* and lose our reputation for toughness and shrewdness.'

221–2. The king's mind is made up; no more words are needed: it is time for action. He has, we notice, allowed Canterbury and the others to speak at length, while he has listened, considered, and decided. *Now are we well resolv'd* reminds us of his *we would be resolv'd.* *Dauphin* was the traditional title of the French king's eldest son.

223. *sinews:* a metaphor for his nobles. He needs their help just as muscles need sinews to transfer power to the limbs.

224. *France being ours . . . awe:* 'If as you say France really should by right be mine, I'll make it bow down to my authority.'

225–8. *or there we'll sit . . . or lay these bones.* We should say 'Either there we'll sit etc.'. Shakespeare often used 'or . . . or . . .' where we now prefer 'either . . . or . . .'.

226. *large and ample empery:* absolute, unchallenged supremacy.

227. *her almost kingly dukedoms.* Some of the French dukedoms were large, powerful, and independent, almost kingdoms in themselves – Burgundy, for example. (In Act V we see the Duke of Burgundy as an independent mediator between the French and English kings.)

228–9. *Or lay these bones . . . them:* 'or (if I can't gain absolute power over France) I'll die in the attempt, and you can throw my body into any ordinary grave, without a proper gravestone or even an epitaph to say whose it is.'

230–3. He repeats the idea of the previous two lines, emphasizing the extreme alternatives he has set himself: glorious success or shameful death and burial.

230. *with full mouth:* eloquently and enthusiastically. Note the contrast with the *Turkish mute* in line 232, whose mouth is tongueless and therefore 'empty' and silent.

The poor mechanic porters crowding in   200
Their heavy burdens at his narrow gate,
The sad-ey'd justice, with his surly hum,
Delivering o'er to executors pale
The lazy yawning drone. I this infer,
That many things, having full reference   205
To one consent, may work contrariously;
As many arrows loosed several ways
Come to one mark, as many ways meet in one
    town,
As many fresh streams meet in one salt sea,
As many lines close in the dial's centre;   210
So many a thousand actions, once afoot,
End in one purpose, and be all well borne
Without defeat. Therefore to France, my liege.
Divide your happy England into four;
Whereof take you one quarter into France,   215
And you withal shall make all Gallia shake.
If we, with thrice such powers left at home,
Cannot defend our own doors from the dog,
Let us be worried, and our nation lose
The name of hardiness and policy.   220

King

Call in the messengers sent from the Dauphin.

[Exeunt some ATTENDANTS*]*

Now are we well resolv'd; and, by God's help
And yours, the noble sinews of our power,
France being ours, we'll bend it to our awe,
Or break it all to pieces; or there we'll sit,   225
Ruling in large and ample empery
O'er France and all her almost kingly dukedoms,
Or lay these bones in an unworthy urn,
Tombless, with no remembrance over them.
Either our history shall with full mouth   230
Speak freely of our acts, or else our grave,

232. *Turkish mute.* The story goes that in Turkey slaves who knew some of their masters' scandalous secrets had their tongues cut out to stop them talking (added to which, they would not have been able to write).

233. *Not worshipp'd . . . epitaph:* 'not distinguished with even a waxen epitaph', a 'silent' grave, without any writing on it at all. *a waxen epitaph.* This may have been a piece of paper fixed in place with wax, perhaps one carved in wax, or even written with wax; in any event it would be easily obliterated. Poor men could afford nothing better in those days. Henry feels that he will not deserve even one of those if he fails in his bid for France.

235. *our fair cousin Dauphin:* diplomatically polite language. Persons of rank spoke this way of each other without necessarily having any blood relationship.

237–40. *May't please your Majesty . . . embassy?* Will you give us permission to speak out frankly what we have to say? Or must we keep to formal diplomatic language and hint indirectly at the Dauphin's message? The Ambassador's anxiety is understandable enough: the message he has to deliver is thoroughly offensive.

241–5. Henry prefers frankness. Here he makes it clear that he is not the sort of man to be upset by plain-speaking: he has his *passion* (temper) as well under control as a convict chained up in prison. The *grace* he claims to have is Christian mildness and mercy – as opposed to the anger of legendary pagan rulers who would kill the bringer of an unwelcome message.

245. *in few:* in a few words.

250–7. The Dauphin, through his Ambassadors, is taunting Henry by reminding him of his wild youth, and by treating him as though he is still the same irresponsible boy. 'This claim of yours is too childish (*you savour too much of your youth*),' he says. 'You obviously have not grown up yet. It is about time you learnt that you cannot get anywhere in France with these playboy tactics: you cannot dance your way into a dukedom.' (A *galliard* is a quick, lively dance, and to *revel* is to have fun dancing and playing games.) 'You'd better stick to your boyish pastimes, and here is a present to encourage you.' Notice that Shakespeare is clever enough to give effective speeches to the enemy too.

258. When the tennis balls are revealed, the court watches in shocked silence to see how the king will react. He pauses for some moments before replying.

259. *We are glad.* Is he really glad? Could he perhaps force a smile here, as though he were enjoying the joke? Or is this just the quietly sarcastic prelude to the angry climax that follows?

Like Turkish mute, shall have a tongueless mouth,
Not worshipp'd with a waxen epitaph.

[Enter AMBASSADORS *of France]*

Now are we well prepar'd to know the pleasure
Of our fair cousin Dauphin; for we hear   235
Your greeting is from him, not from the King.
First Ambassador
    May't please your Majesty to give us leave
    Freely to render what we have in charge;
    Or shall we sparingly show you far off
    The Dauphin's meaning and our embassy?   240
King
    We are no tyrant, but a Christian king,
    Unto whose grace our passion is as subject
    As are our wretches fetter'd in our prisons;
    Therefore with frank and with uncurbed plainness
    Tell us the Dauphin's mind.   245
First Ambassador
                              Thus then, in few.
    Your Highness, lately sending into France,
    Did claim some certain dukedoms in the right
    Of your great predecessor, King Edward the Third.
    In answer of which claim, the Prince our master
    Says that you savour too much of your youth,   250
    And bids you be advis'd there's nought in France
    That can be with a nimble galliard won;
    You cannot revel into dukedoms there.
    He therefore sends you, meeter for your spirit,
    This tun of treasure; and, in lieu of this,   255
    Desires you let the dukedoms that you claim
    Hear no more of you. This the Dauphin speaks.
King
    What treasure, uncle?
Exeter
                              Tennis-balls, my liege.
King
    We are glad the Dauphin is so pleasant with us;
    His present and your pains we thank you for.   260

261–6. The tennis referred to is the original game from which modern lawn tennis developed; it is now known as 'real tennis' but is rarely played, as it requires a special court with *hazards* (openings into which the ball can be struck). Henry treats the tennis balls as a personal challenge to a contest, and uses tennis terms in his reply, but with the double meaning throughout that the 'game' he is going to play against the Dauphin is the war game. A *wrangler* is a stubborn opponent, *courts* are both tennis courts and the homes of the nobility, and *chaces* refers to the second bounce in tennis (i.e. winning shots) and to the 'chase' in hunting a prey or an enemy.

267. *How he comes o'er us with our wilder days:* how he makes fun of me by referring to my wildness in the past.

268. *Not measuring:* not taking into account.

269–70. *We never valu'd . . . living hence.* He means that as a young man he had not had much respect for the king's court and had spent a lot of time away from home. *seat:* throne, i.e. kingdom.

271. *barbarous licence:* unrestrained self-indulgence.

272. *from home:* away from parental control.

273. *keep my state:* behave in a manner befitting a king.

274. *show my sail of greatness.* The image of the sail seems to be chosen to give a picture of majestic, billowing fulness: he is saying that there will be no doubt about the true majesty of his nature when he takes over France, even if there have been doubts so far.

275. *rouse me:* we should say 'rouse myself.' The idea of a lion rousing itself occurs again here, as it did in line 123.

276–7. *For that . . . working-days:* with that prospect in view I have for a time lived an unprincelike sort of life, like a working-class man who plods his way through the week in the expectation of a fuller life at the week-end.

278. *But I will rise there.* He speaks of himself metaphorically as the sun, about to rise in dazzling brilliance.

281. *pleasant:* literally means jocular, fond of a joke, but with a distinctly sarcastic flavour in this context.

mock: ridicule. In the next few lines Henry uses it as both noun and verb to press home the point that the results of the joke will be no laughing matter.

282. *Hath turn'd his balls to gun-stones.* He is going to play the game with cannon-balls rather than tennis-balls. Cannons used to fire round stones.

282–3. *and his son Shall stand sore charged:* it will all be the Dauphin's fault. *wasteful:* destructive (of human life). In fact, Henry had decided to wage war in France before he received the Dauphin's message, but he is now so angry and bitter that he will fight more destructively, and the Dauphin's soul will be severely condemned at the Last Judgement for the suffering his joke has caused. The Last Judgement is the final trial of all men, living and dead, at the end of the world.

284–5. *for many a thousand widows . . . husbands:* this joke of his will joke thousands of women into widowhood.

When we have match'd our rackets to these balls,
We will in France, by God's grace, play a set
Shall strike his father's crown into the hazard.
Tell him he hath made a match with such a wrangler
That all the courts of France will be disturb'd   265
With chaces. And we understand him well,
How he comes o'er us with our wilder days,
Not measuring what use we made of them.
We never valu'd this poor seat of England;
And therefore, living hence, did give ourself   270
To barbarous licence; as 'tis ever common
That men are merriest when they are from home.
But tell the Dauphin I will keep my state,
Be like a king, and show my sail of greatness,
When I do rouse me in my throne of France;   275
For that I have laid by my majesty
And plodded like a man for working-days;
But I will rise there with so full a glory
That I will dazzle all the eyes of France,
Yea, strike the Dauphin blind to look on us.   280
And tell the pleasant Prince this mock of his
Hath turn'd his balls to gun-stones, and his soul
Shall stand sore charged for the wasteful vengeance
That shall fly with them; for many a thousand
     widows
Shall this his mock mock out of their dear husbands;   285
Mock mothers from their sons, mock castles down;

287. *ungotten:* not even conceived yet. He is thinking of the children whose fathers will be killed in the war, some of whom are yet to be conceived.

289. Does Henry at this point pull himself up with the thought that perhaps God would not want him to be so vicious and vengeful? However, *I am coming on* sounds terribly determined (line 291).

293. *a well-hallow'd cause:* a cause God approves of, he has the Archbishop's authority now.

295–6. *His jest . . . laugh at it:* his little joke won't seem so funny when there are thousands more weeping over it than ever laughed at it.

297. *Convey them with safe conduct:* escort the Ambassadors safely back to their own country. As enemies of England, and especially after the provocation of their message, the Ambassadors were in some danger. Henry shows humanity and a proper respect for the diplomatic rules in giving orders for their protection. Nevertheless, we imagine them departing somewhat shakily after the violence of his threats.

300–1. *omit no happy hour . . . expedition:* don't miss any opportunities of speeding up our preparations for this expedition.

303. He puts God first, and everything he does has to have God's blessing.
304. *our proportions:* our part of the national forces.

307. *More feathers to our wings.* More feathers enable birds to fly faster. The emphasis is now on speed: the discussion is over, the decision made, the message sent to the French. Now is the time for action. Henry's urgency sounds infectious, and the Prologue to Act II tells how his people respond.
307. *God before:* with God's guidance.
308. 'We'll sort this Dauphin out under his father's very nose.' *Childe* suggests an adult giving a boy a thrashing to punish him for some offence; doing it *at his father's door* sounds very daring.
309. *task his thought:* think hard (i.e. looking for opportunities to put the plan into action at once). Compare line 6.

And some are yet ungotten and unborn
That shall have cause to curse the Dauphin's scorn.
But this lies all within the will of God,
To whom I do appeal; and in whose name,   290
Tell you the Dauphin, I am coming on,
To venge me as I may and to put forth
My rightful hand in a well-hallow'd cause.
So get you hence in peace; and tell the Dauphin
His jest will savour but of shallow wit,   295
When thousands weep more than did laugh at it.
Convey them with safe conduct. Fare you well.

[Exeunt AMBASSADORS]

Exeter

This was a merry message.

King

We hope to make the sender blush at it.
Therefore, my lords, omit no happy hour   300
That may give furth'rance to our expedition;
For we have now no thought in us but France,
Save those to God, that run before our business.
Therefore let our proportions for these wars
Be soon collected, and all things thought upon   305
That may with reasonable swiftness add
More feathers to our wings; for, God before,
We'll chide this Dauphin at his father's door.
Therefore let every man now task his thought
That this fair action may on foot be brought.   310

[Exeunt]

ACT TWO

PROLOGUE

Stage Direction. *Flourish:* a fanfare of trumpets.

1–2. The spirit of urgency and excitement in the king's last speech in Act I has communicated itself to all the young men of his realm, who are *on fire* with enthusiasm; they have put away the silken clothes they wore for their amorous flirtations (*dalliance*), and have set the armourers to work.

3. *Now thrive the armourers:* The armourers are doing good business now.

honour's thought: looking forward to the honour to be won in the war.

5. All but the humblest foot-soldiers had to come equipped with a horse.

6. *the mirror of all Christian kings:* the king who reflects all that is best in all Christian kings (i.e. Henry himself). *Mirror* was often used figuratively to mean an ideal to be imitated.

7. *Mercuries.* In ancient Roman legend Mercury was the messenger of the gods; wings on his cap and on his sandals enabled him to fly swiftly. The English knights are like him in their haste to follow their king's instructions.

8. *Expectation:* a personification of the hopes that fill the minds of all those going to the war. They see themselves holding swords which are encircled from point to *hilts* (the crossbars which protected the hand) with the crowns and coronets they expect to win.

12. *intelligence:* spies. The word is still used for the Secret Service.

14. *pale policy.* The French are frightened (pale in the face) and their fear has prompted them to try *policy* (an underhand method of thwarting the English plans).

16–17. England is a *model* in the sense that it is only small compared with its inner strength.

18–19. *What mightst thou do . . . natural!* what achievements that would bring honour would you rise to if all your people behaved naturally (i.e. patriotically).

20 *fault:* weakness, a flaw in the English people. It seems the king of France has probed and found the weak spot, a little group of traitors.

21. *hollow bosoms.* The bosom is where one is supposed to have one's feelings. These traitors' bosoms are *hollow* – false, empty, corruptible.

22. *treacherous crowns:* the money paid to bribe the traitors (crowns were coins).

26. *gilt . . . guilt.* This is a pun. *gilt:* gold, i.e. money.

ACT TWO
Prologue

[Flourish. Enter CHORUS*]*

Chorus

    Now all the youth of England are on fire,
    And silken dalliance in the wardrobe lies;
    Now thrive the armourers, and honour's thought
    Reigns solely in the breast of every man;
    They sell the pasture now to buy the horse,   5
    Following the mirror of all Christian kings
    With winged heels, as English Mercuries.
    For now sits Expectation in the air,
    And hides a sword from hilts unto the point
    With crowns imperial, crowns, and coronets,   10
    Promis'd to Harry and his followers.
    The French, advis'd by good intelligence
    Of this most dreadful preparation,
    Shake in their fear and with pale policy
    Seek to divert the English purposes.   15
    O England! model to thy inward greatness,
    Like little body with a mighty heart,
    What mightst thou do that honour would thee do,
    Were all thy children kind and natural!
    But see thy fault! France hath in thee found out   20
    A nest of hollow bosoms, which he fills
    With treacherous crowns; and three corrupted men—
    One, Richard Earl of Cambridge, and the second,
    Henry Lord Scroop of Masham, and the third,
    Sir Thomas Grey, knight of Northumberland,   25
    Have, for the gilt of France – O guilt indeed!—

27. *fearful:* full of fear ('frightened' rather than 'frightening' as it would be today).

28. *this grace of kings:* this most perfect of all kings.

29. 'If this hellish treason succeeds.'

31. *Linger your patience on:* be patient for a little longer.

31–2. *digest The abuse of distance:* make it easy for you to follow the abrupt changes from place to place.

32. *force a play:* compress these far flung events into the narrow limits of a play – (literally, 'stuff a play').

34. *is set:* has set out.

34–40. The chorus talks as though the audience really will be travelling, first to Southampton, then to France, and back again to England. The journey will be so convincing that it will be necessary to charm the sea into calmness; he doesn't want anyone in the audience to be sea-sick – *We'll not offend one stomach with our play.*

41–2. *But . . . scene:* but we shall not shift the scene to Southampton until the king himself appears. It is necessary to explain this because the following scene is not in Southampton but in London.

SCENE I

Now we come down to earth with a bump, from the weighty decision-making and majestic oratory of the king in council to the petty brawling and crude jokes of some of the roughest 'layabouts' in London. The change comes as something of a relief, and moreover reminds us that not everyone in the army is as heroic as *the mirror of all Christian kings.* For these three, Nym, Bardolph, and Pistol, are joining the expedition to France – not with any intention of fighting, but because a war provides many opportunities for looting, stealing, and generally making a quick and easy profit. It is difficult to see how such men can win the rank of Corporal and Lieutenant, but they are associates of Sir John Falstaff, who was formerly a friend of the king and may have had 'influence.'

For the vulgar tone of this conversation Shakespeare drops from blank verse to informal prose, which seems more appropriate, but Pistol speaks in verse form as part of his pretence to be learned and heroic: he seems to have seen a lot of 'heroic' plays, and most of his conversation consists of sayings and phrases that he has picked up but doesn't understand.

3. *Ancient Pistol.* An Ancient was an Ensign, a junior officer or under-lieutenant whose job was to carry the flag into battle. The ranks of all three men are proudly announced in the first three lines, but Pistol and Nym have quarrelled: *are . . . you friends yet?* means 'Haven't you made it up yet?'

4–9. Nym's answer is that he and Pistol are still enemies, but he'll make it up when he feels like it. He has a habit of speaking mysteriously, as though there is a sinister threat underlying his words, but he admits he is too scared to use his *iron* (sword) except with his eyes shut, and its main purpose seems to be to toast cheese. But *it will endure cold* too: it's as good as anybody else's sword for waving around out of its scabbard. *And there's an end* is one of his 'signing off'

Confirm'd conspiracy with fearful France;
And by their hands this grace of kings must die—
If hell and treason hold their promises,
Ere he take ship for France – and in Southampton.   30
Linger your patience on, and we'll digest
The abuse of distance, force a play.
The sum is paid, the traitors are agreed,
The King is set from London, and the scene
Is now transported, gentles, to Southampton;   35
There is the play-house now, there must you sit,
And thence to France shall we convey you safe
And bring you back, charming the narrow seas
To give you gentle pass; for, if we may,
We'll not offend one stomach with our play.   40
But, till the King come forth, and not till then,
Unto Southampton do we shift our scene.

[Exit]

Scene I

London. Before the Boar's Head Tavern, Eastcheap

[Enter CORPORAL NYM *and* LIEUTENANT BARDOLPH*]*

Bardolph
    Well met, Corporal Nym.
Nym
    Good morrow, Lieutenant Bardolph.
Bardolph
    What, are Ancient Pistol and you friends yet?
Nym
    For my part, I care not; I say little, but when time shall
    serve, there shall be smiles – but that shall be as it   5
    may. I dare not fight; but I will wink and hold out
    mine iron. It is a simple one; but what though? It will

remarks, tacked onto the end of statements, *like that's the certain of it* and *that's the rendezvous of it* in his next speech: if they have a meaning at all it is 'That's the way things are and there's no more to be said on the subject.' Such phrases seem to be the ancestors of the catch-phrases of modern comedians.

10. *bestow:* make a present of. Bardolph is anxious to bring Nym and Pistol together so that all three can help each other to the rich harvest that awaits them in France.

14–15. *I will do as I may:* I shall just have to do the other thing.

15. *rest . . . rendezvous.* Both words mean 'the only thing to be done, the last resort, the only choice left,' but, like Pistol, Nym uses words without much idea of their meaning.

18. *troth-plight:* engaged to be married, but in a more solemn way than in modern engagements, less easily broken. Once you had 'plighted your troth' you were as good as married.

19. *I cannot tell:* I don't know what will come of it (also lines 23–4).

19–23. Nym is hinting darkly that he is thinking of murdering Pistol in his sleep. *though patience . . . conclusions* seems to mean that although patience is wearisome it gets its reward in the end – he may have to wait for his chance to deal with his enemy, but it will come.

Stage Direction. *Hostess:* Nell Quickly, the woman they are fighting over, is the landlady of the Boar's Head Tavera.

27–8. *host:* having married the Hostess, Pistol is now presumably the Host, but he considers the title beneath his dignity. Nym seems to be using the word to annoy Pistol, as a way of starting a fight.

28–30. Pistol's roaring, bombastic reply is typical of him. *Base tike* is just a pompous way of saying 'You lousy dog'. When he says *Nor shall my Nell keep lodgers*, he pats her hand, as if to say 'Now she is married to me she can expect to be something better than a mere lodging-house keeper.'

31–4. 'No, I shan't go on doing that much longer, because you can't put up a few honest working girls without everyone jumping to the conclusion that you're running a brothel.' Perhaps she really is running a brothel; perhaps the girls aren't all that 'honest'; but now she is married she has to appear respectable.

35. *well-a-day:* alas.

Lady: an oath, by the mother of Jesus.

toast cheese, and it will endure cold as another man's
sword will; and there's an end.

Bardolph

I will bestow a breakfast to make you friends; and we'll   10
be all three sworn brothers to France. Let't be so, good
Corporal Nym.

Nym

Faith, I will live so long as I may, that's the certain of
it; and when I cannot live any longer, I will do as I
may. That is my rest, that is the rendezvous of it.   15

Bardolph

It is certain, Corporal, that he is married to Nell
Quickly; and certainly she did you wrong, for you were
troth-plight to her.

Nym

I cannot tell; things must be as they may. Men may
sleep, and they may have their throats about them at   20
that time; and some say knives have edges. It must be
as it may; though patience be a tired mare, yet she
will plod. There must be conclusions. Well, I cannot
tell.

[Enter PISTOL *and* HOSTESS*]*

Bardolph

Here comes Ancient Pistol and his wife. Good Corporal,   25
be patient here.

Nym

How now, mine host Pistol!

Pistol

Base tike, call'st thou me host?
Now by this hand, I swear I scorn the term
Nor shall my Nell keep lodgers.   30

Hostess

No, by my troth, not long; for we cannot lodge and
board a dozen or fourteen gentlewomen that live
honestly by the prick of their needles, but it will be
thought we keep a bawdy-house straight. *[*NYM *draws]*
O well-a-day, Lady, if he be not drawn! Now we shall   35

45

37. *offer nothing here:* don't start fighting. Bardolph is the peacemaker throughout.

38. *Pish!* an exclamation of contempt.

39. *Iceland dog:* the dogs brought over from Iceland were said to be long-haired, shaggy, and bad-tempered, all of which may well fit Nym. *prick-ear'd* means with pointed ears.

41–2. *show thy valour, and put up your sword:* she contradicts herself. *Put up* means put away, and Nym could hardly show *valour* by putting his sword away; perhaps she meant 'wisdom'.

43. *shog off:* clear off.

solus: alone – he is telling the Hostess to go away because he wants Pistol on his own. However, Pistol thinks the word *solus* is another dreadful insult.

44. *egregious:* outrageous – we might use 'utter'.

45. *mervailous:* an old form of 'marvellous'.

46–9. Pistol is apparently threatening to thrust the word *solus* back down Nym's throat. *maw* could mean stomach, throat, or mouth; any way it makes nonsense of his intended climax on *And, which is worse, within thy nasty mouth!*

47. *perdy:* a corruption of the French oath 'par Dieu' (by God).

48. *nasty:* disgustingly foul (a much stronger word in Shakespeare's day).

50. *take:* ignite. Here and in *cock* Pistol is playing with his own name: 'I am primed and ready to fire.'

52. *Barbason:* the name of a devil.

conjure me: control me by magical formulae.

53. *humour:* inclination. Strictly, a 'humour' was a fluid in the body which gave a person his particular temperament; there were thought to be four of them corresponding to the four elements (see note on Prologue to Act 1, lines 1–2) but the word was frequently misused, as it is here and again in line 56.

to knock you indifferently well: to give you a damned good hiding. But Nym is too nervous to put it so bluntly.

54. *scour:* to clean vigorously something *foul* – particularly the barrel of a pistol (in this case with his rapier as a cleaning rod).

55. *if you would walk off:* a modern equivalent might be 'come outside for a moment,' (i.e. come and fight).

57. *and that's the humour of it:* another of Nym's 'and that's the way it is' remarks; likewise *in fair terms, in good terms*.

58. *braggart:* boaster.

wight: fellow.

59. *doting:* adoring, but Pistol probably uses it for its alliteration with *death*.

60. *exhale:* draw your sword (but it could also mean 'die' – breathe your last – which seems to be implied in the previous line).

see wilful adultery and murder committed.

Bardolph

Good Lieutenant, good Corporal, offer nothing here.

Nym

Pish!

Pistol

Pish for thee, Iceland dog! thou prick-ear'd cur of
Iceland! 40

Hostess

Good Corporal Nym, show thy valour, and put up
your sword.

Nym

Will you shog off? I would have you solus.

Pistol

'Solus' egregious dog? O viper vile!
The 'solus' in thy most mervailous face; 45
The 'solus' in thy teeth, and in thy throat,
And in thy hateful lungs, yea, in thy maw, perdy;
And, which is worse, within thy nasty mouth!
I do retort the 'solus' in thy bowels;
For I can take, and Pistol's cock is up, 50
And flashing fire will follow.

Nym

I am not Barbason: you cannot conjure me. I have an
humour to knock you indifferently well. If you grow
foul with me, Pistol, I will scour you with my rapier,
as I may, in fair terms; if you would walk off I would 55
prick your guts a little, in good terms, as I may, and
that's the humour of it.

Pistol

O braggart vile and damned furious wight!
The grave doth gape and doting death is near;
Therefore exhale. 60

[PISTOL draws]

Bardolph

Hear me, hear me what I say: he that strikes the

62. *I'll run him up to the hilts:* I'll stick my sword in him up to the hilt.

62–3. *as I am a soldier:* Bardolph's way of saying that he isn't afraid to do it; at all events Nym and Pistol are sufficiently impressed to sheathe their swords pretty smartly.

64. *mickle might:* a lot of force – a stock phrase from the popular ballads. *abate:* be softened.

65. Note the unnatural inverted word order.
66. *tall:* brave.

69. *'Couple a gorge!':* Pistol misquotes the French 'couper la gorge' (cut the throat). Nym's muttered threat has renewed his fury.
71. *hound of Crete:* another shaggy dog, like the Icelandic one in line 39, or possibly the Minotaur of Knossos, a mythical beast, with the body of a man and the head of a bull which fed upon human flesh. *spouse:* wife.
72–5. *to the spital go . . . espouse:* go to the hospital and drag that diseased tart Doll Tearsheet out of the V.D. ward and marry her. Veneral diseases were often treated in the *spital* (hospital) by sweating in a heated tub. *lazar* comes from Lazarus, the leper in the Bible, but was used of the victim of any loathsome disease. A *kite* is a bird of prey with hooked beak and claws, and thus, metaphorically, a prostitute, especially when linked with Cressida, the girl who, in ancient Greek legend, was unfaithful to her lover, the Trojan Troilus, and became a byword for falseness in women. Again note the high-flown language, comically inappropriate to the subject.
76. *quondam:* former. She was Mistress Quickly before she married.
77. *the only she:* the only woman in the world.
pauca: in a few words (Latin again).
78. *Go to:* to hell with you.

Stage Direction: This is Sir John Falstaff's page.
79–80. *and your hostess:* it has been suggested that this should read 'and you, hostess'.
82. *do the office of a warming-pan:* warm the bed up for him. A *warming-pan* was a metal container filled with burning coal and put into a bed to warm it. The boy is making fun of Bardolph's red face.
Faith: indeed (a shortened form of 'in faith' or 'by my faith').
84. *By my troth* (similar to 'by my faith').
he'll yield the crow a pudding: a picturesque way of saying Falstaff hasn't long to live (crows eat dead flesh).
85. *the King has kill'd his heart.* When he became king, Henry spurned his former riotous associates (as explained in Act I, Scene i). Falstaff was particularly heart-broken, partly because he was very fond of Prince Hal and partly because he had hoped for favours when his friend was on the throne.
86. *presently:* now.

first stroke I'll run him up to the hilts, as I am a
soldier.

[Draws]

Pistol

An oath of mickle might; and fury shall abate.

[PISTOL and NYM sheathe their swords]

Give me thy fist, thy fore-foot to me give;   65
Thy spirits are most tall.

Nym

I will cut thy throat one time or other, in fair terms;
that is the humour of it.

Pistol

'Couple a gorge!'
That is the word. I thee defy again.   70
O hound of Crete, think'st thou my spouse to get?
No; to the spital go,
And from the powd'ring tub of infamy
Fetch forth the lazar kite of Cressid's kind,
Doll Tearsheet she by name, and her espouse.   75
I have, and I will hold, the quondam Quickly
For the only she; and – pauca, there's enough.
Go to.

[Enter the BOY]

Boy

Mine host Pistol, you must come to my master; and
your hostess – he is very sick, and would to bed. Good   80
Bardolph, put thy face between his sheets, and do the
office of a warming-pan. Faith, he's very ill.

Bardolph

Away, you rogue.

Hostess

By my troth, he'll yield the crow a pudding one of
these days: the King has kill'd his heart. Good husband,   85
come home presently.

[Exeunt HOSTESS and BOY]

90. *Let floods . . . howl on!* Does this mean anything? Is Pistol saying 'we won't kill each other just yet'? Or is it another of his 'quotations', ranted out for the sake of alliteration?

95. *As manhood shall compound:* 'let's decide whether I'm going to pay up by fighting it out like men.'
push home: fight to a decision. But at the first sign of intervention from Bardolph both men again sheathe their swords, and Pistol even, eventually, agrees to pay.

99. *an:* if.

101. *Prithee put up:* 'I beg you, put your sword away.' *Prithee:* is a corruption of 'I pray thee'.
103. *noble*: equivalent to 33 pence at that time. It would hurt Pistol's pride to pay up in full.
present pay: hard cash, and immediate payment, as opposed to the liquor and friendship which he also offers.
105. *combine:* bind us together.
106. *I'll live . . . me:* 'we'll help each other to make a living.' Pistol is obviously proposing a sort of brotherhood of thieves.
107. *sutler:* a camp-follower who sold provisions to the army – and made a lot of money by doing so. But a sutler was not a member of the army, as Pistol seems to be; *I shall sutler be* is probably wishful thinking.

Bardolph

Come, shall I make you two friends? We must to France together; why the devil should we keep knives to cut one another's throats?

Pistol

Let floods o'erswell, and fiends for food howl on!   90

Nym

You'll pay me the eight shillings I won of you at betting?

Pistol

Base is the slave that pays.

Nym

That now I will have; that's the humour of it.

Pistol

As manhood shall compound: push home.   95

[PISTOL and NYM draw]

Bardolph

By this sword, he that makes the first thrust I'll kill him; by this sword, I will.

Pistol

Sword is an oath, and oaths must have their course.

[Sheathes his sword]

Bardolph

Corporal Nym, an thou wilt be friends, be friends; an thou wilt not, why then be enemies with me too. 100 Prithee put up.

Nym

I shall have my eight shillings I won of you at betting?

Pistol

A noble shalt thou have, and present pay;
And liquor likewise will I give to thee,
And friendship shall combine, and brotherhood.   105
I'll live by Nym and Nym shall live by me.
Is not this just? For I shall sutler be

113. *As ever you come of women:* literally, 'If you were born the sons of women' (i.e. if you're human). We might say 'if you've got any human feelings'. Hostess is in a panic because Falstaff is dying.

115. *quotidian tertain.* A *quotidian* is an illness which causes bouts of fever every day, but a *tertian* causes them on alternate days. She contradicts herself: she obviously doesn't understand the medical terms.

117. *run bad humours on the knight:* made Falstaff ill by being so cruel to him.

120. *fracted and corroborate.* Pistol means broken, but *fracted* (having a part displaced) hardly describes a broken heart, and *corroborate* (to make stronger) is even more absurd. He uses the words because they sound impressive.

122. *he passes some humours and careers:* 'you never know what the king's going to do next, but when he does it he goes flat out.' Again, this seems to be what Nym means; we can only guess, but it is in fact a fairly accurate description of Henry. *humours* seems to mean 'whims and fancies' here; but Shakespeare is making fun of the way the word was used in his day to mean almost anything. In *The Merry Wives of Windsor* Nym carries this to even more ridiculous lengths. 'To pass a career' was to ride a horse flat out for a short distance.

123. *condole:* we should say 'condole with' (sympathize with). Pistol may have meant 'console'.

123. *we will live:* old Sir John may die, but we're going to have a good time. Pistol puts his arms round his mates and leads them into the Tavern, their happy anticipation of the future only slightly dimmed by the sad news about Falstaff.

SCENE II

1. *these traitors:* the ones mentioned in the Prologue to this Act. The king has been informed of their plot to kill him, but is waiting for the right moment before arresting them (as we see later in this scene). Meanwhile he is behaving as though he trusts them, casually mingling with them and chatting as though he were in no danger. Bedford speaks angrily – the alliteration of *trust these traitors* is spat out – and indeed all three nobles express disgust in these first eleven lines.

2. *apprehended by and by:* arrested soon.

Unto the camp, and profits will accrue.
Give me thy hand.

Nym [Sheathing his sword]
I shall have my noble? 110

Pistol
In cash most justly paid.

Nym [Shaking hands]
Well, then, that's the humour of't.

[Re-enter HOSTESS]

Hostess
As ever you come of women, come in quickly to Sir
John. Ah, poor heart! he is so shak'd of a burning
quotidian tertian that it is most lamentable to behold. 115
Sweet men, come to him.

Nym
The King hath run bad humours on the knight; that's
the even of it.

Pistol
Nym, thou hast spoke the right;
His heart is fracted and corroborate. 120

Nym
The King is a good king, but it must be as it may; he
passes some humours and careers.

Pistol
Let us condole the knight; for, lambkins, we will live.

[Exeunt]

Scene II

Southampton. A council-chamber

[Enter EXETER, BEDFORD, and WESTMORELAND]

Bedford
Fore God, his Grace is bold, to trust these traitors.

Exeter
They shall be apprehended by and by.

3. *smooth and even:* unruffled.

4–5. *As if allegiance . . . loyalty:* as if the thought of being disloyal had never entered their heads.

7. The traitors do not know that news of the plot has leaked.

8. *Nay, but:* a way of introducing an exclamation. We might say 'It's unbelievable!'

his bedfellow refers to Scroop who had been a particularly close friend of Henry's – see lines 93–102.

9. Henry had shown so much kindness to Scroop that Scroop must have become tired of it. *dull'd and cloy'd* usually referred to the appetite losing its edge and then turning to sickness as a result of over-eating.

12. The wind is in the right direction for the journey to France and the king is anxious to go aboard. In his last council meeting before sailing he pretends he wants to discuss prospects in the war, but his real purpose appears later.

14. *And you, my gentle knight:* addressed to Grey. Calling him *gentle* (noble) is part of Henry's act; his conversation with the traitors is full of irony.

17–18. *Doing the execution . . . assembled them:* Destroying the French army and achieving the purpose for which I have mustered them.

18. *in head:* in a body.

20. *well persuaded:* convinced.

21–2. *We carry not . . . ours:* 'there is not a single man coming with me who is not one hundred per cent on my side.' An interesting bit of dramatic irony: the audience know full well that the very men the king is talking to are not *in a fair consent*, but his remark is still true, because they will not in fact be making the trip.

23–4. Even this is true: he will not be leaving the traitors behind, because they will be dead. The treble negative *Nor . . . not . . . not* is confusing; as often in Shakespeare it is one too many, and should be a double negative, with the positive meaning 'Everyone we leave behind wishes *etc.*'

25. All three traitors now put on a thoroughly nauseating display of sham loyalty and obsequiousness: if we hated them for their treachery we now despise them for their hypocrisy.

fear'd here means respected.

Westmoreland
    How smooth and even they do bear themselves,
    As if allegiance in their bosoms sat,
    Crowned with faith and constant loyalty!   5
Bedford
    The King hath note of all that they intend,
    By interception which they dream not of.
Exeter
    Nay, but the man that was his bedfellow,
    Whom he hath dull'd and cloy'd with gracious favours—
    That he should, for a foreign purse, so sell   10
    His sovereign's life to death and treachery!

      [Trumpets sound. Enter the KING, SCROOP,
        CAMBRIDGE, GREY, *and* ATTENDANTS*]*

King
    Now sits the wind fair, and we will aboard.
    My Lord of Cambridge, and my kind Lord of Masham,
    And you, my gentle knight, give me your thoughts.
    Think you not that the pow'rs we bear with us   15
    Will cut their passage through the force of France,
    Doing the execution and the act
    For which we have in head assembled them?
Scroop
    No doubt, my liege, if each man do his best.
King
    I doubt not that, since we are well persuaded   20
    We carry not a heart with us from hence
    That grows not in a fair consent with ours;
    Nor leave not one behind that doth not wish
    Success and conquest to attend on us.
Cambridge
    Never was monarch better fear'd and lov'd   25
    Than is your Majesty. There's not, I think, a subject
    That sits in heart-grief and uneasiness
    Under the sweet shade of your government.

30. *steep'd their galls in honey:* turned their former bitterness into sweetness and become your friends.
gall: (bile) a very bitter body fluid, which was thought to cause bitter feelings.
31. *create:* created, made up.
33–5. *And shall forget . . . worthiness:* I shall forget how to write my own name before I forget to give a suitable reward to those who deserve it. *office* here means the work the hand usually does, *quittance:* suitable reward, *desert:* what is deserved (the noun from the verb 'to deserve'). Again, dramatic irony – he is about to reward them suitably.
36–8. *So service . . . services:* With the hope of such rewards and appreciation as you have just mentioned, your servants will work untiringly to be constantly useful to you. Scroop is really grovelling, and it is all the more sickening because we know his *desert* exactly.

39. *We judge no less:* 'I'm sure you're right.'
40. *Enlarge:* set free.
committed: arrested.
41. *rail'd against our person:* shouted abuse at me.
42. *set him on:* made him do it.
43. *on his more advice:* now that he's sobered up and thought better of it.

44–6. *That's mercy . . . kind:* 'that's merciful of you, but also rather over-confident. You really ought to punish him, in case other people, seeing him get away with it, follow his example.'
sufferance: 'being tolerated'.

47. *O, let us yet be merciful.* The king is leading the traitors further into the trap.

49–50. 'You will be acting mercifully if you spare his life, even though you punish him severely.' A harsh attitude which will ensure that he, Grey, will get no mercy when his turn comes.

52. *heavy orisons:* powerful arguments.
53–6. *If little faults . . . that man:* 'If I can't turn a blind eye to trivial offences like this that are only the result of a bit too much to drink, there will be no punishment severe enough for really serious crimes that have been carefully and deliberately planned in cold blood. I still (*yet*) insist on setting that man free.'

Grey

    True: those that were your father's enemies

    Have steep'd their galls in honey, and do serve you   30

    With hearts create of duty and of zeal.

King

    We therefore have great cause of thankfulness,

    And shall forget the office of our hand

    Sooner than quittance of desert and merit

    According to the weight and worthiness.   35

Scroop

    So service shall with steeled sinews toil,

    And labour shall refresh itself with hope,

    To do your Grace incessant services.

King

    We judge no less. Uncle of Exeter,

    Enlarge the man committed yesterday   40

    That rail'd against our person. We consider

    It was excess of wine that set him on;

    And on his more advice we pardon him.

Scroop

    That's mercy, but too much security.

    Let him be punish'd, sovereign, lest example   45

    Breed, by his sufferance, more of such a kind.

King

    O, let us yet be merciful!

Cambridge

    So may your Highness, and yet punish too.

Grey

    Sir,

    You show great mercy if you give him life,

    After the taste of much correction.   50

King

    Alas, your too much love and care of me

    Are heavy orisons 'gainst this poor wretch!

    If little faults proceeding on distemper

    Shall not be wink'd at, how shall we stretch our eye

    When capital crimes, chew'd, swallow'd, and digested,   55

57–8. *dear care And tender preservation.* Would the king say this with obvious sarcasm, or would he try to say it as though he meant it?

60. *the late commissioners:* the officials recently appointed (*late*) to govern the country in the king's absence. The three traitors are not really so privileged: the king has chosen this highly dramatic way of handing them the warrants for their arrest.

62. *it:* the document confirming the appointment as commissioner.

68. *know I know your worthiness:* these papers will show you that I know exactly what you're worth. He says this quite innocently, then turns to other matters. But the irony of his words is immediately clear to the traitors, who turn pale with horror as they read their death-warrants.

72. *complexion:* colour in the cheeks.

74–5. *cowarded and chas'd your blood Out of appearance:* made your blood run like a coward out of sight.

78. *quick:* alive and active.
but late: a little while ago.

79. *counsel:* advice.

81. *your own reasons turn into your bosoms:* a few minutes ago you yourselves were arguing against mercy, and now your own arguments are going to be the death of you. Note how the king has led the traitors into this position.

Appear before us? We'll yet enlarge that man,
Though Cambridge, Scroop, and Grey, in their dear
    care
And tender preservation of our person,
Would have him punish'd. And now to our French
    causes:
Who are the late commissioners?   60
Cambridge
I one, my lord.
Your Highness bade me ask for it to-day.
Scroop
So did you me, my liege.
Grey
And I, my royal sovereign.
King
Then, Richard Earl of Cambridge, there is yours;   65
There yours, Lord Scroop of Masham; and, Sir
    Knight,
Grey of Northumberland, this same is yours.
Read them, and know I know your worthiness.
My Lord of Westmoreland, and uncle Exeter,
We will aboard to-night. Why, how now, gentlemen? 70
What see you in those papers, that you lose
So much complexion? Look ye how they change!
Their cheeks are paper. Why, what read you there
That have so cowarded and chas'd your blood
Out of appearance?
Cambridge
                    I do confess my fault,   75
And do submit me to your Highness' mercy.
Grey, Scroop
To which we all appeal.
King
The mercy that was quick in us but late
By your own counsel is suppress'd and kill'd.
You must not dare, for shame, to talk of mercy;   80
For your own reasons turn into your bosoms
As dogs upon their masters, worrying you.
See you, my princes and my noble peers,

84. *These English monsters!* To the Elizabethans, *monsters* were the hideously deformed creatures sometimes displayed for public entertainment as freaks (the modern word is 'monstrosities') but they were usually associated with distant lands; these monsters are more remarkable because they are English.

85–7. *You know . . . honour:* 'you know how ready I was in my regard for him to see that he was given everything a man of his position should have.'

88. *light . . . lightly.* The Elizabethan audience would see the point of this play on words more easily than we do: *light* meant not only light in weight or colour but also 'easily gained' (like a loose woman, for example). Here it suggests that Cambridge was an easy target for the French bribes, which were worthless compared with the soul that he gave in return.

89. *practices:* plots.

90. *Hampton:* Southampton.

91. *This knight:* he turns to Grey now, who is just as indebted to him as Cambridge. *bounty:* generosity.

94. *Ingrateful.* The modern word is ungrateful.

95. *didst bear the key of all my counsels:* knew all my secrets. Scroop had been a particularly close and confidential friend.

97–8. *That almost . . . use:* 'you might have turned me into gold for yourself if you had wanted to take advantage of our friendship.'

99–101. The king finds it difficult to believe that Scroop could be bribed to hurt even his little finger, let alone murder him.

102. *gross:* plainly visible.

104–9. The main idea in this difficult passage is that whereas usually nobody is surprised to find that a man with treason in his heart wants to commit murder, Scroop does astonish everybody because he of all people should feel a natural desire to protect the king.

yoke-devils. This suggests that treason and murder are two devils yoked together (harnessed together) like a couple of oxen pulling a cart; they are obliged to work together (*sworn to either's purpose*). *admiration* used to mean 'surprise and wonder', and *whoop* is an exclamation of surprise.

proportion in this context means 'what one would naturally expect'.

108–9. 'Made treason and murder things to be looked at in incredulous horror.'

111. *That wrought . . . preposterously:* prevailed on you so unnaturally.

112. *got the voice:* won the prize (*voice* here means vote).

113. *suggest by treasons:* tempt men by suggesting treason to them.

114–16. *Do botch . . . piety:* dress the damnable act up to look attractive, reasonable, even glossily pious.

botch and bungle suggests that the devils do the job very clumsily, they just throw a rough-and-ready disguise together, but in Scroop's case it wasn't necessary even to do that.

fetch'd means 'derived'.

117. *temper'd:* worked on.

119. *to dub thee with the name of traitor:* to give you the new title of 'traitor'. To *dub* is to confer a special rank on a person, particularly a knighthood.

These English monsters! My Lord of Cambridge
   here—
You know how apt our love was to accord   85
To furnish him with all appertinents
Belonging to his honour; and this man
Hath, for a few light crowns, lightly conspir'd,
And sworn unto the practices of France
To kill us here in Hampton; to the which   90
This knight, no less for bounty bound to us
Than Cambridge is, hath likewise sworn. But, O,
What shall I say to thee, Lord Scroop, thou cruel,
Ingrateful, savage, and inhuman creature?
Thou that didst bear the key of all my counsels,   95
That knew'st the very bottom of my soul,
That almost mightst have coin'd me into gold,
Wouldst thou have practis'd on me for thy use—
May it be possible that foreign hire
Could out of thee extract one spark of evil   100
That might annoy my finger? 'Tis so strange
That, though the truth of it stands off as gross
As black and white, my eye will scarcely see it.
Treason and murder ever kept together,
As two yoke-devils sworn to either's purpose,   105
Working so grossly in a natural cause
That admiration did not whoop at them;
But thou, 'gainst all proportion, didst bring in
Wonder to wait on treason and on murder;
And whatsoever cunning fiend it was   110
That wrought upon thee so preposterously
Hath got the voice in hell for excellence;
And other devils that suggest by treasons
Do botch and bungle up damnation
With patches, colours, and with forms, being fetch'd 115
From glist'ring semblances of piety;
But he that temper'd thee bade thee stand up,
Gave thee no instance why thou shouldst do treason,
Unless to dub thee with the name of traitor.

120–4. Henry's feelings about Scroop prompt him to refer again and again to hell and the devils; he seems to feel that, whereas other traitors have motives, Scroop has no motive other than sheer evil. The devil who tempted him hardly had to try. *gull'd:* 'made a fool of'. *Tartar:* another name for hell (from Tartarus, the fiery region in classical mythology). *lion gait* echoes a verse in the Bible in which the devil is seen as a 'roaring lion', who 'walketh about, seeking whom he may devour'. (Peter 1, 8).

123. *legions:* of the damned.

125–6. *O, how hast thou . . . affiance!* Scroop's behaviour means that all trust between people will now be tainted with suspicion. The king returns to this theme later in lines 138–40.

126–36. Scroop has every good quality, or so it seemed.

130. *spare in diet:* restrained in eating habits, not a glutton.

131. *or of mirth or anger:* either of mirth or of anger.

132. *not swerving with the blood:* stable, not moody or subject to violent changes of feeling.

133. *Garnish'd and deck'd in modest complement.* This probably refers to all the external signs of personality, such as dress, looks, manners, talents, and accomplishments. It suggests a man whose inner character is *garnish'd and deck'd* (pleasingly fitted out) with an outward attractiveness that is not pretentious and showy but does make him a complete man.

134–5. *Not working . . . neither:* not trusting his senses unless they supported each other, and even then only when their evidence was a cold certainty. *purged:* purified, rid of any foreign matter; *purged judgment* is free from prejudice and unclouded by strong feelings.

136. 'You seemed to be just as refined and free from vice as these men I have described.' A *bolt* was a sieve for sifting flour, to get rid of coarse grains and impurities.

138. *the full-fraught man and best indued:* the man who is best endowed with good qualities and valuable gifts. The idea here is similar to that in lines 126–7: if a man as perfect as Scroop can't be trusted, from now on every man, no matter how trustworthy he seems, will be under suspicion.

139. *I will weep for thee.* At several moments during his remarks to Scroop, Henry seems on the verge of tears, which is natural enough on finding a loved and trusted friend plotting to kill him.

141. *Another fall of man.* The original *fall of man* was Adam's sin in the Garden of Eden, since when all men have been sinful. This sin of Scroop's will also affect all men (as explained in lines 126–7 and 139) and seems as horrifying as Adam's. *Their faults are open.* With the ruthless insistence on justice that was characteristic of him, the king masters his feelings and passes the cold judgment which condemns the traitors to death.

142. *to the answer of the law:* to receive the punishment required by law.

If that same demon that hath gull'd thee thus   120
Should with his lion gait walk the whole world,
He might return to vasty Tartar back,
And tell the legions 'I can never win
A soul so easy as that Englishman's'.
O, how hast thou with jealousy infected   125
The sweetness of affiance! Show men dutiful?
Why, so didst thou. Seem they grave and learned?
Why, so didst thou. Come they of noble family?
Why, so didst thou. Seem they religious?
Why, so didst thou. Or are they spare in diet,   130
Free from gross passion or of mirth or anger,
Constant in spirit, not swerving with the blood,
Garnish'd and deck'd in modest complement,
Not working with the eye without the ear,
And but in purged judgment trusting neither?   135
Such and so finely bolted didst thou seem;
And thus thy fall hath left a kind of blot
To mark the full-fraught man and best indued
With some suspicion. I will weep for thee,
For this revolt of thine, methinks, is like   140
Another fall of man. Their faults are open.
Arrest them to the answer of the law;

143. *And God acquit them of their practices!* May God spare them eternal punishment for their sins.

150. *discover'd:* revealed.

151–3. Scroop sounds genuinely repentant (as do the other two); no doubt he is considerably moved by Henry's passionate condemnation, and now regrets his treason and asks forgiveness for it, although he knows he is going to be executed anyway. He does not expect mercy for his body, but perhaps his soul will be forgiven. When Cambridge and Grey echo this feeling (they *rejoice* in the discovery of their plot) we are satisfied that all England is in harmony again, and that the king's words in lines 20–4 are true after all.

154–6. Cambridge admits that the French bribe was in his case only an added incentive to his real intention, which was to put his brother-in-law, the Earl of March, on the throne. (March had a better claim than King Henry. Nevertheless, a king was sacred, the Lord's Anointed', and treason was a kind of blasphemy.)

158. *in sufferance:* in suffering my punishment. *rejoice:* rejoice at.

159. *Beseeching:* begging, imploring.

160–4. Grey claims to be as happy about the discovery of the treason as any *faithful* (utterly loyal) subject would be. Like Scroop, he asks for his body to be punished but his fault forgiven.

165. *quit:* acquit, forgive. They may hope for mercy from God, but not from the king.

167. *an enemy proclaim'd:* an enemy against whom we have officially declared war, i.e. France.

168. *the golden earnest of our death:* an advance payment pledging the conspirators to kill the king.

170. *servitude:* slavery, or subjection to a foreign power. But this would not have been the result of putting the English Earl of March on the throne. The king seems to be exaggerating here and in the following lines, although no doubt some form of civil war would have followed his assassination.

173–4. *Touching our person . . . tender:* 'I am not interested in any purely personal revenge for the threat on my life; but I do have to guard the security of my country so carefully . . .'

And God acquit them of their practices!

Exeter

I arrest thee of high treason, by the name of Richard
Earl of Cambridge.   145

I arrest thee of high treason, by the name of Henry
Lord Scroop of Masham.

I arrest thee of high treason, by the name of Thomas
Grey, knight, of Northumberland.

Scroop

Our purposes God justly hath discover'd,   150
And I repent my fault more than my death;
Which I beseech your Highness to forgive,
Although my body pay the price of it.

Cambridge

For me, the gold of France did not seduce,
Although I did admit it as a motive   155
The sooner to effect what I intended;
But God be thanked for prevention,
Which I in sufferance heartily will rejoice,
Beseeching God and you to pardon me.

Grey

Never did faithful subject more rejoice   160
At the discovery of most dangerous treason
Than I do at this hour joy o'er myself,
Prevented from a damned enterprise.
My fault, but not my body, pardon, sovereign.

King

God quit you in his mercy! Hear your sentence.   165
You have conspir'd against our royal person,
Join'd with an enemy proclaim'd, and from his coffers
Receiv'd the golden earnest of our death;
Wherein you would have sold your king to slaughter,
His princes and his peers to servitude,   170
His subjects to oppression and contempt,
And his whole kingdom into desolation.
Touching our person seek we no revenge;
But we our kingdom's safety must so tender,

178–9. *The taste whereof . . . endure:* 'and I hope God gives you the patience to endure the pain of death.'

180. *dear:* very serious.

181. Henry seems to have no difficulty in switching his mind at once to the subject of the war. The past is over and done with: now for the future. A lesser man might have been too emotionally disturbed by the previous episode to be able to think clearly about anything else for some time.

182. *Shall be to you as us like glorious:* 'shall bring as much glory to you as to me'.

like: alike.

183. *We doubt not of:* I am confident we shall have.

186–7. *we doubt not . . . way:* I am confident now that every obstacle has been cleared from our path.

rub. This is a term from bowls, a game in which large wooden balls are rolled along the grass towards a target; any unevenness in the surface of the grass which diverts the ball is called a *rub*.

188–9. *let us deliver . . . God:* let us ask God for his blessing on our army.

190. *straight in expedition:* immediately in motion.

191. *Cheerly to sea:* let us joyfully put to sea.

the signs of war advance: raise the flags and banners carried by the army.

192. *No king . . . France:* 'I don't want to be king of England unless I am also King of France.' Notice the contrast between this mood of joyful anticipation and the sombre pessimism of a few moments ago. The new mood is emphasized by an exciting *flourish* on the trumpets.

SCENE III

1–2. The three rogues and the boy are setting off to join the king's forces at Southampton; the hostess wants to accompany her husband part of the way, as far as Staines.

3. *earn:* grieve (a variation of 'yearn'). He is grieving because Falstaff is dead.

4. *blithe:* gay.

rouse thy vaunting veins: stir up your enthusiasm.

vaunting veins. This is another of Pistol's meaningless alliterations; he probably means 'blood', the 'humour' which was thought to produce spirit and optimism (see note on Act II, Scene i, line 53). He is trying to cheer his comrades up.

7. *wheresome'er:* wherever. Falstaff having been the man he was, there is a fair chance that he is in hell.

Whose ruin you have sought, that to her laws   175
We do deliver you. Get you therefore hence,
Poor miserable wretches, to your death;
The taste whereof God of his mercy give
You patience to endure, and true repentance
Of all your dear offences. Bear them hence.   180

[Exeunt CAMBRIDGE, SCROOP, and GREY, guarded]

Now, lords, for France; the enterprise whereof
Shall be to you as us like glorious.
We doubt not of a fair and lucky war,
Since God so graciously hath brought to light
This dangerous treason, lurking in our way   185
To hinder our beginnings; we doubt not now
But every rub is smoothed on our way.
Then, forth, dear countrymen; let us deliver
Our puissance into the hand of God,
Putting it straight in expedition.   190
Cheerly to sea; the signs of war advance;
No king of England, if not king of France!

[Flourish. Exeunt.]

Scene III

Eastcheap. Before the Boar's Head tavern

[Enter PISTOL, HOSTESS, NYM, BARDOLPH, and BOY]

Hostess
    Prithee, honey-sweet husband, let me bring thee to
    Staines.
Pistol
    No; for my manly heart doth earn.
    Bardolph, be blithe; Nym, rouse thy vaunting veins;
    Boy, bristle thy courage up. For Falstaff he is dead,   5
    And we must earn therefore.
Bardolph
    Would I were with him, wheresome'er he is, either in
    heaven or in hell!

9. *Arthur's bosom:* heaven, but she has confused the Biblical expression 'Abraham's bosom' (Luke 22, 16) with the legend of King Arthur.

10–11. *'A made a finer end . . . christom child:* He died as peacefully as if he had been an innocent baby. *finer* seems to be another of Hostess's slips of the tongue, and *christom* is a mispronunciation of 'chrisom'. (A 'chrisom child' was one who died within a month of being baptized.) Note that she often says 'a' for 'he'. In spite of her comic language, the Hostess's genuine emotion comes through.

16–17. *'a babbl'd of green fields:* perhaps Falstaff was dreaming, as he approached death, of the 'green pastures' of Psalm 23, and talking incoherently about them.

19–20. *'a should not think of God:* she means he should not worry yet about the need to make his peace with God before dying. In her clumsy way she was trying to reassure him that he would live for a long time. Her account is full of unconscious humour, which would seem quite appropriate to an audience who had grown to love the rogueries of Falstaff in *Henry IV*.

26. *of sack:* against sack. *Sack* is a name for a sherry-type wine to which Falstaff had been addicted and which had probably been partly responsible for his illness.

28. Bardolph unkindly suggests that Falstaff also blamed his association with women for his condition, and although the Hostess denies it the boy confirms it.

30–1. *incarnate . . . carnation:* *incarnate* means in bodily form, disguised as human beings, but the Boy is better educated than the Hostess, who misunderstands it as *carnation* (the colour of flesh).

33. *the devil would have him about women:* the devil would take his soul as punishment for his immoral dealings with women.

34. *in some sort . . . handle women:* make some sort of mention of women, (but of course the Hostess is again unconsciously using words which can be understood in a different meaning).

35–6. *the Whore of Babylon:* a whore is a prostitute, but the expression *Whore of Babylon* was often used in Shakespeare's time for the Church of Rome; probably the Hostess mistook Falstaff's comments on it as talk about women. *rheumatic:* Hostess's word for delirious (lunatic perhaps?).

Hostess

Nay, sure, he's not in hell: he's in Arthur's bosom, if
ever man went to Arthur's bosom. 'A made a finer end, 10
and went away an it had been any christom child; 'a
parted ev'n just between twelve and one, ev'n at the
turning ô th' tide; for after I saw him fumble with the
sheets, and play with flowers, and smile upon his
fingers' end, I knew there was but one way; for his 15
nose was as sharp as a pen, and 'a babbl'd of green
fields. 'How now, Sir John!' quoth I 'What, man, be ô
good cheer.' So 'a cried out 'God, God, God!' three or
four times. Now I, to comfort him, bid him 'a should
not think of God; I hop'd there was no need to trouble 20
himself with any such thoughts yet. So a' bade me lay
more clothes on his feet; I put my hand into the bed
and felt them, and they were as cold as any stone;
then I felt to his knees, and so upward and upward,
and all was as cold as any stone. 25

Nym

They say he cried out of sack.

Hostess

Ay, that 'a did.

Bardolph

And of women.

Hostess

Nay, that 'a did not.

Boy

Yes, that a' did, and said they were devils incarnate. 30

Hostess

'A could never abide carnation; 'twas a colour he never
lik'd.

Boy

'A said once the devil would have him about women.

Hostess

'A did in some sort, indeed, handle women; but then
he was rheumatic, and talk'd of the Whore of 35
Babylon.

37–9. Another cheeky comment by the boy on the colour of Bardolph's nose (the first was in Act II, Scene i, lines 81–2).

40. *the fuel:* the alcohol that Falstaff had given Bardolph; this, as strong drink is said to do, had turned his nose red, and this apparently was the only payment Bardolph ever received for his services.

42. *Shall we shog?* Shall we get going?

45. *chattels:* possessions (now in his wife's safekeeping).

46. *Let senses rule.* Pistol's parting words to his wife are on the theme of looking after herself and his property, keeping her wits about her and not trusting anyone. ***Pitch and Pay*** means 'Payment by cash; no credit.'

48. *straws . . . wafer-cakes:* things easily broken.

49. *Holdfast:* holding on to what you've got, from the proverb: 'Brag (boast) is a good dog, but Holdfast is a better.'

50. *Caveto* (ka-vee'to): wariness (a Latin word which strictly means 'be wary').

51. *clear thy crystals:* dry your eyes.

Yoke-fellows in arms: fellow soldiers.

53. Pistol is presumably referring, with pretended ferocity, to the blood of the French enemy, but knowing what we do about his intention to make money we may interpret it as the lifeblood (i.e. money) of his own troops.

54. The Boy's reply sounds apprehensive, as if he were saying 'And that won't do us much good.' Later in the play (Act III, Scene ii) he openly expresses his regret at ever having allied himself with these three.

58. *Let housewifery appear; keep close:* Pistol commands his wife to devote her time to looking after the house, and not to go out where she might get into mischief. And so saying he leads his little party off on an enterprise which is nothing but mischief.

Boy

Do you not remember a' saw a flea stick upon
Bardolph's nose, and 'a said it was a black soul burning
in hell?

Bardolph

Well, the fuel is gone that maintain'd that fire: that's   40
all the riches I got in his service.

Nym

Shall we shog? The King will be gone from Southampton.

Pistol

Come, let's away. My love, give me thy lips.
Look to my chattels and my moveables;   45
Let senses rule. The word is 'Pitch and Pay'.
Trust none;
For oaths are straws, men's faiths are wafer-cakes,
And Holdfast is the only dog, my duck.
Therefore, Caveto be thy counsellor.   50
Go, clear thy crystals. Yoke-fellows in arms,
Let us to France, like horse-leeches, my boys,
To suck, to suck, the very blood to suck.

Boy

And that's but unwholesome food, they say.

Pistol

Touch her soft mouth and march.   55

Bardolph

Farewell, hostess.

[Kissing her]

Nym

I cannot kiss, that is the humour of it; but, adieu.

Pistol

Let housewifery appear; keep close, I thee command.

Hostess

Farewell; adieu.

[Exeunt]

SCENE IV

King Charles VI of France, whom we now meet, suffered from bouts of insanity, and although Shakespeare has made him seem more or less sane in this play we inevitably find ourselves comparing him unfavourably with his English counterpart. He is old and feeble, and has little control over his son the Dauphin; he has heard about the great gatherings of men and arms that have been going on in the south of England, and about the failure of his plot to have Henry assassinated, and now that the English army is on its way he seems to be almost quaking with fear; above all, when he can bring himself to make a decision, it does not seem to receive unquestioning respect.

2–3. *And more than carefully . . . defences:* 'It is a matter of extreme and anxious concern to me that our defences are effective.'

6. *dispatch:* promptness of action.

7. *line:* strengthen, reinforce.

8. *means defendant:* means of defence, ramparts, weapons etc.

9. *England:* here used to refer to the king of England.

10. *gulf:* whirlpool, a striking simile for the frightening strength and speed of the English.

11–14. *It fits us . . . fields:* It would therefore be common sense to take whatever precautions are indicated by our respect for the English, remembering those previous occasions when they thrashed us because we didn't take them seriously enough. He is referring to the English victories at Crécy (1346) and Poitiers (1356).

fatal: deadly because underestimated (*neglected*).

14. *redoubted:* literally 'dreaded', but we should say 'respected'.

15. *most meet we arm us:* quite right that we should arm ourselves.

16–25. The Dauphin has already indicated his contempt for Henry in the message he sent with the tennis balls in Act I, Scene ii, and now he resents his father's talk of fearing the English. 'By all means let's be ready for war – any country, no matter how peaceful, should be prepared – but let us not imagine that we have anything to fear from the English.'

17. *Though war nor no known quarrel.* Shakespeare's negatives are sometimes confusing. We should say 'Though neither war nor any known quarrel'.

18. *musters:* companies of soldiers who can be called on when needed. Modern services have the term 'muster-parade', in which the men are counted and inspected.

20. *As were a war in expectation:* as though a war were expected.

25. *a Whitsun morris-dance:* a dance often performed in England at Whitsun (Whitsunday in the Christian calendar is the seventh Sunday after Easter). As the dancers blackened their faces for the occasion they were thought to represent Moors; hence 'Moorish' and eventually 'morris'.

26–9. An echo of his earlier remarks about Henry, who, the Dauphin thinks, is too idle and childish to be worth worrying about.

26. *idly king'd:* ruled by such a frivolous fellow.

Scene IV

France. The King's palace

[Flourish. Enter the FRENCH KING, *the* DAUPHIN, *the*
DUKES OF BERRI *and* BRITAINE, *the* CONSTABLE, *and*
OTHERS]*

French King
    Thus comes the English with full power upon us;
    And more than carefully it us concerns
    To answer royally in our defences.
    Therefore the Dukes of Berri and of Britaine,
    Of Brabant and of Orleans, shall make forth,   5
    And you, Prince Dauphin, with all swift dispatch,
    To line and new repair our towns of war
    With men of courage and with means defendant;
    For England his approaches makes as fierce
    As waters to the sucking of a gulf.   10
    It fits us, then, to be as provident
    As fear may teach us, out of late examples
    Left by the fatal and neglected English
    Upon our fields.
Dauphin
              My most redoubted father,
    It is most meet we arm us 'gainst the foe;   15
    For peace itself should not so dull a kingdom,
    Though war nor no known quarrel were in question,
    But that defences, musters, preparations,
    Should be maintain'd, assembled, and collected,
    As were a war in expectation.   20
    Therefore, I say, 'tis meet we all go forth
    To view the sick and feeble parts of France;
    And let us do it with no show of fear—
    No, with no more than if we heard that England
    Were busied with a Whitsun morris-dance;   25
    For, my good liege, she is so idly king'd,

27. *sceptre:* a gold rod set with jewels which traditionally the king carries as a symbol of his royal authority.

28. *humorous:* unbalanced.

29. *O peace:* 'hey, wait a minute'.

31. *Question your Grace the late ambassadors:* let your Grace ask the ambassadors who recently returned from England.

32. *great state:* impressive dignity.

34–5. *How modest in exception . . . resolution:* how restrained when expressing disagreement, yet how frightening in his firm steadfastness.

36. *vanities forespent:* previous foolishness.

37. *the Roman Brutus:* one of the first consuls of Rome (much earlier than the Brutus who assassinated Julius Caesar), who pretended to be stupid in order to disguise his plans for the liberation of Rome from the tyrant Tarquin.

39. *ordure:* dung, the mulch put round delicate plants to protect and nourish them. The Constable's point is similar to Ely's strawberry idea in Act I, Scene i, lines 60–4 but more logically expressed: the dung is filthy in itself, but it is put down deliberately for the sake of the precious life underneath.

40. *first spring:* show early growth (when there is still a danger of frost).

41. *Well, 'tis not so:* you can say what you like, but you're wrong and I'm right – typical of the Dauphin's brash arrogance, which we in the audience are able to recognize because we know that the Constable is right. He appears here and elsewhere in the play as a wise and experienced statesman, in contrast to the Dauphin.

42–8. The Dauphin concedes that it is better to over-estimate an enemy so that the defences are at least adequate. Planning defence too weakly would be to make the same mistake as a miser who spoils his clothes by trying to economize on cloth.

46. *Which of:* which being of, i.e. if these are.

48. *Think we King Harry strong:* Let us assume that King Henry's army is powerful.

49. *look you:* make sure that you.

50. *The kindred . . . us:* his ancestors got their training by killing us. Hawks and hounds were *flesh'd* (given flesh to eat) to develop their appetite for hunting.

51. *bred out of that bloody strain:* an offspring of that bloodthirsty family.

52. 'That harried us on our own ground.'

53–64. In Act I, Scene ii, lines 105–114 Canterbury glowed with pride as he told this same story about Edward III watching the Black Prince proving himself at the Battle of Crécy; now we hear the other side's view. For the French King it was a shameful disaster he can never forget; even the *Black* in the victor's name has a special horrifying meaning for him; the English soundly defeated the young men who were the pride of France; and his voice quivers with anguish at the thought of the same thing happening again. *the work of nature* and *the patterns that by God etc.*, are expressions that suggest that these young men were perfect, the result of twenty years' careful training.

Her sceptre so fantastically borne
By a vain, giddy, shallow, humorous youth,
That fear attends her not.

Constable

              O peace, Prince Dauphin!
You are too much mistaken in this king.   30
Question your Grace the late ambassadors
With what great state he heard their embassy,
How well supplied with noble counsellors,
How modest in exception, and withal
How terrible in constant resolution,   35
And you shall find his vanities forespent
Were but the outside of the Roman Brutus,
Covering discretion with a coat of folly;
As gardeners do with ordure hide those roots
That shall first spring and be most delicate.   40

Dauphin

Well, 'tis not so, my Lord High Constable;
But though we think it so, it is no matter.
In cases of defence 'tis best to weigh
The enemy more mighty than he seems;
So the proportions of defence are fill'd;   45
Which of a weak and niggardly projection
Doth like a miser spoil his coat with scanting
A little cloth.

French King

            Think we King Harry strong;
And, Princes, look you strongly arm to meet him.
The kindred of him hath been flesh'd upon us;   50
And he is bred out of that bloody strain
That haunted us in our familiar paths.
Witness our too much memorable shame

54. *struck:* joined.

57. *mountain sire:* suggesting superhuman might and grandeur.

62–3. *stem . . . stock.* The *stock* is the main trunk of a tree or plant, from which the *stem* grows. (The meaning of 'stem' changed slightly: nowadays we use the word for the main trunk.)

64. *The native mightiness and fate of him:* his inborn strength and the great things that men of his family seem destined to do. Thus Shakespeare has built his hero up by showing us the attitudes of his enemies. The Constable has a healthy and well-informed admiration for him and the king has been conditioned to fear anyone of Henry's family. Their attitudes show how ill-founded is the Dauphin's scorn.

66. *crave:* beg.

67. *We'll give them present audience:* 'I'll see them now.' An *audience* in this context is a formal interview granted by a person of high authority (especially a king or the Pope).

68. Another hunting metaphor, echoing lines 50–1, and also Henry's reference to *chaces* (with the pun on 'chases') in Act I, Scene ii, line 266.

69–71. The Dauphin takes up the hunting image: he wants his father to stop running away and to fight the English, like a hunted deer turning to attack the hounds with its horns. *spend their mouths.* This refers to the way hounds howl and bark excitedly when they are 'in full cry' after their prey.

72. *Take up the English short:* 'nip the English attack in the bud.' (Don't let them get into their stride.) As before, the Dauphin is rashly overconfident; he seems to think it is no problem to turn the English back.

74–5. *Self-love . . . self-neglecting:* 'It may be wrong to think too much of oneself, but it is not nearly as bad as not bothering to take precautions.'

Stage Direction. *Re-enter Lords, with Exeter and Train:* indicating that the stage fills up now with members of the French court and the English Ambassador and his *Train* (escort of friends and assistants). Exeter's message is firm, clear-cut and frighteningly to the point, in contrast with the sneering irrelevance of the French Ambassadors in Act I, Scene ii, lines 246–57. Henry's demand is the demand of God: the French crown should be his because God gave it to him, and because the *law of nature* (logic) *and of nations* (the normal, accepted way of doing things) are on his side. The French King has merely *borrowed* it; the time has come to give it back to the rightful owner.

78. *divest:* strip off.

When Cressy battle fatally was struck,
And all our princes captiv'd by the hand   55
Of that black name, Edward, Black Prince of Wales;
Whiles that his mountain sire – on mountain standing,
Up in the air, crown'd with the golden sun—
Saw his heroical seed, and smil'd to see him,
Mangle the work of nature, and deface   60
The patterns that by God and by French fathers
Had twenty years been made. This is a stem
Of that victorious stock; and let us fear
The native mightiness and fate of him.

[Enter a MESSENGER]

Messenger
Ambassadors from Harry King of England   65
Do crave admittance to your Majesty.
French King
We'll give them present audience. Go and bring them.

[Exeunt MESSENGER and certain LORDS]

You see this chase is hotly followed, friends.
Dauphin
Turn head and stop pursuit; for coward dogs
Most spend their mouths when what they seem to
    threaten   70
Runs far before them. Good my sovereign,
Take up the English short, and let them know
Of what a monarchy you are the head.
Self-love, my liege, is not so vile a sin
As self-neglecting.

[Re-enter LORDS, with EXETER and TRAIN]

French King
             From our brother of England?   75
Exeter
From him, and thus he greets your Majesty:
He wills you, in the name of God Almighty,
That you divest yourself, and lay apart

77

80. *'longs:* belongs.

82–4. *And all wide-stretched . . . France:* and all the dominions that go with it.
the ordinance of times. The practice that has become established over the years
and is now generally accepted.
85. *no sinister nor no awkward claim:* not an illegal or fabricated claim.
86–7. The claim has not been dragged out of the forgotten past, or pieced
together from outdated history books: it is based on recent history and is right
up-to-date.
88. *this most memorable line:* this highly significant family tree.

89. *demonstrative:* it proves the claim conclusively.
90. *Willing you overlook:* asking you to examine.
91. *evenly derived:* directly descended.

94. *indirectly:* illegally.
95. *native:* natural, legal (by birth).
97. *constraint:* force, compulsion: 'If you won't give us the crown we'll have
to take it by force.'
100. *Jove.* Another name for Jupiter, the supreme ruler over all the gods and
men in Roman mythology, who expressed anger by hurling thunderbolts. A
tremendous hyperbole for Henry's fury.
101. *requiring:* asking.
102. The Hebrews, and so as the Elizabethans who studied the Bible closely,
thought that the bowels were the source of emotions, of tenderness, pity and
mercy. The phrase 'in the bowels of Christ' occurs in the Bible (Philippians I,
8) with the same meaning as *in the bowels of the Lord* here: 'with the sort of
mercy and compassion that Jesus demonstrated.' The appeal is for the sake of
those who will be swallowed up by the war if the crown is not handed over
peacefully.
105–6. *on your head Turning:* putting the blame on you for . . . Compare
Henry's reply to the Dauphin in Act I, Scene ii, lines 281–8. His attitude is quite
uncompromising: he is utterly certain of the rightness of his claim, is
determined to go to any lengths to achieve it, will have no scruples about any
suffering caused in the process, and is confident that God will blame the French
for everything because they should have given in peacefully and made
the war unnecessary.
107. *privy:* probably a misprint for 'pining' or 'prived' (deprived).

The borrowed glories that by gift of heaven,
By law of nature and of nations, 'longs   80
To him and to his heirs – namely, the crown,
And all wide-stretched honours that pertain,
By custom and the ordinance of times,
Unto the crown of France. That you may know
'Tis no sinister nor no awkward claim,   85
Pick'd from the worm-holes of long-vanish'd days,
Nor from the dust of old oblivion rak'd,
He sends you this most memorable line,

[Gives a paper]

In every branch truly demonstrative;
Willing you overlook this pedigree.   90
And when you find him evenly deriv'd
From his most fam'd of famous ancestors,
Edward the Third, he bids you then resign
Your crown and kingdom, indirectly held
From him, the native and true challenger.   95
French King
Or else what follows?
Exeter
Bloody constraint; for if you hide the crown
Even in your hearts, there will he rake for it.
Therefore in fierce tempest is he coming,
In thunder and in earthquake, like a Jove,   100
That if requiring fail, he will compel;
And bids you, in the bowels of the Lord,
Deliver up the crown; and to take mercy
On the poor souls for whom this hungry war
Opens his vasty jaws; and on your head   105
Turning the widow's tears, the orphans' cries,
The dead men's blood, the privy maidens' groans,
For husbands, fathers, and betrothed lovers,
That shall be swallowed in this controversy.
This is his claim, his threat'ning, and my message;   110
Unless the Dauphin be in presence here,

112. *To whom . . . too:* for whom I also have a special message. The word *greeting* is sarcastic.

113. *For us:* as for me (as opposed to the Dauphin). Notice the French king's indecisiveness in contrast to Henry's prompt and forthright reply to the French Ambassadors in Act I, Scene ii. He wants time, perhaps to work out some compromise or some offer which will appease the English.

114. *intent:* intention.

115–16. Perhaps the Dauphin is nervous of admitting his presence, knowing what sort of message he is going to receive.

117. *slight regard:* very little respect, a very low opinion.

118–19. *And anything . . . prize you at:* and any other expression of disapproval that is appropriate to the great king who sends it; that's what he thinks of you.

120. *an if: an* is an old word for 'if'. Both are used here for emphasis.

121. *in grant of all demands at large:* by granting all our demands in full. Doing so would of course soften Henry's desire to pay the Dauphin back for his *bitter mock*.

123–6. *He'll call . . . ordinance:* he'll get his own back with such a violent barrage of gunfire that the caves and hollow caverns of France will echo the noise, shouting curses at you for your offence and turning your joke back on you.

ordinance: artillery (the modern word is 'ordnance').

127. *fair return:* a friendly and conciliatory reply.

129. *odds:* quarrels, war.

To that end. This suggests that the Dauphin sent the tennis balls deliberately to provoke a quarrel.

131. *Paris balls.* Tennis was associated with Paris.

132. *Louvre:* the French king's palace.

133. *mistress court:* supreme court.

136. *greener days:* younger days (like a plant still fresh, not yet old and brown).

137. *masters.* This meant 'possesses' in Elizabethan times, but the word also conveys something of the authority and self-possession of Henry's maturity.

137–8. *Now he weighs the . . . grain:* 'he makes full use of every second – not frittering away his time on trivialities.

grain: an old measure, one fifteenth of a gramme, a very tiny quantity.

138. *that you shall read:* you'll find that out.

140. Once again the French King fails to give the manly and forthright reply that the situation demands.

141. *Dispatch us:* 'send us on our way'. Exeter doesn't want to be kept waiting; moreover his next words suggest contempt for the French King's procrastination.

To whom expressly I bring greeting too.
French King
    For us, we will consider of this further;
    To-morrow shall you bear our full intent
    Back to our brother of England.
Dauphin
                          For the Dauphin: 115
    I stand here for him. What to him from England?
Exeter
    Scorn and defiance, slight regard, contempt,
    And anything that may not misbecome
    The mighty sender, doth he prize you at.
    Thus says my king: an if your father's Highness   120
    Do not, in grant of all demands at large,
    Sweeten the bitter mock you sent his Majesty,
    He'll call you to so hot an answer of it
    That caves and womby vaultages of France
    Shall chide your trespass and return your mock   125
    In second accent of his ordinance.
Dauphin
    Say, if my father render fair return,
    It is against my will; for I desire
    Nothing but odds with England. To that end,
    As matching to his youth and vanity,   130
    I did present him with the Paris balls.
Exeter
    He'll make your Paris Louvre shake for it,
    Were it the mistress court of mighty Europe;
    And be assur'd you'll find a difference,
    As we his subjects have in wonder found,   135
    Between the promise of his greener days
    And these he masters now. Now he weighs time
    Even to the utmost grain; that you shall read
    In your own losses, if he stay in France.
French King
    To-morrow shall you know our mind at full.   140
Exeter
    Dispatch us with all speed, lest that our king

143. *is footed*: has set foot.

145–6. The usual triumphant *flourish* on the trumpets as the king adjourns his council cannot disguise his uninspiring leadership. These last words are a feeble attempt to defend his lack of decision.

Come here himself to question our delay;
For he is footed in this land already.

French King

You shall be soon dispatch'd with fair conditions.
A night is but small breath and little pause   145
To answer matters of this consequence.

[Flourish. Exeunt]

ACT THREE

PROLOGUE

2. celerity: speed. Some time has passed before the king's next appearance, actually in battle, and the Chorus fills in the intervening details.

4. well-appointed: fully equipped for war.

5. Embark his royalty: 'go on board with his royal attendants and equipment.' **brave:** 'making a fine show'.

6. the young Phœbus is the early-morning sun; Phœbus is another name for Apollo, the ancient Greek sun-god, and Shakespeare's imagination sees the **streamers** (long, pointed flags or pennons) actually **fanning** the face of the god.

7. Play with your fancies: exercise your imagination. And Shakespeare enables us to do so by providing a series of marvellously vivid details of sight, sound, and feeling that bring this voyage to life.

8. hempen tackle: the rigging of the ships (ropes made of hemp).

9–10. The **whistle** was used to give orders, and here it provides an orderly sound for our imaginations to hear among the general confusion.

threaden: woven of linen thread.

11. Borne: billowing out.

12. bottoms: the hulls of ships, but the word is used for the ships themselves.

13. the lofty surge: the high waves.

14. rivage: shore.

18. A grappling-iron or grapnel is an iron hook used in boarding ships; the audience are asked to attach themselves to the back of the ships, i.e. to follow them in imagination.

19. as dead midnight still: as quiet as if it were permanently the middle of the night (because all the young men have gone to France).

21. Either past . . . puissance: people who have passed the prime of life or haven't reached it yet.

22–3. Every young man approaching maturity, even if he has only the beginnings of a beard, has joined the army.

24. cull'd and choice-drawn cavaliers: carefully selected knights.

25. therein: in your thoughts.

26–7. Harfleur was a fortified French town **girded** (encircled) with a strong defensive wall, which is now threatened by the English cannons.

ACT THREE

Prologue

[Flourish. Enter CHORUS]

Chorus

Thus with imagin'd wing our swift scene flies,
In motion of no less celerity
Than that of thought. Suppose that you have seen
The well-appointed King at Hampton pier
Embark his royalty; and his brave fleet   5
With silken streamers the young Phœbus fanning.
Play with your fancies; and in them behold
Upon the hempen tackle ship-boys climbing;
Hear the shrill whistle which doth order give
To sounds confus'd; behold the threaden sails,   10
Borne with th' invisible and creeping wind,
Draw the huge bottoms through the furrowed sea,
Breasting the lofty surge. O, do but think
You stand upon the rivage and behold
A city on th' inconstant billows dancing;   15
For so appears this fleet majestical,
Holding due course to Harfleur. Follow, follow!
Grapple your minds to sternage of this navy
And leave your England as dead midnight still,
Guarded with grandsires, babies, and old women,   20
Either past or not arriv'd to pith and puissance;
For who is he whose chin is but enrich'd
With one appearing hair that will not follow
These cull'd and choice-drawn cavaliers to France?
Work, work your thoughts, and therein see a siege;   25
Behold the ordnance on their carriages,
With fatal mouths gaping on girded Harfleur.

29–31. This is presumably the answer for which Exeter had to wait at the end of the last scene: the French King has offered to give his daughter to be Henry's wife, and *to dowry* (as a wedding-gift) some small and worthless territories.

32. *The offer likes not.* Henry is not impressed by this offer, and the battle goes on.

32–3. Gunners had to be *nimble* because firing a gun was extremely hazardous in those early days. They fixed a match in the end of a long stick known as the linstock, applied ('touched') it to the charge in the touch hole, and then took cover.

Stage Direction. An *alarum* was a call, often on a trumpet, to tell soldiers to advance, fire etc. *Chambers* were small cannon. There is a good opportunity here for sound effects.

35. *eke out:* supplement, fill in the gaps in the performance.

SCENE I

The English, besieging the walled town of Harfleur, have opened up a gap in the wall and are trying to force their way through it. The first attempts, it seems, have failed, and King Henry stirs his men to renewed efforts, speaking from a raised position from which he surveys them as they crowd round him, amid the machinery, smoke, and noise of war.

There are seven scenes in this act and eight in the next. In the Elizabethan theatre, with no curtain to bring down between scenes, this would give the impression of fast and exciting action.

1. *breach:* a hole or gap in the wall.

3. *so becomes:* is so appropriate or suitable to.

8. *Disguise fair nature . . . rage:* let your anger turn your natural good-looks into grimness; *favour* used to mean face.

9. *lend . . . aspect:* make your eyes gleam terrifyingly.

10–14. Two vivid similes depict the profile of an angry, threatening face with the eyes shining fiercely out from beneath a contracted and overhanging brow. *portage* refers to the gun-ports in the sides of a ship, through which cannons were fired, *a galled rock* is an eroded cliff, one that has been worn away by the sea below so that the upper part juts out: *o'erwhelm* means overhang, *jutty* means jut out beyond, and *confounded* means hollowed out. Notice how the rhythm and alliteration of *Swill'd with the wild and wasteful ocean* convey the movement of the sea against rocks.

16. *bend up:* stretch up.

18. *Whose blood . . . war-proof:* whose blood is inherited from fathers who proved themselves in war.

fet: fetched, got.

Suppose th' ambassador from the French comes back;
Tells Harry that the King doth offer him
Katherine his daughter, and with her to dowry   30
Some petty and unprofitable dukedoms.
The offer likes not; and the nimble gunner
With linstock now the devilish cannon touches,

[Alarum, and chambers go off]

And down goes all before them. Still be kind,
And eke out our performance with your mind.

[Exit]

Scene I

France. Before Harfleur

*[Alarum. Enter the KING, EXETER, BEDFORD,
GLOUCESTER, and soldiers with scaling-ladders]*

King

Once more unto the breach, dear friends, once more;
Or close the wall up with our English dead.
In peace there's nothing so becomes a man
As modest stillness and humility;
But when the blast of war blows in our ears,   5
Then imitate the action of the tiger:
Stiffen the sinews, summon up the blood,
Disguise fair nature with hard-favour'd rage;
Then lend the eye a terrible aspect;
Let it pry through the portage of the head   10
Like the brass cannon: let the brow o'erwhelm it
As fearfully as doth a galled rock
O'erhang and jutty his confounded base,
Swill'd with the wild and wasteful ocean.
Now set the teeth and stretch the nostril wide;   15
Hold hard the breath, and bend up every spirit
To his full height. On, on, you noblest English,
Whose blood is fet from fathers of war-proof—

19. *like so many Alexanders:* they all fought as tirelessly and as successfully as Alexander the Great himself.

21. *argument:* opposition.

22–3. 'Prove by your courage now that you really are the sons of those valiant fathers; don't shame your mothers by suggesting you were begotten by other men.'

24. *Be copy:* be an example. *men of grosser blood:* men of inferior breeding.

25–8. The *yeomen* were freemen farmers (not serfs or forced levies), who served as foot-soldiers during war; Henry at this point notices a group of them listening to him, and addresses them in farming language. *The mettle of your pasture:* 'the quality of your upbringing' (good grass produces good cattle), *let us swear That you are worth your breeding:* 'prove to us that the care that went into breeding you was worthwhile'.

29–30. Good psychology: *mean and base* are at the opposite end of the class structure from *noble*, and the yeomen were in between, above serfs but below gentlemen. Henry raises not only the yeomen but all the soldiers listening to him to the level of nobility; indeed this speech does no doubt make their eyes shine with *noble lustre*.

31. *slips:* leashes for holding grey hounds (hunting dogs) at the start of a hunt; they could be quickly released ('slipped').

32. *The game's afoot:* the quarry is on the run.

33. *Follow your spirit.* The soldiers' minds are already there in the thick of the battle, and now their bodies must follow. (A similar idea was mentioned in Act I, Scene ii, lines 128–30.)

upon this charge: when you charge this time. The king himself leads the charge, roaring the battle-cry as he goes.

SCENE II

1. *On, on* etc.: As the king and his charging followers surge back towards the heat of battle, they leave behind, unnoticed, a little nest of shrinking cowards. Bardolph makes some sort of effort to get the others to fight.

2. Bardolph was a Lieutenant in Act II.

2–3. *the knocks . . . lives:* 'the fighting is too fierce for my liking, and speaking for myself I've only got one life to lose.'

4–5. *that is the very plain-song of it:* that is the simple truth of the matter, but it is just another variation on Nym's continuous theme. *plain song:* a simple melody sung in unison without variations.

Fathers that like so many Alexanders
Have in these parts from morn till even fought,   20
And sheath'd their swords for lack of argument.
Dishonour not your mothers; now attest
That those whom you call'd fathers did beget you.
Be copy now to men of grosser blood,
And teach them how to war. And you, good yeomen,   25
Whose limbs were made in England, show us here
The mettle of your pasture; let us swear
That you are worth your breeding – which I doubt not;
For there is none of you so mean and base
That hath not noble lustre in your eyes.   30
I see you stand like greyhounds in the slips,
Straining upon the start. The game's afoot:
Follow your spirit; and upon this charge
Cry 'God for Harry, England, and Saint George!'

[Exeunt. Alarum, and chambers go off]

Scene II

Before Harfleur

[Enter NYM, BARDOLPH, PISTOL, and BOY]

Bardolph

On, on, on, on, on! to the breach, to the breach!

Nym

Pray thee, Corporal, stay; the knocks are too hot, and
for mine own part I have not a case of lives. The
humour of it is too hot; that is the very plain-song of
it.   5

Pistol

The plain-song is most just; for humours do abound.
Knocks go and come; God's vassals drop and die;

And sword and shield
In bloody field
Doth win immortal fame.   10

12. *fame.* Pistol has just referred bravely (but of course hypocritically) to the fame to be won in battle. The Boy is just as scared but more honest: he'd exchange his fame for safety.

14–18. Pistol sings, and the Boy adds a witty comment on his singing. *duly* seems to mean quickly. *truly:* in tune. Pistol might fly like a bird but he certainly can't sing like one.

20. *Avaunt, you cullions!* 'Get going, you swine!' (The literal meaning of *cullions* was testicles, but it was used as a general term of vulgar abuse.)

21. Fluellen is a Welsh Captain, but as he drives the three rascals off to the battle, whacking their backsides with the flat of his sword, he seems like a *great duke*; they all cower before him, squealing for mercy; *men of mould* are presumably men made of clay, i.e. mere humans in contrast to the *great duke*, who seems to be some sort of god.

24. *bawcock:* a compliment, from 'beau coq' (French for 'fine fellow'), and *sweet chuck* was a term of endearment used by lovers: Pistol is trying everything to wheedle round Fluellen.

lenity: mildness, mercy, gentleness.

25–6. *good humours . . . bad humours.* Nym is squealing pathetically and of course using his favourite word, but if there is a meaning it is that the *good humours* are, ironically, the blows of Fluellen's sword, and the *bad humours* are the anger and terror the cowards feel as a result.

27–8. We have already noticed the Boy's wit and honesty; now we hear how shrewdly he sums up the *three swashers* (blustering boasters) whom he serves.

28–30. *but all they three . . . do not amount to a man:* 'even if all three of them were servants of mine I could not call them "my man," because three freaks like them added together wouldn't make one man.'

30. *For Bardolph:* as for Bardolph.

white-liver'd: cowardly. The liver was thought to be the source of courage; if it had no blood in it it could produce no courage. But Bardolph is *red-fac'd* – his face is braver than his liver: he looks fierce but never fights.

33. *a killing tongue and a quiet sword:* in a good man it would be the other way round, of course. Instead of breaking his sword in fighting Pistol *breaks words* instead: he flings them about, misusing them, and also 'breaks his word' (doesn't keep promises).

Boy

 Would I were in an alehouse in London! I would give
 all my fame for a pot of ale and safety.

Pistol

 And I:

> If wishes would prevail with me,
> My purpose should not fail with me,   15
> But thither would I hie.

Boy

> As duly, but not as truly,
> As bird doth sing on bough.

[Enter FLUELLEN]

Fluellen

 Up to the breach, you dogs!
 Avaunt, you cullions!   20

[Driving them forward]

Pistol

 Be merciful, great duke, to men of mould.
 Abate thy rage, abate thy manly rage;
 Abate thy rage, great duke.
 Good bawcock, bate thy rage. Use lenity, sweet chuck.

Nym

 These be good humours. Your honour wins bad 25
 humours.

[Exeunt all but BOY]

Boy

 As young as I am, I have observ'd these three swashers.
 I am boy to them all three; but all they three, though
 they would serve me, could not be man to me; for
 indeed three such antics do not amount to a man. For 30
 Bardolph, he is white-liver'd and red-fac'd; by the
 means whereof 'a faces it out, but fights not. For Pistol,
 he hath a killing tongue and a quiet sword; by the
 means whereof 'a breaks words and keeps whole
 weapons. For Nym, he hath heard that men of few 35

41. *purchase:* used to mean plunder, a more or less legal acquisition for soldiers in war. These three pretend that their petty thefts are legitimate. The *lute-case* (a lute is a musical instrument), worthless without its contents, is a good example of the absourd lengths to which they will go to make a little profit. A *league* is about three miles.

46. *carry coals:* a colloquial phrase for 'get up to any dishonest work,' but the Boy may also mean that they will finish up using the *fire-shovel* they have stolen to help stoke the fires of hell.

46–9. 'They want me to slide into men's pockets as easily as their gloves and handkerchiefs do (into theirs), but being a pickpocket goes against my nature and it's nothing but an insult to expect me to do it.'

50. *pocketing up of wrongs* has two meanings: (1) the obvious one of 'putting stolen goods in my pocket' and (2) the colloquial meaning it used to have of 'putting up with insults'.

51–2. *goes against my weak stomach:* makes me sick; *and therefore I must cast it up:* and so I'd better spew it out (i.e. leave them). However, in spite of his resolve to *seek some better service*, which commands our admiration, the Boy appears again later in the play, still in the 'service' of Pistol.

54. *presently:* at once.

55. *mines:* tunnels which the attackers have dug under the town walls, either to provide a way into the town or to make the walls collapse.

57. Fluellen's speech is peculiar in various ways, and of course it has a strong Welsh accent. *mines is* is typical of his unconventional grammer, and he also tends to 'unvoice' voiced consonants, e.g. *plow* for 'blow' in line 63, Cheshu for 'Jesu' (Jesus), and so on. Another stock trick of the stage Welshman is the repeated use of 'look you'.

59–60. *the concavities of it is not sufficient:* the mines aren't deep enough; a silly mistake and quite contrary to *the disciplines of the war* (the accepted rules of warfare), in which Fluellen is a great believer.

60. *athversary:* adversary (enemy).

61. *discuss:* explain.

60–4. Fluellen means that the enemy has dug countermines four yards underneath the mines. A *countermine* was dug by the defenders to cut off or collapse the attackers' mine.

words are the best men, and therefore he scorns to
say his prayers lest 'a should be thought a coward;
but his few bad words are match'd with as few good
deeds; for 'a never broke any man's head but his
own, and that was against a post when he was drunk.   40
They will steal anything, and call it purchase.
Bardolph stole a lute-case, bore it twelve leagues, and
sold it for three halfpence. Nym and Bardolph are
sworn brothers in filching, and in Calais they stole
a fire-shovel; I knew by that piece of service the men   45
would carry coals. They would have me as familiar
with men's pockets as their gloves or their hand-
kerchers; which makes much against my manhood,
if I should take from another's pocket to put into
mine; for it is plain pocketing up of wrongs. I must   50
leave them and seek some better service; their villainy
goes against my weak stomach, and therefore I must
cast it up.

[Exit]

[Re-enter FLUELLEN, GOWER following]

Gower

Captain Fluellen, you must come presently to the
mines; the Duke of Gloucester would speak with   55
you.

Fluellen

To the mines! Tell you the Duke it is not so good to
come to the mines; for, look you, the mines is not
according to the disciplines of the war; the concavities
of it is not sufficient. For, look you, th' athversary –   60
you may discuss unto the Duke, look you – is digt
himself four yard under the countermines; by Cheshu,
I think 'a will plow up all, if there is not better
directions.

Gower

The Duke of Gloucester, to whom the order of the   65

70. *he is an ass, as in the world:* he is as big a fool as anyone in the world. *I will verify as much in his beard:* Fluellen will happily say the same thing to the Irishman's face; indeed he soon does, as we shall see. His low opinion may be deserved, or it may be the result of traditional Welsh/Irish rivalry.

71. *directions:* knowledge.

72–3. The Romans were considered good models, especially by those who thought gunpowder was of no benefit in war. Shakespeare, besides making Fluellen's speech comic, is also laughing at his fierce insistence on outdated tactics.

than is a puppy-dog: 'than a puppy-dog has.'

Stage Direction. *Macmorris* is the very same Irishman under discussion, and as he is accompanied by a Scotsman we now have the complete quartet of an Englishman (Gower), an Irishman, a Scotsman, and a Welshman, the conventional company for some knockabout (rough) comedy.

76. *falorous:* valorous (brave).

77. *of great expedition and knowledge.* Jamy has considerable knowledge of the *aunchiant* (ancient, i.e. Roman) wars at his finger tips.

79–80. *he will maintain his argument.* Fluellen, like many Welshmen, loves an argument, and sets great store by a man's ability to argue well. This can lead him into mistaken judgments of people; later in the play he is completely hoodwinked for a time by the 'arguments' of Pistol, of all people.

81. *pristine:* ancient.

82–3. *gud day* and *God-den* are dialect expressions for 'Good day' or 'Good evening'; here and in the rest of the scene Shakespeare is trying to bring out the contrasts in the accents.

85. *pioneers:* the soldiers who are digging the mines. *given o'er:* given up, stopped work.

86. *tish:* Macmorris says 'sh' for 's' (*tish* means 'it is'), in contrast to Jamy, whose 'sall' means 'shall'.

siege is given, is altogether directed by an Irishman – a
very valiant gentleman, i' faith.

Fluellen

It is Captain Macmorris, is it not?

Gower

I think it be.

Fluellen

By Cheshu, he is an ass, as in the world: I will verify   70
as much in his beard; he has no more directions in
the true disciplines of the wars, look you, of the Roman
disciplines, than is a puppy-dog.

[Enter MACMORRIS *and* CAPTAIN JAMY]

Gower

Here 'a comes; and the Scots captain, Captain Jamy,
with him.   75

Fluellen

Captain Jamy is a marvellous falorous gentleman, that
is certain, and of great expedition and knowledge in
th' aunchiant wars, upon my particular knowledge of
his directions. By Cheshu, he will maintain his argument as well as any military man in the world, in the   80
disciplines of the pristine wars of the Romans.

Jamy

I say gud day, Captain Fluellen.

Fluellen

God-den to your worship, good Captain James.

Gower

How now, Captain Macmorris! Have you quit the
mines? Have the pioneers given o'er?   85

Macmorris

By Crish, la, tish ill done! The work ish give over, the
trompet sound the retreat. By my hand, I swear, and
my father's soul, the work ish ill done; it ish give over;
I would have blowed up the town, so Chrish save me,
la, in an hour. O, tish ill done, tish ill done; by my   90
hand, tish ill done!

92–3. *voutsafe:* vouchsafe (kindly and graciously give).

96. *friendly communication.* Fluellen tries to sound friendly but as he says this he is glaring fiercely into the Irishman's eyes, challenging him to the sort of argument that might lead to blows.

100–2. Very roughly Jamy's is saying, 'That's a good idea, and I'll make the odd contribution to the discussion myself from time to time'.

106. *beseech'd:* besieged.

108. *so God sa' me:* may God not save me if what I say isn't true.

112. *mess:* mass, service of the Eucharist.
113. *de:* do.
lig i' th' grund: lie in the ground (i.e. 'I'll do good service or die in the attempt.').
114. *ay, or go to death* merely says the same as 'lie in the ground'; a repetition with a comic effect which Shakespeare is fond of.
pay't: pay it, do my service.
115–16. *the breff and the long:* the long and the short of it (i.e. all there is to it)'.
116–17. *Marry . . . tway:* by Jove, I should love to hear a really good argument between you two. *Marry* is an oath, by Mary, mother of Christ.
119–20. As soon as Fluellen mentions *your nation*, Macmorris jumps to the conclusion that he is going to attack the Irish, and promptly loses his temper, as Irishmen are popularly supposed to do. *Of my nation?* he says, 'What about my nation? Is some rotten bastard going to mock my nation?' And so on.

Fluellen

Captain Macmorris, I beseech you now, will you voutsafe me, look you, a few disputations with you, as
partly touching or concerning the disciplines of the
war, the Roman wars, in the way of argument, look   95
you, and friendly communication; partly to satisfy my
opinion, and partly for the satisfaction, look you, of
my mind, as touching the direction of the military
discipline, that is the point.

Jamy

It sall be vary gud, feith, gud captains bath; and I sall 100
quit you with gud leve, as I may pick occasion; that
sall I, marry.

Macmorris

It is no time to discourse, so Chrish save me. The day
is hot, and the weather, and the wars, and the King,
and the Dukes; it is no time to discourse. The town is 105
beseech'd, and the trumpet call us to the breach; and
we talk and, be Chrish, do nothing. 'Tis shame for us
all, so God sa' me, 'tis shame to stand still; it is shame,
by my hand; and there is throats to be cut, and works
to be done; and there ish nothing done, so Chrish sa' 110
me, la.

Jamy

By the mess, ere theise eyes of mine take themselves
to slomber, ay'll de gud service, or I'll lig i' th' grund
for it; ay, or go to death. And I'll pay't as valorously
as I may, that sall I suerly do, that is the breff and the 115
long. Marry, I wad full fain heard some question 'tween
you tway.

Fluellen

Captain Macmorris, I think, look you, under your
correction, there is not many of your nation—

Macmorris

Of my nation? What ish my nation? Ish a villain, and 120
a bastard, and a knave, and a rascal. What ish my
nation? Who talks of my nation?

124. *peradventure:* perhaps.

125–6. *use me . . . use me:* treat me with the friendliness that you ought.

132. *you will mistake each other:* you are determined to misunderstand each other.

134. *parley:* a truce for talks. Here the townspeople of Harfleur have blown a trumpet call to indicate to the English that they want to talk, in fact to surrender, as the next scene shows.

136. *to be required:* to be found.

SCENE III

Stage Direction. *the walls* could be the small gallery which, in Shakespeare's theatre, covered the inner stage. The Governor would be up there, with Henry below, not in armour now but in formal robes, as it is a time of truce and negotiation. The curtained entrance to the inner stage would be the city gates.

1. *How yet . . . town?* what is the Governor's intention now?
2. *This . . . admit:* this is your last chance to talk.

4. *proud of destruction:* seeking the honour of death.

Fluellen

Look you, if you take the matter otherwise than is
meant, Captain Macmorris, peradventure I shall think
you do not use me with that affability as in discre- 125
tion you ought to use me, look you; being as good
a man as yourself, both in the disciplines of war and
in the derivation of my birth, and in other
particularities.

Macmorris

I do not know you so good a man as myself; so Chrish 130
save me, I will cut off your head.

Gower

Gentlemen both, you will mistake each other.

Jamy

Ah! that's a foul fault.

[A parley sounded]

Gower

The town sounds a parley.

Fluellen

Captain Macmorris, when there is more better oppor- 135
tunity to be required, look you, I will be so bold as to
tell you I know the disciplines of war; and there is an
end.

[Exeunt]

Scene III

Before the gates of Harfleur

[Enter the GOVERNOR *and some citizens on the walls.
Enter the* KING *and all his train before the gates]*

King

How yet resolves the Governor of the town?
This is the latest parle we will admit;
Therefore to our best mercy give yourselves
Or, like to men proud of destruction,
Defy us to our worst; for, as I am a soldier,   5

6. *becomes:* suits.

7. *batt'ry:* assault.

8. *half-achieved:* half-captured. He won't call the attack off until the town is nothing but a pile of ashes.

11. *flesh'd:* accustomed to bloodshed (compare Act II, Scene iv, line 50).

11–14. As in Act I, Scene ii and Act II, Scene iv, the horrors of war are vividly described and the French are told it will be their fault if such horrors come about, because they should have submitted peacefully to the English demands. If Harfleur does not give in now, Henry will give his men complete freedom to rape and murder to their heart's content. *with conscience wide as hell:* with a conscience so open that nothing will seem sinful, not even hell itself.

fresh fair virgins and *flow'ring infants:* phrases that poetically emphasize the beauty and innocence that will be destroyed.

15. *What is it then to me . . . ?* 'what will I care . . . ?'

16–18. War is likened to Satan, *the prince of fiends*, bathed in flames and sooty faced like the soldiers committing all the hideous cruelties of sacking a city. *fell:* cruel.

20–1. *fall into the hand . . . violation:* 'suffer violent rape.'

22–3. *What rein . . . career?* The passions of his men, once they have been aroused, will be as impossible to control as a horse that has bolted and is charging away down a hill. *career* had a similar meaning in Act II, Scene i, line 122.

24–7. *We may as bootless . . . ashore:* Once my soldiers have been let loose in the city they'll get so worked up that trying to stop them plundering the place would be about as successful as ordering a whale to come ashore. *bootless:* useless. The *Leviathan* was a legendary sea-monster, sometimes taken to refer to a whale.

28. *Take pity of:* have pity on.

29. *in my command:* under my control.

30–2. The contrast between disciplined soldiers and the insane mob they will become when given freedom to plunder is further emphasized by this vivid image of the cool, clean breeze keeping the filthy clouds away.

heady murder: headstrong, uncontrolled, blood-lust. *spoil:* plunder.

And these evil passions are *contagious*, like a poison that spreads rapidly from man to man.

33. *look to see:* you can expect to see.

34. *blind and bloody:* blinded with the lust for blood.

35. *Defile the locks:* literally 'dirty the hair'; we visualize blood-stained soldiers dragging the girls off by the hair.

38. *spitted:* a spit is a pointed stick which is stuck through meat to be roasted, so that it can be turned over the fire. A *pike* is a weapon consisting of an iron point on the end of a long wooden pole.

40. *break the clouds:* i.e. with their howling; a hyperbole (exaggeration).

40–1. When Herod heard of the birth of Jesus, in his fear he ordered all of the male children in the land to be killed.

A name that in my thoughts becomes me best,
If I begin the batt'ry once again,
I will not leave the half-achieved Harfleur
Till in her ashes she lie buried.
The gates of mercy shall be all shut up,   10
And the flesh'd soldier, rough and hard of heart,
In liberty of bloody hand shall range
With conscience wide as hell, mowing like grass
Your fresh fair virgins and your flow'ring infants.
What is it then to me if impious war,   15
Array'd in flames, like to the prince of fiends,
Do, with his smirch'd complexion, all fell feats
Enlink'd to waste and desolation?
What is't to me when you yourselves are cause,
If your pure maidens fall into the hand   20
Of hot and forcing violation?
What rein can hold licentious wickedness
When down the hill he holds his fierce career?
We may as bootless spend our vain command
Upon th' enraged soldiers in their spoil,   25
As send precepts to the Leviathan
To come ashore. Therefore, you men of Harfleur,
Take pity of your town and of your people
Whiles yet my soldiers are in my command;
Whiles yet the cool and temperate wind of grace   30
O'erblows the filthy and contagious clouds
Of heady murder, spoil, and villainy.
If not – why, in a moment look to see
The blind and bloody soldier with foul hand
Defile the locks of your shrill-shrieking daughters;   35
Your fathers taken by the silver beards,
And their most reverend heads dash'd to the walls;
Your naked infants spitted upon pikes,
Whiles the mad mothers with their howls confus'd
Do break the clouds, as did the wives of Jewry   40
At Herod's bloody-hunting slaughtermen.
What say you? Will you yield, and this avoid?

43. *guilty in defence*. As before, Henry insists that the people will only have themselves to blame if they don't surrender and are massacred as a result.

44–7. The Governor of Harfleur has applied to the Dauphin for help, but has today received the message that the Dauphin has not yet collected a big enough army to drive the English away. The town can't hold out on its own any longer, and has no choice but to surrender.

succours: help.

returns us: answers us.

Stage Direction. The governor goes away from the walls (the gallery) down to the inner stage.

54. *Use mercy to them all*. Having threatened the most terrible consequences if the town didn't surrender, Henry demands good behaviour from his men when it does – another illustration of his fair-mindedness and insistence on absolute justice.

55–6. Shakespeare here gives a brief hint of the historical fact that the siege of Harfleur was nearly disastrous for Henry's expedition: it took too long and many men were lost both in battle and to a disease which swept through the army. Marching to Calais was really a retreat, hence *we will retire to Calais*. (Calais was an English possession at that time.)

58. *are we addrest:* 'we are prepared'.

SCENE IV

A light-hearted interlude in which the French princess, Katherine, knowing that she may be asked to marry the king of England, tries to learn a little English. Her lady-in-waiting, Alice, has difficulty in remembering some of the words, and her pronunciation is distinctly odd; the result is a variation of the playing around with words that seems to have been so popular with Shakespeare's audience. The appearance of the young princess also provides a pleasant break from the rather harsh masculinity of the preceding scenes. The French has been 'corrected' (more or less) by successive editors.

Or, guilty in defence, be thus destroy'd?

Governor

Our expectation hath this day an end:
The Dauphin, whom of succours we entreated,   45
Returns us that his powers are yet not ready
To raise so great a siege. Therefore, great King,
We yield our town and lives to thy soft mercy.
Enter our gates; dispose of us and ours;
For we no longer are defensible.   50

[*Exit* GOVERNOR]

King

Open your gates. Come, uncle Exeter,
Go you and enter Harfleur; there remain,
And fortify it strongly 'gainst the French;
Use mercy to them all. For us, dear uncle,
The winter coming on, and sickness growing   55
Upon our soldiers, we will retire to Calais.
To-night in Harfleur will we be your guest;
To-morrow for the march are we addrest.

[*Flourish. The* KING *and his* TRAIN *enter the town*]

Scene IV

Rouen. The French King's palace

[*Enter* KATHERINE *and* ALICE]

Katherine

Alice, tu es été en Angleterre, et tu parles bien le
langage.

Alice

Un peu, madame.

Katherine

Je te prie, m'enseignez; il faut que j'apprenne à parler.
Comment appelez-vous la main en Anglais?   5

6. *de hand:* the hand. French people often have difficulty in pronouncing English 'the'.

15–16. Katherine runs through the three nouns she has learnt, and on hearing her mangled rendering Alice assures her 'You pronounce them very well, madam – extremely good English.'

Alice

La main? Elle est appelée de hand.

Katherine

De hand. Et les doigts?

Alice

Les doigts? Ma foi, j'oublie les doigts; mais je me souvi-
endrai. Les doigts? Je pense qu'ils sont appelés de
fingres; oui, de fingres.   10

Katherine

La main, de hand; les doigts, de fingres. Je pense que
je suis le bon écolier; j'ai gagné deux mots d'Anglais
vîtement. Comment appelez-vous les ongles?

Alice

Les ongles? Nous les appelons de nails.

Katherine

De nails. Ecoutez; dites-moi si je parle bien: de hand,   15
de fingres, et de nails.

Alice

C'est bien dit, madame; il est fort bon Anglais.

Katherlne

Dites-moi l'Anglais pour le bras.

Alice

De arm, madame.

Katherine

Et le coude?   20

Alice

D'elbow.

Katherine

D'elbow. Je m'en fais la répétition de tous les mots que
vous m'avez appris dès à présent.

Alice

Il est trop difficile, madame, comme je pense.

Katherine

Excusez-moi, Alice; écoutez: d'hand, de fingre, de nails, 25
d'arma, de bilbow.

Alice

D'elbow, madame.

33–5. Again, after Katherine has said 'sin' for 'chin', Alice compliments her, 'Really, madam, you pronounce the words as well as the native English-speakers themselves.'

47. *count:* Alice is trying to say 'gown.' The words 'foot' and 'count' together, as pronounced by Alice, shock Katherine deeply, because to her (and to the English audience) they sound like words a princess should never even hear, let alone learn to say. Nevertheless, she does recite again all the words she has learnt so far – with increasing embarrassment, as now *count* comes at the end of a list of parts of the body.

Katherine

O Seigneur Dieu, je m'en oublie! D'elbow. Comment appelez-vous le col?

Alice

De nick, madame.   30

Katherine

De nick. Et le menton?

Alice

De chin.

Katherine

De sin. Le col, de nick; le menton, de sin.

Alice

Oui. Sauf votre honneur, en vérité, vous prononcez les mots aussi droit que les natifs d'Angleterre.   35

Katherine

Je ne doute point d'apprendre, par la grace de Dieu, et en peu de temps.

Alice

N'avez-vous pas déjà oublié ce que je vous ai enseigné?

Katherine

Non, je reciterai à vous promptement: d'hand, de   40
fingre, de mails—

Alice

De nails, madame.

Katherine

De nails, de arm, de ilbow.

Alice

Sauf votre honneur, d'elbow.

Katherine

Ainsi dis-je; d'elbow, de nick, et de sin. Comment   45
appelez-vous le pied et la robe?

Alice

Le foot, madame; et le count.

Katherine

Le foot et le count. O Seigneur Dieu! ils sont mots de son mauvais, corruptible, gros, et impudique, et

57. 'That's enough for one lesson; let's go to dinner.'

SCENE V

History helps us to understand this scene. By the time Henry had captured Harfleur his army was severely weakened; the sensible thing to do was to return to England direct from Harfleur before the French army could gather its full strength and destroy him completely. This advice was in fact given, but to Henry it seemed like an admission of failure, whereas a march to Calais would at least appear to be a continuation of his campaign. But Calais was two hundred miles away and in his path were forests, marshes, swollen rivers and fortified towns – a hazardous march for a sick army hoping to feed off the countryside, made even more dangerous by the imminent threat of a full-scale attack by the French. However, Henry's faith in God's protection led him to attempt it.

Here the French nobles express their astonishment at Henry's recklessness and their urgent desire to destroy him and his army now.

5–26. The Dauphin and the Duke of Britaine (Brittany) are furious that their people are being put to shame by the daring of the English, who are, according to them, only *Norman bastards*, the offspring of the love-affairs of the English women with the Normans who invaded England with William the Conqueror in 1066. The Constable finds it difficult to believe that a race with a climate as deplorable as England's can show such unusual spirit.

5–9. Grafting, which the Dauphin uses for his metaphor, consists of inserting a shoot (*scion*) of a delicate plant in the main trunk (*stock*) of a stronger one; in this way a beautiful rose, for example, may be grafted on to an ordinary but vigorous stock and thus benefit from the latter's strength. To the Dauphin's annoyance the *scions* (Normans grafted on to English stock) are doing better than their *grafters* or parent stock (the French).

6. *luxury:* lust.

11. *Mort Dieu, ma vie!:* French oaths, literally 'Death of God, my life!'

13. *a slobb'ry and a dirty farm:* a slimy, muddy farm.

14. *nook-shotten:* a contemptuous reference to the English coastline, 'full of silly little inlets'.

Albion is a poetical name for England.

non pour les dames d'honneur d'user: je ne voudrais 50
prononcer ces mots devant les seigneurs de France pour
tout le monde. Foh! le foot et le count! Néanmoins,
je reciterai une autre fois ma leçon ensemble: d'hand,
de fingre, de nails, d'arm, d'elbow, de nick, de sin, de
foot, le count. 55

Alice
Excellent, madame!

Katherine
C'est assez pour une fois: allons-nous à dîner.

[*Exeunt*]

Scene V

The French King's palace

[*Enter the* KING OF FRANCE, *the* DAUPHIN, DUKE OF
BRITAINE, *the* CONSTABLE OF FRANCE *and* OTHERS]

French King
'Tis certain he hath pass'd the river Somme.

Constable
And if he be not fought withal, my lord,
Let us not live in France; let us quit all,
And give our vineyards to a barbarous people.

Dauphin
O Dieu vivant! Shall a few sprays of us, 5
The emptying of our fathers' luxury,
Our scions, put in wild and savage stock,
Spirt up so suddenly into the clouds,
And overlook their grafters?

Britaine
Normans, but bastard Normans, Norman bastards! 10
Mort Dieu, ma vie! if they march along
Unfought withal, but I will sell my dukedom
To buy a slobb'ry and a dirty farm
In that nook-shotten isle of Albion.

15. *Dieu de batailles:* God of battles. *mettle:* spirit, courage.

17. *as in despite.* The sun is personified as shining feebly on England because it despises the English people.

18–26. Heat is equivalent to spirit, courage, and vitality, coldness to dullness and cowardice. The French, great makers and drinkers of wine, believe that it warms the blood, giving them courage; they despise people who have only 'cold' drinks. Constable wonders how the English, who drink *barley-broth* (beer), which is nothing more than *sodden* (i.e. boiled) *water, A drench for sur-rein'd jades* (medicine forced down the throats of over-worked horses), can appear hotter than the French.

23. *like roping icicles:* i.e. frozen into inactivity.

24–5. *whiles a more frosty people . . . fields:* the 'cold' English are showing all the courage at the moment.

26. *Poor . . . lords:* 'The fields are rich, but we can consider them poor in the quality of the men they have produced.'

28. *madams:* wives. The Dauphin, and later Britaine, paint a pathetic picture of domestic strife, with the French ladies ridiculing their husbands for their inactivity.

29–31. *Our mettle . . . warriors:* 'our stock has exhausted its vigour, and it's time to start a new breed, preferably a cross with the English, as it worked so well last time'.

32–5. *They bid us . . . runaways:* 'they tell us to go and teach dancing to the English, because we've shown such skill in jumping in fear and running away from danger that we should be pretty good at lively dances'. The *lavolta* was a dance that involved leaping high in the air, and the *coranto* another with a fast running step. *our grace is only in our heels* has the double meaning of (i) 'the only thing we're any good at is dancing' and (ii) 'we have shown distinction only in the speed with which we take to our heels (run away).'

37. *England:* the king of England.

38. *spirit of honour:* sense of honour.

47. *For your great seats . . . shames:* 'as becomes the high positions you occupy rid yourselves of the great shame that lies on you.'

Constable

    Dieu de batailles! where have they this mettle?   15
    Is not their climate foggy, raw, and dull;
    On whom, as in despite, the sun looks pale,
    Killing their fruit with frowns? Can sodden water,
    A drench for sur-rein'd jades, their barley-broth,
    Decoct their cold blood to such valiant heat?   20
    And shall our quick blood, spirited with wine,
    Seem frosty? O, for honour of our land,
    Let us not hang like roping icicles
    Upon our houses' thatch, whiles a more frosty people
    Sweat drops of gallant youth in our rich fields—   25
    Poor we call them in their native lords!

Dauphin

    By faith and honour,
    Our madams mock at us and plainly say
    Our mettle is bred out, and they will give
    Their bodies to the lust of English youth   30
    To new-store France with bastard warriors.

Britaine

    They bid us to the English dancing-schools
    And teach lavoltas high and swift corantos,
    Saying our grace is only in our heels
    And that we are most lofty runaways.   35

French King

    Where is Montjoy the herald? Speed him hence;
    Let him greet England with our sharp defiance.
    Up, Princes, and, with spirit of honour edged
    More sharper than your swords, hie to the field:
    Charles Delabreth, High Constable of France;   40
    You Dukes of Orleans, Bourbon, and of Berri,
    Alençon, Brabant, Bar, and Burgundy;
    Jaques Chatillon, Rambures, Vaudemont,
    Beaumont, Grandpré, Roussi, and Fauconbridge,
    Foix, Lestrake, Bouciqualt, and Charolois;   45
    High dukes, great princes, barons, lords and knights,
    For your great seats now quit you of great shames.

48. *Bar:* stop him from going any further.

49. *pennons:* small flags.

50–2. Two images are worked in together: first the simile, the French sweeping down on the English like an avalanche in the Alps, then the personification of the Alps as a haughty lord treating inferiors with contempt.

low vassal seat: a position of humble subordination to a superior being.

void his rheum: 'empty his mouth and nose of phlegm'.

55–60. Constable speaks as though he and his fellow nobles have been waiting some time for this decision by the French king.

This becomes the great: 'This is the sort of action we expect from a great man,' but it would be said with joy and relief, as we might say 'At last you've done the right thing.' He is sorry it wasn't done before because now the English are so enfeebled that they won't be able to give the good fight that the Constable seems to want.

60. *achievement:* a way out of the difficulty.

64–6. In spite of these lines, the Dauphin does in fact appear in the battle scenes later on.

SCENE VI

1–2. Henry has sent a small force ahead to capture a bridge that his army has to cross. Fluellen, returning with the news that the bridge is now safe in English hands, meets Gower, who is just ahead of the main body.

Bar Harry England, that sweeps through our land
With pennons painted in the blood of Harfleur.
Rush on his host as doth the melted snow   50
Upon the valleys, whose low vassal seat
The Alps doth spit and void his rheum upon;
Go down upon him, you have power enough,
And in a captive chariot into Rouen
Bring him our prisoner.

Constable

This becomes the great.   55
Sorry am I his numbers are so few,
His soldiers sick and famish'd in their march;
For I am sure, when he shall see our army,
He'll drop his heart into the sink of fear,
And for achievement offer us his ransom.   60

French King

Therefore, Lord Constable, haste on Montjoy,
And let him say to England that we send
To know what willing ransom he will give.
Prince Dauphin, you shall stay with us in Rouen.

Dauphin

Not so, I do beseech your Majesty.   65

French King

Be patient, for you shall remain with us.
Now forth, Lord Constable and Princes all,
And quickly bring us word of England's fall.

[Exeunt]

Scene VI

The English camp in Picardy

[Enter CAPTAINS, *English and Welsh,* GOWER *and*
FLUELLEN]

Gower

How now, Captain Fluellen! Come you from the
bridge?

5. Exeter was left in charge of Harfleur (Act III, Scene iii), but has now rejoined the marching army and has led the advance party to the bridge.

6. *magnanimous:* showing great courage. *Agamemnon* was the commander of the ancient Greek army that attacked Troy. The story of this war is told in the *Iliad* by Homer.

9–10. *not . . . any hurt in the world:* not injured in any way.

12. *aunchient:* Fluellen's pronunciation of 'Ancient,' the rank which Pistol was said to hold in Act II, Scene i.

14–15. *estimation:* reputation.

15–16. *gallant service:* by Pistol! It seems unbelievable. The explanation comes later in the scene (line 63).

21–2. Pistol is trying to wheedle a favour out of Fluellen, because Fluellen has influence in high places.

23–4. *I have merited . . . hands:* 'I deserve his good opinion (because I have served him well).'

25–6. A laughable description of Bardolph. *buxom:* vigorous.

27–38. The thought of Fortune sends Pistol off on to one of his rhetorical and alliterative descriptions, but in Fluellen he has a rival who not only likes airing his knowledge but also has a good deal more to air than Pistol has. Fortune, we learn, is depicted as blind (utterly indifferent to people); she may drive a wheel (which lifts men up on high one minute, then grinds them down the next. *fickle, inconstant, mutability,* and *variation* all refer to this habit of changing her mind without reason); or she may push an ever-rolling stone which destroys anything which happens, by ill-fortune, to lie in its path.

Fluellen

I assure you there is very excellent services committed
at the bridge.

Gower

Is the Duke of Exeter safe?   5

Fluellen

The Duke of Exeter is as magnanimous as Agamemnon; and a man that I love and honour with my
soul, and my heart, and my duty, and my live, and
my living, and my uttermost power. He is not – God
be praised and blessed! – any hurt in the world, but   10
keeps the bridge most valiantly, with excellent discipline. There is an aunchient Lieutenant there at the
bridge – I think in my very conscience he is as valiant
a man as Mark Antony; and he is a man of no estimation in the world; but I did see him do as gallant   15
service.

Gower

What do you call him?

Fluellen

He is call'd Aunchient Pistol.

Gower

I know him not.

[*Enter* PISTOL]

Fluellen

Here is the man.   20

Pistol

Captain, I thee beseech to do me favours.
The Duke of Exeter doth love thee well.

Fluellen

Ay, I praise God; and I have merited some love at
his hands.

Pistol

Bardolph, a soldier, firm and sound of heart,   25
And of buxom valour, hath by cruel fate
And giddy Fortune's furious fickle wheel,

38. *moral:* personification.

40. *pax:* a piece of wood or metal with Christ's picture on it, which people kissed at communion services to receive peace. The history books mention a soldier who stole a 'pyx', a box in which the consecrated wafers for communion were kept, and it seems possible that 'pax' is a mistake for 'pyx', though Shakespeare himself must have known the difference. It is significant that Henry's discipline was so good that this sort of theft was rare, and indeed the execution of the culprit shows how ruthlessly the king's orders were carried out.

43. *hemp:* rope.

47. *vital thread:* the thread of life.

48. 'with a bit of cheap rope.'

49. *requite:* reward. Pistol is really offering Fluellen a bribe to stop justice taking its proper course.

50. *partly understand:* he pretends not to understand about the bribe.

55. *to use his good pleasure:* to punish him as he thought fit. Even if his own brother were the culprit Fluellen would not speak up for him.

56. *for discipline ought to be used.* To Fluellen discipline is more important than family feeling and sentimentality.

57–9. The *figo* and *the fig of Spain* were terms of abuse accompanied by a coarse gesture. Pistol is furious, not only because his 'friend' has turned him down, but also because he has lost a lot of face in having his bribe rejected.

That goddess blind.

That stands upon the rolling restless stone—

Fluellen

By your patience, Aunchient Pistol. Fortune is painted 30
blind, with a muffler afore her eyes, to signify to you
that Fortune is blind; and she is painted also with a
wheel, to signify to you, which is the moral of it, that
she is turning, and inconstant, and mutability, and
variation; and her foot, look you, is fixed upon a 35
spherical stone, which rolls, and rolls, and rolls. In
good truth, the poet makes a most excellent description
of it: Fortune is an excellent moral.

Pistol

Fortune is Bardolph's foe, and frowns on him;
For he hath stol'n a pax, and hanged must 'a be— 40
A damned death!
Let gallows gape for dog; let man go free,
And let not hemp his windpipe suffocate.
But Exeter hath given the doom of death
For pax of little price. 45
Therefore, go speak – the Duke will hear thy voice;
And let not Bardolph's vital thread be cut
With edge of penny cord and vile reproach.
Speak, Captain, for his life, and I will thee requite.

Fluellen

Aunchient Pistol, I do partly understand your 50
meaning.

Pistol

Why then, rejoice therefore.

Fluellen

Certainly, Aunchient, it is not a thing to rejoice at; for
if, look you, he were my brother, I would desire the
Duke to use his good pleasure, and put him to execu- 55
tion; for discipline ought to be used.

Pistol

Die and be damn'd! and figo for thy friendship!

61. *an arrant counterfeit rascal:* 'an absolute crook.'

62. *a bawd:* one who arranges meetings between men and prostitutes (nowadays a 'pimp').

A *cutpurse* was a pickpocket; men used to wear their purses on a string from their belts, and it was fairly easy to cut the string.

63–4. Now we see why Fluellen spoke so highly of Pistol earlier in the scene: Pistol had merely *talked* bravely.

64–6. Fluellen's words sound menacing, as though he intends to take Pistol to task when the time suits him.

67. *gull:* idiot.

68. *to grace himself:* to give himself airs, putting on a big act. Gower goes on to give a delightful description of the way bogus soldiers like Pistol impress an *ale-wash'd* and extremely gullible audience in London.

70. *are perfect in:* they can rattle the names off without hesitation.

71. *learn . . . by rote:* learn by heart. *services:* actions, exploits.

72. *sconce:* a small fort.

74. *what terms the enemy stood on:* what conditions the enemy demanded. (The sort of information only important officers would really know.)

75. *con . . .: learn off pat the jargon of war.*

76. *they trick up . . . oaths:* they mix all this carefully learned knowledge with all the latest phrases and catch words. The type is still clearly recognizable today.

76–7. They go to the extent of imitating the fashions of their commanders, and making sure their military dress shows unmistakable signs of a desperate campaign. And the effect they create in the right company is wonderful – which does not say much for the company.

79–81. Gower gently points out that Fluellen has been a little gullible. *slanders of the age* are people who bring disgrace upon this particular generation.

84. *a hole in his coat:* an opportunity to show him up.

86. *I must speak with him from the pridge:* I must give him the news about events at the bridge.

Fluellen
    It is well.
Pistol
    The fig of Spain!

                            [Exit]

Fluellen
    Very good.   60
Gower
    Why, this is an arrant counterfeit rascal; I remember
    him now – a bawd, a cutpurse.
Fluellen
    I'll assure you, 'a utter'd as prave words at the pridge
    as you shall see in a summer's day. But it is very well;
    what he has spoke to me, that is well, I warrant you,   65
    when time is serve.
Gower
    Why, 'tis a gull, a fool, a rogue, that now and then
    goes to the wars to grace himself, at his return into
    London, under the form of a soldier. And such fellows
    are perfect in the great commanders' names; and they   70
    will learn you by rote where services were done – at
    such and such a sconce, at such a breach, at such a
    convoy; who came off bravely, who was shot, who
    disgrac'd, what terms the enemy stood on; and this
    they con perfectly in the phrase of war, which they   75
    trick up with new-tuned oaths; and what a beard of
    the General's cut and a horrid suit of the camp will
    do among foaming bottles and ale-wash'd wits is
    wonderful to be thought on. But you must learn to
    know such slanders of the age, or else you may be   80
    marvellously mistook.
Fluellen
    I tell you what, Captain Gower, I do perceive he is
    not the man that he would gladly make show to the
    world he is; if I find a hole in his coat I will tell him
    my mind. *[Drum within]* Hark you, the King is coming;   85
    and I must speak with him from the pridge.

Stage Direction. *his poor soldiers* reminds us that the king is now accompanied by a sick, weary, ragged shambles of an army.

90–1. *is gone off:* have retreated. Notice that Fluellen *can* speak to the point.
92. *passages:* skirmishes, fights. The English soldiers under the Duke of Exeter have fought well to win the bridge. *th'athversary:* the adversary, enemy.

97–100. The French have lost many men in the battle, but the only English loss is Bardolph, for disciplinary reasons. *marry* is another form of oath by Mary, the mother of Jesus.
100–5. A wonderful description of Bardolph's features, which we already knew from the Boy's jokes were flaming red. *bubukles* and *whelks* are boils and pimples, and we gather that his lips blew like bellows to fan the fire of his nose. But he is already dead, apparently, although Pistol was pleading for him a few minutes ago: *his fire's out* has the double meaning that his life is finished and his face doesn't flame any more. We have to accept that sometimes a playwright needs to compress events into a shorter length of actual stage time than they would take in real life.
106. *We would have . . . cut off.* The king does indeed know Bardolph, but he shows no emotion. He is determined to be fair to the local people, and to punish ruthlessly any one convicted of the brutality and thieving that invading armies usually indulged in.
110–12. *for when lenity . . . winner:* 'I am more likely to succeed in my ambitions in France by being kind to the people than by being cruel to them.' The image is a personification of *lenity* (gentleness) and *cruelty* playing against each other at dice, with a kingdom as the stake.
Stage Direction. Montjoy, the French herald, enters in his official costume accompanied by an escort and a trumpeter. (*Tucket* is a brief trumpet call announcing the arrival of an important messenger.)
113. *habit:* coat. The herald was easily recognizable by the special coat he wore, which had his crest embroidered on it. But one would expect a mere herald to make his first remarks to a king a little more respectful: 'You know who I am, of course,' he says. 'All right then, if you say so, I know who you are,' the king replies. 'What have you come to tell me?'

[Drum and colours Enter the KING *and his poor*
SOLDIERS, *and* GLOUCESTER]

God pless your Majesty!
King

How now, Fluellen! Cam'st thou from the bridge?
Fluellen

Ay, so please your Majesty. The Duke of Exeter has
very gallantly maintain'd the pridge; the French is gone   90
off, look you, and there is gallant and most prave
passages. Marry, th' athversary was have possession of
the pridge; but he is enforced to retire, and the Duke
of Exeter is master of the pridge; I can tell your Majesty
the Duke is a prave man.   95
King

What men have you lost, Fluellen!
Fluellen

The perdition of th' athversary hath been very great,
reasonable great; marry, for my part, I think the Duke
hath lost never a man, but one that is like to be
executed for robbing a church – one Bardolph, if your 100
Majesty know the man; his face is all bubukles, and
whelks, and knobs, and flames o' fire; and his lips
blows at his nose, and it is like a coal of fire, sometimes
plue and sometimes red; but his nose is executed and
his fire's out.   105
King

We would have all such offenders so cut off. And we
give express charge that in our marches through the
country there be nothing compell'd from the villages,
nothing taken but paid for, none of the French
upbraided or abused in disdainful language; for when 110
lenity and cruelty play for a kingdom the gentler game-
ster is the soonest winner.

[Tucket. Enter MONTJOY]

Montjoy

You know me by my habit.

118–21. The French king's message begins with an attempt to justify his slowness to act so far. *advantage . . . rashness* means 'it is better tactics to wait for a good moment to attack than to rush recklessly into battle.' This sounds admirable, but ironically the opportunity the French did eventually choose, at Agincourt, was probably the worst tactical moment they could have chosen.

120–1. *we thought not good to bruise an injury till it were full ripe:* 'we thought it best not to try to squeeze the poison out of the boil until it had come to a head,' (they preferred to let the English wear themselves out before destroying them).

122. *cue.* The end of one actor's speech is the *cue* for the next speaker to begin. So far the French have been 'slow on their cue,' pausing too long before joining in the drama, but now they are going to act promptly. This metaphor from drama is continued in *our voice is imperial.* Now they are going to take charge and act everybody else off the stage.

124. *sufferance:* patience.

124–32. The French have such a tremendous advantage over the enfeebled English army that they are in a position to make this haughty demand for ransom; if the English pay they will be allowed to return home, if not they will be destroyed utterly. The sum to be paid will have to bear some proportion to the losses the French have suffered, but it would be impossible to compensate them fully: Henry hasn't enough money in his exchequer to do it, and anyway the French blood that has been spilt is irreplaceable – the whole English race couldn't produce enough blood of the same quality.

134–5. *So far . . . office:* 'that's what my king told me to say, and I've done my job.'

137–8. *Montjoy* is not his personal name, but the title of the chief herald of France. Henry recognizes it and compliments him on the very frank way he does the job.

140–1. *But could be willing . . . impeachment:* 'but I would prefer to march on to Calais without having to stop and fight.'

141. *sooth:* truth.

143. *an enemy of craft and vantage:* 'an enemy who is full of guile and also has considerable superiority over me.'

King

    Well then, I know thee; what shall I know of thee?

Montjoy

    My master's mind.   115

King

    Unfold it.

Montjoy

    Thus says my king. Say thou to Harry of England:
Though we seem'd dead we did but sleep; advantage
is a better soldier than rashness. Tell him we could
have rebuk'd him at Harfleur, but that we thought not 120
good to bruise an injury till it were full ripe. Now we
speak upon our cue, and our voice is imperial: England
shall repent his folly, see his weakness, and admire our
sufferance. Bid him therefore consider of his ransom,
which must proportion the losses we have borne, the 125
subjects we have lost, the disgrace we have digested;
which, in weight to re-answer, his pettiness would bow
under. For our losses his exchequer is too poor; for th'
effusion of our blood, the muster of his kingdom too
faint a number; and for our disgrace, his own person 130
kneeling at our feet but a weak and worthless satisfaction. To this add defiance; and tell him, for conclusion,
he hath betrayed his followers, whose condemnation
is pronounc'd. So far my king and master; so much
my office.   135

King

    What is thy name? I know thy quality.

Montjoy

    Montjoy.

King

    Thou dost thy office fairly. Turn thee back,
And tell thy king I do not seek him now,
But could be willing to march on to Calais   140
Without impeachment; for, to say the sooth—
Though 'tis no wisdom to confess so much
Unto an enemy of craft and vantage—

144–9. Another scornful reference to the inferiority of French soldiers: when the English soldier is fully fit he is as good as three Frenchmen.

149–51. Henry pretends to repent of bragging, but makes it clear that he only brags in answer to the arrogant boasting of Montjoy's message – he has caught the infection from the French. They, however, with the exception of the Constable, don't realize they are being so boastful, the next scene bears this out, whereas Henry recognizes his bragging as something for which he must repent.

153. *trunk:* body. The only ransom he offers is his body, which of course the French will have to capture in battle.

155–7. *Yet, God before . . . way:* in spite of our weakness, with God as our leader we intend to march on, even if the king of France himself and another equally powerful enemy, too, try to stop us.

157. *There's for thy labour:* here's some money for your trouble. And he throws Montjoy a bag of gold as a token of his respect for Montjoy's courage in speaking out as he did.

158. *well advise himself:* consider carefully.

159–65. *If we may pass . . . master:* 'Our condition being what it is, we would prefer not to fight, but we are not afraid to fight if we have to and if we do we shall make this French earth red with French blood.

166–7. With Henry's defiant words ringing in his ears Montjoy departs, but as soon as he has gone Gloucester's remark reveals just how anxious the English really feel.

My people are with sickness much enfeebled;
My numbers lessen'd; and those few I have   145
Almost no better than so many French;
Who when they were in health, I tell thee, herald,
I thought upon one pair of English legs
Did march three Frenchmen. Yet forgive me, God,
That I do brag thus; this your air of France   150
Hath blown that vice in me; I must repent.
Go, therefore, tell they master here I am;
My ransom is this frail and worthless trunk;
My army but a weak and sickly guard;
Yet, God before, tell him we will come on,   155
Though France himself and such another neighbour
Stand in our way. There's for thy labour, Montjoy.
Go, bid thy master well advise himself.
If we may pass, we will; if we be hinder'd,
We shall your tawny ground with your red blood   160
Discolour; and so, Montjoy, fare you well.
The sum of all our answer is but this:
We would not seek a battle as we are;
Nor as we are, we say, we will not shun it.
So tell your master.   165

Montjoy

I shall deliver so. Thanks to your Highness.

[Exit]

Gloucester

I hope they will not come upon us now.

King

We are in God's hand, brother, not in theirs.
March to the bridge, it now draws toward night;
Beyond the river we'll encamp ourselves,   170
And on to-morrow bid them march away.

[Exeunt]

SCENE VII

It is the night before the battle. The French nobles are on edge, impatient for the next day to dawn. The thought of losing the battle does not enter their heads; they are interested only in their own armour, their horses, their courage, the impression they will create on the battlefield, and the number of English prisoners they will capture.

1–11.Note the recurrence of remarks such as *Would it were day! Will it never be morning?* These lines are spoken with many pauses and sighs of impatience, as though the French nobles are trying to think of something to say to relieve the monotony of waiting. They also show Shakespeare, in a theatre which could not be darkened, reminding his audience that it is a night scene.

9. *of both:* with both horse and armour.

11–18. The Dauphin will not change his horse for any ordinary horse that merely walks (*treads but*) on four legs (*pasterns*) for his flying horse is like Pegasus, with flaming nostrils, or like a tennis ball bouncing.
Pegasus: a winged horse in ancient Greek mythology. *as if his entrails were hairs.* Tennis balls used to be stuffed with hair. *Hermes* was an ancient Greek god who charmed the monster Argus with the music of his pipe.
19. *the colour of the nutmeg:* a light reddish-brown colour. It was thought to indicate a good, agile horse.
20. *And of the heat of the ginger:* he has the spirit of ginger horses, which were thought to be fiery. The Dauphin's horse seems to combine all the best qualities of all types. *Perseus* was the mythical hero who cut off the Medusa's head, among other famous exploits.
21–2. *the dull elements:* see the note on Act I, Prologue, line 1. All four elements were thought to be present in everything, but a greater proportion of air and fire would produce more life and spirit.

Scene VII

The French camp near Agincourt

[Enter the CONSTABLE OF FRANCE, *the* LORD RAMBURES,
the DUKE OF ORLEANS, *the* DAUPHIN, *with* OTHERS*]*

Constable

Tut! I have the best armour of the world. Would it
were day!

Orleans

You have an excellent armour; but let my horse have
his due.

Constable

It is the best horse of Europe.   5

Orleans

Will it never be morning?

Dauphin

My Lord of Orleans and my Lord High Constable, you
talk of horse and armour?

Orleans

You are as well provided of both as any prince in the
world.   10

Dauphin

What a long night is this! I will not change my horse
with any that treads but on four pasterns. Ça, ha! he
bounds from the earth as if his entrails were hairs; le
cheval volant, the Pegasus, chez les narines de feu!
When I bestride him I soar, I am a hawk. He trots   15
the air; the earth sings when he touches it; the basest
horn of his hoof is more musical than the pipe of
Hermes.

Orleans

He's of the colour of the nutmeg.

Dauphin

And of the heat of the ginger. It is a beast for Perseus: 20
he is pure air and fire; and the dull elements of earth
and water never appear in him, but only in patient

24. *jades:* poor worn-out horses – a contemptuous term used by the Dauphin for all other horses.

25–6. The Constable is tired of the Dauphin's boasting. We might say 'All right, we admit it: it's a marvellous horse. Now shut up.' *absolute:* perfect.

27. A *palfrey* is a small horse used for riding, not a war-horse.

32. *lodging:* lying down.

32–3. *vary deserved praises on my palfrey:* maintain a continuous and ever-varying sequence of praises on my horse (a metaphor from music).

33. *fluent:* flowing and continuous.

35. *argument for them all:* sufficient subject matter for every grain of sand to be able to say something different.

36. *reason on:* hold forth on.

38–9. *to lay apart their particular functions:* to stop doing what they ought to be doing.

39. *writ:* wrote.

43–67. The Dauphin's declaration *my horse is my mistress* sets off one of the sequences of double-meanings and plays on words that Shakespeare and his audience loved. Many of the words can be used of lovers and of horses, and this new conversational game reawakens the Constable's interest, and his wit.

44. *bears well:* carries her rider well.

45–6. *Me well . . . mistress:* she carries me well, and me only, which is exactly what a good and faithful mistress should do.

particular: belonging to oneself exclusively.

47. *shrewdly:* sharply.

stillness while his rider mounts him; he is indeed a
horse, and all other jades you may call beasts.

Constable

Indeed, my lord, it is a most absolute and excellent 25
horse.

Dauphin

It is the prince of palfreys: his neigh is like the bid-
ding of a monarch, and his countenance enforces
homage.

Orleans

No more, cousin. 30

Dauphin

Nay, the man hath no wit that cannot, from the rising
of the lark to the lodging of the lamb, vary deserved
praise on my palfrey. It is a theme as fluent as the sea:
turn the sands into eloquent tongues, and my horse
is argument for them all; 'tis a subject for a sovereign 35
to reason on, and for a sovereign's sovereign to ride
on; and for the world – familiar to us and unknown
– to lay apart their particular functions and wonder at
him. I once writ a sonnet in his praise and began thus:
'Wonder of nature'— 40

Orleans

I have heard a sonnet begin so to one's mistress.

Dauphin

Then did they imitate that which I compos'd to my
courser; for my horse is my mistress.

Orleans

Your mistress bears well.

Dauphin

Me well; which is the prescript praise and perfection 45
of a good and particular mistress.

Constable

Nay, for methought yesterday your mistress shrewdly
shook your back.

Dauphin

So perhaps did yours.

50. *bridled:* the bridle is the rider's means of controlling the horse, and the horse may resent it and try to shake the rider off. The Constable's mistress was under no such compulsion and did not try to shake him off.

51. *belike:* probably.

52. *kern of Ireland:* an Irish soldier who wore a tunic or kilt and no trousers. *French hose* was loose, wide breeches, and *strait strossers* means narrow trousers, but of course the Dauphin means the tight skin of bare legs.

54. *You have . . . horsemanship:* you seem to know all about this kind of riding.

56. *foul bogs:* hazards for riders, but the Dauphin is referring metaphorically to the dangers of loose morals.

57. *to my mistress:* as my mistress.

58. *I had as lief have my mistress a jade:* Constable is playing on the two uses of *jade:* (1) a poor, old, worn-out horse, and (ii) an unpleasant woman. *as lief:* 'as willingly'.

63–4. *Le chien . . . bourbier:* 'The dog is turned to his own vomit again; and the sow that was washed to her wallowing in the mire.' (2 *Peter* ii, 22). A proverb which the Dauphin uses to illustrate the way the Constable makes use of any remark for his own advantage.

67. *so little kin to the purpose:* so irrelevant.

68–9. Feeling that the argument is getting a little too heated, Rambures tactfully changes the subject.

70–2. The stars are probably some form of engraved decoration on the Constable's armour. In saying he hopes some will fall, the Dauphin seems to be hoping the Constable himself will receive a buffeting that will (as it were) shake some of them off. The reply *And yet my sky shall not want* means 'And yet there will be no shortage of stars in my sky' or 'Even if I am killed I shall still have plenty of glory and honour.'

Constable
    Mine was not bridled.   50

Dauphin
    O, then belike she was old and gentle; and you rode
    like a kern of Ireland, your French hose off and in your
    strait strossers.

Constable
    You have good judgment in horsemanship.

Dauphin
    Be warn'd by me, then: they that ride so, and ride not   55
    warily, fall into foul bogs. I had rather have my horse
    to my mistress.

Constable
    I had as lief have my mistress a jade.

Dauphin
    I tell thee, Constable, my mistress wears his own
    hair.   60

Constable
    I could make as true a boast as that, if I had a sow to
    my mistress.

Dauphin
    'Le chien est retourné à son propre vomissement, et
    la truie lavée au bourbier.' Thou mak'st use of
    anything.   65

Constable
    Yet do I not use my horse for my mistress, or any such
    proverb so little kin to the purpose.

Rambures
    My Lord Constable, the armour that I saw in your tent
    to-night – are those stars or suns upon it?

Constable
    Stars, my lord.   70

Dauphin
    Some of them will fall to-morrow, I hope.

Constable
    And yet my sky shall not want.

73. *a many:* far too many.

77. *his desert:* all the praises he deserves.

78–81. The Dauphin's ***my way shall be paved with English faces*** is a presumptuous boast, and the Constable uses its words to rebuke him for it: 'I would not make a remark like that in case there turned out to be too many faces and I were put to shame (*fac'd out*).'

81. *would fain be:* very much want to be.

82. *about the ears of the English:* fighting the English (continuing the play on *faces*).

83–5. Rambures wants a game of dice with English prisoners as the stake, the loser to pay his debts tomorrow after the battle has been won and the prisoners taken.

go to hazard: 'gamble.' But the more sensible, less presumptuous Constable points out that they haven't got the prisoners yet, and have to 'go to hazard' (run the risks of battle) to get them.

89. After the Dauphin's exit, the Constable's opinion of him becomes even more obvious: he clearly doesn't expect the Dauphin to kill any Englishmen in battle.

91. *tread out the oath:* obliterate it. The Constable thinks the oath should not have been made and had better now be forgotten, because the Dauphin is not in fact ***a gallant prince***.

93. *Doing . . . doing:* if as you say he is active then he must do something, but he never does anything.

Dauphin

That may be, for you bear a many superfluously, and
'twere more honour some were away.

Constable

Ev'n as your horse bears your praises, who would trot   75
as well were some of your brags dismounted.

Dauphin

Would I were able to load him with his desert! Will it
never be day ? I will trot to-morrow a mile, and my
way shall be paved with English faces.

Constable

I will not say so, for fear I should be fac'd out of my   80
way; but I would it were morning, for I would fain be
about the ears of the English.

Rambures

Who will go to hazard with me for twenty prisoners?

Constable

You must first go yourself to hazard ere you have
them.   85

Dauphin

'Tis midnight; I'll go arm myself.

[Exit]

Orleans

The Dauphin longs for morning.

Rambures

He longs to eat the English.

Constable

I think he will eat all he kills.

Orleans

By the white hand of my lady, he's a gallant prince.   90

Constable

Swear by her foot, that she may tread out the oath.

Orleans

He is simply the most active gentleman of France.

Constable

Doing is activity, and he will still be doing.

95–6. The Dauphin won't do any harm to the English either, and so will maintain his reputation for never doing harm.

100. *car'd not:* didn't care.

104. *lackey:* valet – the only person the Dauphin has struck bravely, because of course the valet can't hit back.
104. *hooded* and *bate:* terms from falconry. The hawk was kept hooded so that it could not see or fly away, until the creature being hunted was sighted; when the hood was removed from a badly trained hawk it would beat its wings before being released and fall off the falconer's wrist.
bate: The Dauphin's courage is like an inferior hawk; it spends most of the time subdued under a hood and when the hood is removed, goes off ineffectually.
106–16. A battle of words, mostly proverbs.

111–12. *'A pox of the devil':* 'May the devil get a good dose of the pox.' This is what is *due* to the devil (Constable's answer to the previous proverb quoted by Orleans). *Pox* might be any unpleasant skin-disease (chicken-pox, small-pox), but especially syphilis.
113–14. *You are the better . . . soon shot:* just as it's easy for a fool to fire his weapon too soon (and leave himself defenceless) so you have an easy and worthless superiority at quoting proverbs.

115. *shot over:* i.e. missed the target. 'You are wrong.'

Orleans

He never did harm that I heard of.

Constable

Nor will do none to-morrow: he will keep that good   95
name still.

Orleans

I know him to be valiant.

Constable

I was told that by one that knows him better than you.

Orleans

What's he?

Constable

Marry, he told me so himself; and he said he car'd not 100
who knew it.

Orleans

He needs not; it is no hidden virtue in him.

Constable

By my faith, sir, but it is; never anybody saw it but
his lackey. 'Tis a hooded valour, and when it appears
it will bate.   105

Orleans

Ill-wind never said well.

Constable

I will cap that proverb with 'There is flattery in
friendship'.

Orleans

And I will take up that with 'Give the devil his due'.

Constable

Well plac'd! There stands your friend for the devil; 110
have at the very eye of that proverb with 'A pox of
the devil!'

Orleans

You are the better at proverbs by how much 'A fool's
bolt is soon shot'.

Constable

You have shot over.   115

116. *overshot:* beaten.

124. *peevish:* silly, annoying, irritating.

125–6. *to mope . . . knowledge:* 'to come blundering with his half-witted followers so far away from places he knows and things he understands.'

127. *apprehension:* intelligent understanding of the situation.

132–6. English mastiff dogs had a reputation for bear-baiting, the sport of tying a bear to a post and setting dogs on it. But Orleans thinks they are just stupid and ignorant rather than courageous – rather like the English army.

134. *winking:* 'with their eyes shut.'

138. *Just, just!* Exactly! A good point.
sympathise with: resemble. The Englishmen are like their dogs in their apparently brave but utterly senseless aggressiveness.

Orleans

'Tis not the first time you were overshot.

[Enter a MESSENGER]

Messenger

My Lord High Constable, the English lie within fifteen hundred paces of your tents.

Constable

Who hath measur'd the ground?

Messenger

The Lord Grandpré.   120

Constable

A valiant and most expert gentleman. Would it were day! Alas, poor Harry of England! he longs not for the dawning as we do.

Orleans

What a wretched and peevish fellow is this King of England, to mope with his fat-brain'd followers so far 125 out of his knowledge!

Constable

If the English had any apprehension, they would run away.

Orleans

That they lack; for if their heads had any intellectual armour, they could never wear such heavy 130 head-pieces.

Rambures

That island of England breeds very valiant creatures; their mastiffs are of unmatchable courage.

Orleans

Foolish curs, that run winking into the mouth of a Russian bear, and have their heads crush'd like rotten 135 apples! You may as well say that's a valiant flea that dare eat his breakfast on the lip of a lion.

Constable

Just, just! and the men do sympathise with the mastiffs in robustious and rough coming on, leaving

140. *wits:* brains.
140–2. English courage was thought to derive from the vast amounts of beef they were reputed to eat. *iron and steel:* weapons.

143. *shrewdly out of beef:* there is a serious shortage of beef in the English camp.

145. *stomachs:* two meanings: (i) appetite for food (ii) inclination and courage for fighting. The lack of beef will give the English the first and take away the second.

147–8. The scene ends on a note of typical boasting and overconfidence.

their wits with their wives; and then give them great 140
meals of beef and iron and steel; they will eat like
wolves and fight like devils.

Orleans

Ay, but these English are shrewdly out of beef.

Constable

Then shall we find to-morrow they have only stomachs
to eat, and none to fight. Now is it time to arm. Come, 145
shall we about it?

Orleans

It is now two o'clock; but let me see – by ten
We shall have each a hundred Englishmen.

[Exeunt]

ACT FOUR

PROLOGUE

1. *entertain conjecture of:* imagine.

2. *the poring dark:* darkness which strains the eyes. The audience need to be vividly reminded that it is still night (see note on Act III, Scene vii, lines 1–11).

4. *the foul womb of night.* Shakespeare's *Macbeth* provides a very full demonstration of this sense of the evil quality of darkness (see particularly *Macbeth* Act II, Scene i, lines 49–56). Later in this Prologue (line 21) night is compared to *a foul and ugly witch*.

5. *stilly:* very quietly. With the sort of quietness that seems to emphasize the surrounding silence.

6–14. We know from the previous scene (lines 117–8) that the two armies are encamped within fifteen hundred paces of each other – well under a mile; so close, in fact, that the sentries can almost pick out their opposite numbers' whispered messages. The men sitting by their fires can look across and see the faces of their enemies *umber'd* (shadowy, as though tinted dark brown) in the light of their fires; horses neigh at each other, as though already threatening; and from the tents on both sides comes the noise of the armourers putting the finishing touches to the armour, a kind of signal (*note*) that a great battle is imminent. These real details enable us to comprehend and in some way experience an utterly extraordinary situation: thousands of men waiting for daylight so that they can kill each other, but in the meantime sitting peacefully near each other, almost sharing each other's company and thoughts, united in the tense quietness of this fateful night.

12. *accomplishing:* completing the armouring of.

17. *secure in soul:* feeling completely confident.

18. *over-lusty:* excessively cheerful and hearty and optimistic.

19. They are playing dice for English prisoners, as explained in the last scene (line 83).

20. *chide:* scold, rebuke.

tardy-gaited: slow-moving (as though a *cripple*).

Again, in the last scene we saw the French nobles repeatedly complaining about the length of the night.

22–8. *poor condemned English, Like sacrifices . . . gesture sad . . . lanklean cheeks . . . horrid ghosts.* Notice the contrast with the *over-lusty* French. The English *inly ruminate* (turn over and over in their minds) *the morning's danger*, while the French play dice, *their gesture sad:* their forlorn bearing; they sit with their heads slumped forward lifelessly, this mood of hopelessness *investing* ('clothing,' i.e. hanging over) everything about them, the undernourished faces and ragged old clothes, and giving them the appearance of ghosts in the moonlight (*horrid:* hair raising). The *gazing moon* watches from her great distance, sympathetically perhaps, but too detached to be able to help.

ACT FOUR

Prologue

[Enter CHORUS]

Chorus

Now entertain conjecture of a time
When creeping murmur and the poring dark
Fills the wide vessel of the universe.
From camp to camp, through the foul womb of night,
The hum of either army stilly sounds,   5
That the fix'd sentinels almost receive
The secret whispers of each other's watch.
Fire answers fire, and through their paly flames
Each battle sees the other's umber'd face;
Steed threatens steed, in high and boastful neighs   10
Piercing the night's dull ear; and from the tents
The armourers accomplishing the knights,
With busy hammers closing rivets up,
Give dreadful note of preparation.
The country cocks do crow, the clocks do toll,   15
And the third hour of drowsy morning name.
Proud of their numbers and secure in soul,
The confident and over-lusty French
Do the low-rated English play at dice;
And chide the cripple tardy-gaited night   20
Who like a foul and ugly witch doth limp
So tediously away. The poor condemned English,
Like sacrifices, by their watchful fires
Sit patiently and inly ruminate
The morning's danger; and their gesture sad   25
Investing lank-lean cheeks and war-worn coats
Presenteth them unto the gazing moon

28–31. *who will behold him . . . Let him cry:* let anyone who sees . . . cry.

34. *And calls them brothers, friends:* an example of what we call 'the common touch,' the ability to be natural and at ease even with the humblest subordinate, which was a valuable part of Henry's great qualities of leadership.

35–6. 'You would not know from the king's face that he is surrounded by such a formidable enemy.'

37–8. 'Nor has being awake all night made him look in the least bit pale.'

39–40. *over-bears attaint With cheerful semblance:* covers his feelings of fear and fatigue with cheerful smiles.

41. *That:* with the result that.

43. *largess:* the generous distribution of gifts to all and sundry by a king or some other important person, usually on special occasions. The gift here is not money but comfort, but it is *universal*, like the sun, shining on all alike.

45. *mean and gentle all:* common soldiers and gentlemen and knights and nobles, all alike.

46. *as may unworthiness define:* 'what I can only describe inadequately as.'

47. *A little touch of Harry.* Henry cures the foreboding of his men just as Jesus (or other miracle-workers) cured disease with a mere *touch*.

50. *foils:* rapiers; the kind of sword used in fencing, not real battleswords.

51. *Right ill-dispos'd:* thoroughly incorrectly handled.

53. *Minding:* imagining.

mock'ries: imitations. In this case the imitations are laughably inadequate, but the audience are asked to use them as a basis for the work of their imaginations, just as they were asked to do in the Prologue to Act I.

So many horrid ghosts. O, now, who will behold
The royal captain of this ruin'd band
Walking from watch to watch, from tent to tent,   30
Let him cry, 'Praise and glory on his head!'
For forth he goes and visits all his host;
Bids them good morrow with a modest smile,
And calls them brothers, friends, and countrymen.
Upon his royal face there is no note   35
How dread an army hath enrounded him;
Nor doth he dedicate one jot of colour
Unto the weary and all-watched night;
But freshly looks, and over-bears attaint
With cheerful semblance and sweet majesty;   40
That every wretch, pining and pale before,
Beholding him, plucks comfort from his looks;
A largess universal, like the sun,
His liberal eye doth give to every one,
Thawing cold fear, that mean and gentle all   45
Behold, as may unworthiness define,
A little touch of Harry in the night.
And so our scene must to the battle fly;
Where – O for pity! – we shall much disgrace
With four or five most vile and ragged foils,   50
Right ill-dispos'd in brawl ridiculous,
The name of Agincourt. Yet sit and see,
Minding true things by what their mock'ries be.

[Exit]

Scene I

France. The English camp at Agincourt

[Enter the KING, BEDFORD, *and* GLOUCESTER]

King
    Gloucester, 'tis true that we are in great danger;
    The greater therefore should our courage be.
    Good morrow, brother Bedford. God Almighty!

4–12. At once we are given an illustration of the cheerfulness mentioned just now by the Chorus: Henry remarks, in the chill, nervous darkness of early morning, that there is something good in evil things, if men will only look for it and draw it out, for their *bad neighbour* (the French Army) has not only made them get up early, which is good for the health and for business, it has also, like a conscience or a preacher, persuaded them to prepare their souls for the possibility of death.

15. *churlish:* rough.

16. *likes me:* pleases me.
17. As the king himself has to sleep on the ground too, Erpingham can comfort himself with the thought that he is living like a king.

18–23. *'Tis good . . . legerity:* it's a good thing for men to accept hardships as a result of seeing others suffer, for it helps them to feel content and easy in their minds, and that in turn enables the body to work more cheerfully and nimbly. *slough:* the outer skin which a snake periodically casts (sheds).

26. *Do:* give.
anon: in a little while.
27. *Desire . . . pavilion:* 'ask them all to come to my tent.'

29–32. Henry refuses Erpingham's offer to accompany him because he wants to meditate alone for a time, perhaps pray; but the cloak he has borrowed (line 24) has a full hood, and when he is left alone he pulls the hood close round his head so that no-one can recognize him. This enables him to mingle with his men without embarrassing them, and also provides the dramatist with some opportunities for humour and dramatic irony.

There is some soul of goodness in things evil,
Would men observingly distil it out; 5
For our bad neighbour makes us early stirrers,
Which is both healthful and good husbandry.
Besides, they are our outward consciences
And preachers to us all, admonishing
That we should dress us fairly for our end. 10
Thus may we gather honey from the weed,
And make a moral of the devil himself.

[Enter ERPINGHAM*]*

Good morrow, old Sir Thomas Erpingham:
A good soft pillow for that good white head
Were better than a churlish turf of France. 15
Erpingham
Not so, my liege; this lodging likes me better,
Since I may say 'Now lie I like a king'.
King
'Tis good for men to love their present pains
Upon example; so the spirit is eased;
And when the mind is quicken'd, out of doubt 20
The organs, though defunct and dead before,
Break up their drowsy grave and newly move
With casted slough and fresh legerity.
Lend me thy cloak, Sir Thomas. Brothers both,
Commend me to the princes in our camp; 25
Do my good morrow to them, and anon
Desire them all to my pavilion.
Gloucester
We shall, my liege.
Erpingham
Shall I attend your Grace?
King
                              No, my good knight:
Go with my brothers to my lords of England; 30
I and my bosom must debate awhile,
And then I would no other company.

35. *Qui va là?* who goes there? (Pistol has to assume some form of affectation, so he speaks in French.)

37. *Discuss unto me:* tell me.
38. *popular:* just a member of the crowd, undistinguished.

39. *gentleman of a company:* a sort of non-commissioned officer, rather superior to the ordinary soldiers.

40.*Trail'st . . . pike?* An affected way of asking 'Are you an infantry-man?' The pike was usually carried near the heavy end, where the metal point was, with the other trailing on the ground.
41. *Even so:* 'Yes, just as you say.'

44. *bawcock:* fine fellow (as in Act III, Scene ii, line 24). Pistol reels off a string of affectionate compliments, little knowing that he is actually talking to the subject of them. *a heart of gold* implies perfection, as gold was the perfect blend of the four elements. We might say 'an absolutely first-class fellow'.
45. *imp:* child.
48. *lovely bully:* adorable fellow, but the Irish 'darling boy' is a nearer modern version.
49. *le Roy* is a pun on the French 'le roi' (the king), made funnier by Pistol's response.

Erpingham
    The Lord in heaven bless thee, noble Harry!

    [Exeunt all but the KING]

King
    God-a-mercy, old heart! thou speak'st cheerfully.

    [Enter PISTOL]

Pistol
    Qui va là?   35
King
    A friend.
Pistol
    Discuss unto me: art thou officer,
    Or art thou base, common, and popular?
King
    I am a gentleman of a company.
Pistol
    Trail'st thou the puissant pike?   40
King
    Even so. What are you?
Pistol
    As good a gentleman as the Emperor.
King
    Then you are a better than the King.
Pistol
    The King's a bawcock and a heart of gold,
    A lad of life, an imp of fame;   45
    Of parents good, of fist most valiant.
    I kiss his dirty shoe, and from heart-string
    I love the lovely bully. What is thy name?
King
    Harry le Roy.
Pistol
    Le Roy! a Cornish name; art thou of Cornish crew?   50
King
    No, I am a Welshman.

54–5. The *leek*, a vegetable of the onion family, is the national emblem of the Welsh, who wear it on their national day, St David's Day (March 1st). Pistol is still squirming from Fluellen's rebuke in Act III, Scene vi.
pate: head.
56. *in your cap:* the leek was worn in the cap. Henry, knowing the relative courage of the two men, gives Pistol a strong warning of Fluellen's probable reaction.

60. *figo:* the same coarse gesture that Pistol directed at Fluellen in the earlier scene (Act III, Scene vi).

63. *sorts well with:* suits. The king is amused by the way Pistol tries to terrify him with his last threatening remark *My name is Pistol call'd.* Does he say *It sorts well with your fierceness* in a mocking way, or with perfect seriousness as though to humour Pistol?

65. *speak fewer:* 'don't talk so much.' In fact poor Gower hardly says a word, while Fluellen's rebuke goes on and on.
66. *admiration:* surprise.
67. *prerogatifes:* prerogatives are privileges, but Fluellen means conventions, the proper and accepted ways of doing things.
69. *Pompey the Great* was a famous Roman general, one of Fluellen's models for correct military behaviour. (Compare his reference to the Roman disciplines in Act III, Scene ii, line 72.)
70. *tiddle-taddle . . . pibble-pabble:* idle chatter.
72–4. *ceremonies . . . cares . . . forms . . . sobriety . . . modesty.* All these add up to 'the proper, correct, and dignified way to behave in war.'

Pistol

    Know'st thou Fluellen?

King

    Yes.

Pistol

    Tell him I'll knock his leek about his pate Upon Saint
    Davy's day.   55

King

    Do not you wear your dagger in your cap that day,
    lest he knock that about yours.

Pistol

    Art thou his friend?

King

    And his kinsman too.

Pistol

    The figo for thee, then!   60

King

    I thank you; God be with you!

Pistol

    My name is Pistol call'd.

[Exit]

King

    It sorts well with your fierceness.

[Enter FLUELLEN and GOWER]

Gower

    Captain Fluellen!

Fluellen

    So! in the name of Jesu Christ, speak fewer. It is the   65
    greatest admiration in the universal world, when the
    true and aunchient prerogatifes and laws of the wars
    is not kept: if you would take the pains but to examine
    the wars of Pompey the Great, you shall find, I warrant
    you, that there is no tiddle-taddle nor pibble-pabble   70
    in Pompey's camp; I warrant you, you shall find the
    ceremonies of the wars, and the cares of it, and the

75. *the enemy is loud:* Gower makes the obvious and sensible observation. The French are, as we have seen, having quite a party, and silence seems to be unnecessary anyway.

76–7. *prating coxcomb:* chattering idiot. Clowns used to wear caps that resembled the comb on a cock's head (a cock's comb) and *coxcomb* came to be used for any showy, conceited fool.

82–3. The king appreciates that Fluellen, even if he is odd in his ways, is a thoroughly reliable and earnest soldier. Compare this comment with the earlier one on Pistol (line 63).

Stage Direction. *Enter three soldiers.* In Shakespeare's theatre, without sophisticated lighting and scenery, they would of course have to enter; if they had been on the stage all of the time they would know about the king's disguise and would not be taken in by it. But it is easier for us to visualize them sitting them by their fire, talking gloomily about the approaching day, with the king standing in the shadows nearby until they challenge him.

86–7. Bates's remark that the English do not want the day to dawn reminds us sharply of the French nobles' longing for it in Act III, scene vii.

forms of it, and the sobriety of it, and the modesty of it, to be otherwise.

Gower

Why, the enemy is loud; you hear him all night.   75

Fluellen

If the enemy is an ass, and a fool, and a prating coxcomb, is it meet, think you, that we should also, look you, be an ass, and a fool, and a prating coxcomb? In your own conscience, now?

Gower

I will speak lower.   80

Fluellen

I pray you and beseech you that you will.

[Exeunt GOWER *and* FLUELLEN*]*

King

Though it appear a little out of fashion,
There is much care and valour in this Welshman.

[Enter three soldiers: JOHN BATES, ALEXANDER COURT,
and MICHAEL WILLIAMS*]*

Court

Brother John Bates, is not that the morning which breaks yonder?   85

Bates

I think it be; but we have no great cause to desire the approach of day.

Williams

We see yonder the beginning of the day, but I think we shall never see the end of it. Who goes there?

King

A friend.   90

Williams

Under what captain serve you?

King

Under Sir Thomas Erpingham.

Williams

A good old commander and a most kind gentleman.

94. *estate:* state, predicament.

95–6. *Even as men . . . tide:* 'he thinks we are like men shipwrecked on a sandbank, who expect to be swept away by the next high tide.' Erpingham was cheerful enough in the early part of this scene, but perhaps that was just a pose he assumed to cover his real misgivings. But Henry's main purpose in revealing Erpingham's fears is to test the morale of his soldiers.

98. *nor it is not meet he should:* and it would not be right for him to tell the king.

99. *the King is but a man as I am.* Henry is disguised as an ordinary soldier, and there is some ironic humour for the audience in the way he talks of the king as someone else. This irony adds to the force of what he says in this speech: 'the king is an ordinary man beneath the royal exterior, just like you and me and anyone else.'

100. *element:* sky.

101. *shows:* appears.

102. *his ceremonies:* all the dignities that go with being king: the clothes, ornaments, buildings, formalities, courtesies, pomp, and ritual. Strip these away, and you find an ordinary man.

103–5. *and though his affections . . . wing:* 'and although his emotions are usually on a higher plane than ours, they have just the same effect on him as ours do on us.' The metaphor is from falconry again: *higher mounted* means 'soaring higher', and *stoop* is the word for the hawk's rapid dive on its prey.

106. *reason of fears:* reasons for being afraid.

107. *be of the same relish:* are of the same kind (taste the same).

107–9. *yet, in reason . . . fear:* so it is sensible that nobody should say or do anything to make him so afraid that his fear becomes visible. We now understand why the king thought it *not meet* that Erpingham should tell his fears; we see too the importance the king attaches to his own example of courage and cheerfulness.

111–13. *He may show . . . neck:* Bates sees the point about the king making a show of courage to inspire his army, but thinks that beneath the show the king secretly wishes he were somewhere else, even in the icy Thames.

113–14. *and so I would he were . . . here:* 'and I wish to goodness he was there, and me with him, no matter how much harm it did us, as long as we were out of this mess.'

115. *I will speak my conscience:* 'I will say what I honestly believe.' Another example of dramatic irony. We in the audience know that he is not speaking his *conscience of the King* so much as speaking as the king from his own conscience.

120–2. *I dare-say . . . minds:* 'I don't suppose you really hate him so much that you wish he were here on his own; you're just saying that to find out what the rest of us think.'

I pray you, what thinks he of our estate?

King

Even as men wreck'd upon a sand, that look to be 95
wash'd off the next tide.

Bates

He hath not told his thought to the King?

King

No; nor it is not meet he should. For though I speak
it to you, I think the King is but a man as I am: the
violet smells to him as it doth to me; the element 100
shows to him as it doth to me; all his senses have but
human conditions; his ceremonies laid by, in his
nakedness he appears but a man; and though his
affections are higher mounted than ours, yet, when
they stoop, they stoop with the like wing. Therefore, 105
when he sees reason of fears, as we do, his fears, out
of doubt, be of the same relish as ours are; yet, in
reason, no man should possess him with any appearance of fear, lest he, by showing it, should dishearten
his army. 110

Bates

He may show what outward courage he will; but I
believe, as cold a night as 'tis, he could wish himself
in Thames up to the neck; and so I would he were,
and I by him, at all adventures, so we were quit here.

King

By my troth, I will speak my conscience of the King: 115
I think he would not wish himself anywhere but where
he is.

Bates

Then I would he were here alone; so should he be sure
to be ransomed, and a many poor men's lives saved.

King

I dare say you love him not so ill to wish him here 120
alone, howsoever you speak this, to feel other men's
minds; methinks I could not die anywhere so contented
as in the King's company, his cause being just

126–9. Hearing their new companion mention the justice and honour of the king's cause, these thoughtful soldiers begin to wonder whether in fact it is just and honourable. But Bates very shrewdly points out that it is better for them not to ask such questions; it is better for ignorant soldiers to remain ignorant, so that they cannot be held responsible for knowingly doing wrong. Better to obey blindly, so that all blame will be put on the one who gives the orders.

130–42. *a heavy reckoning to make:* a great deal to answer for. A *reckoning* is an account or bill. Williams's point is that the king will be held responsible for all the men who die fighting his battle for him, and whereas God might forgive him for causing so much bloodshed in a good cause, He will punish him severely *if the cause be not good.*

123. *latter day:* the Day of Judgment, the day on which, according to the Bible, God will judge all men.

136–7. *rawly left:* suddenly left to cope with life without the help of a father, without preparation or training.

137–9. *I am afeard . . . argument?* 'I'm afraid there are few men who die in a state of grace on a battlefield – it's impossible to feel kind and forgiving when you're busy killing.' To *die well* (in a state of grace) is to die at peace with God and the world, so that the soul can pass straight into God's presence, whereas to die in a state of sin might lead to everlasting torment: that is what these Christian soldiers would have been brought up to believe. However, Williams seems to think that all blame will rest entirely on the king, because he gives the orders to fight and his orders have to be obeyed. An excellent example of an effective theatrical stroke that Shakespeare was master of; putting common sense into the mouths of common people.

141–2. *who to disobey . . . subjection:* and it just wouldn't be right to disobey the king.

143–81. Williams' accusation is really serious – laying on the king the responsibility not only for his soldiers' deaths on earth but also for their punishment in the life after death. The king in fact takes it very much to heart, although the depth of his feeling does not appear until he is left on his own later in the scene (lines 226–80). For the time being he restrains his feelings and in a long and closely reasoned argument persuades Williams to change his views.

144. *do sinfully miscarry:* dies in a state of sin. *imputation:* blame.

148–9. *die in many irreconcil'd iniquities:* die in a state of sin, with many sins on his conscience for which he has not yet obtained God's forgiveness.

149–50. *you may call . . . damnation:* 'you may argue that the master's business is the reason for the servant going to hell.'

151. *bound to answer:* legally responsible for.

153–4. *for they purpose . . . services:* for they do not engage them knowing they will die when they engage them to serve.

154–7. *Besides . . . soldiers:* besides, no king, no matter how pure and righteous his cause is, can ever go into battle with entirely pure and righteous soldiers. *the arbitrement of swords:* reaching a decision by fighting to see who is right.

and his quarrel honourable.

Williams

That's more than we know.   125

Bates

Ay, or more than we should seek after; for we know
enough if we know we are the King's subjects. If his
cause be wrong, our obedience to the King wipes the
crime of it out of us.

Williams

But if the cause be not good, the King himself hath a   130
heavy reckoning to make when all those legs and arms
and heads, chopp'd off in a battle, shall join together
at the latter day and cry all 'We died at such a place'
– some swearing, some crying for a surgeon, some upon
their wives left poor behind them, some upon the debts 135
they owe, some upon their children rawly left. I am
afeard there are few die well that die in a battle; for
how can they charitably dispose of anything when
blood is their argument? Now, if these men do not die
well, it will be a black matter for the King that led   140
them to it; who to disobey were against all proportion
of subjection.

King

So, if a son that is by his father sent about merchandise
do sinfully miscarry upon the sea, the imputation of
his wickedness, by your rule, should be imposed upon   145
his father that sent him; or if a servant, under his
master's command transporting a sum of money, be
assailed by robbers and die in many irreconcil'd iniquities, you may call the business of the master the author
of the servant's damnation. But this is not so: the King 150
is not bound to answer the particular endings of his
soldiers, the father of his son, nor the master of his
servant; for they purpose not their death when they
purpose their services. Besides, there is no king, be his
cause never so spotless, if it come to the arbitrement   155
of swords, can try it out with all unspotted soldiers:

158–9. *some, of beguiling virgins . . . perjury:* some have been guilty of seducing virgins by promising to marry them and not keeping the promise.

159–62. *some, making the wars . . . robbery:* some soldiers go to war to avoid punishment for the crimes they have committed in peace-time.

162–72. The king's point here is that when such criminals as he has described die in battle they are being punished by God for the crimes they have got away with up to that time: God uses war as *His beadle* (a beadle was a parish officer who kept order in the parish by punishing petty criminals, sometimes by whipping them).

165–7. *so that . . . quarrel:* so that men's previous offences against the king's laws are punished later in the king's wars.

167–9. *Where they feared . . . perish:* after committing their crimes they feared punishment by death but were lucky enough to escape with their lives; later in wartime when they hope they will be safe from the law they die.

169. *unprovided:* i.e. not provided with God's grace and forgiveness.

172. *visited:* punished.

174. *mote:* a tiny speck of dust. The king says that a man approaching battle should clean every spot from his conscience by confessing his sins and asking God's forgiveness for them all. Then if he dies in battle *death is to him advantage*, because his soul will be saved; and if he doesn't die the time spent on preparing for death will not have been wasted but *blessedly lost* (well-used).

178–81. *and in him that escapes . . . prepare:* and he who escapes death would be quite justified in thinking God had rewarded him for his devotion by allowing him to live to praise God and to show others the right way to approach death.

182–3. Williams now says the exact opposite of what he said in lines 139–41; he has changed his views completely as a result of the king's argument.

184–5. Bates hopes he won't be killed so that there will not be any question of the king being responsible for his death. But he's not a coward: he is determined to *fight lustily* (vigorously, heartily).

187–9. Williams is a cynic. He suggests that the king is a hypocrite who won't keep his word when the real test comes.

some peradventure have on them the guilt of premedi-
tated and contrived murder; some, of beguiling virgins
with the broken seals of perjury; some, making the
wars their bulwark, that have before gored the gentle 160
bosom of peace with pillage and robbery. Now, if these
men have defeated the law and outrun native punishment, though they can outstrip men they have no
wings to fly from God: war is His beadle, war is His
vengeance; so that here men are punish'd for before- 165
breach of the King's laws in now the King's quarrel.
Where they feared the death they have borne life away;
and where they would be safe they perish. Then if
they die unprovided, no more is the King guilty of
their damnation than he was before guilty of those 170
impieties for the which they are now visited. Every
subject's duty is the King's; but every subject's soul is
his own. Therefore should every soldier in the wars
do as every sick man in his bed – wash every mote
out of his conscience; and dying so, death is to him 175
advantage; or not dying, the time was blessedly lost
wherein such preparation was gained; and in him that
escapes it were not sin to think that, making God so
free an offer, He let him outlive that day to see His
greatness, and to teach others how they should 180
prepare.

Williams

'Tis certain, every man that dies ill, the ill upon his
own head – the King is not to answer for it.

Bates

I do not desire he should answer for me, and yet I
determine to fight lustily for him.   185

King

I myself heard the King say he would not be ransom'd.

Williams

Ay, he said so, to make us fight cheerfully; but when
our throats are cut he may be ransom'd, and we ne'er
the wiser.

191–3. *You pay him then . . . monarch:* 'You try to punish him for breaking his word then!' As if a mere commoner like you could mean anything to a king: what would he care if an insignificant thing like you didn't trust him? It's like imagining you can hurt someone with a toy gun. An *elder-gun* was a toy gun made from a hollowed-out stick of elder-wood.

197. *Your reproof is something too round.* Williams is right, of course: it was foolish for a commoner to say what the king said. But he does speak very aggressively, and the king must be a little nettled at having his remark ridiculed in this way, on top of all that has gone before. *round:* rude, rough.

198. *convenient:* this is not a convenient time for a quarrel, and so the two agree to fight it out after the battle.

200. *I embrace it:* I accept it.

202. *gage:* a pledge to fight, usually a glove thrown down by one contestant and picked up by the other as a symbol of challenge offered and accepted.

209. *take:* strike.

212. *take:* catch.

King

    If I live to see it, I will never trust his word after.   190

Williams

    You pay him then! That's a perilous shot out of an
elder-gun, that a poor and a private displeasure can do
against a monarch! You may as well go about to turn
the sun to ice with fanning in his face with a peacock's
feather. You'll never trust his word after! Come, 'tis a 195
foolish saying.

King

    Your reproof is something too round; I should be angry
with you, if the time were convenient.

Williams

    Let it be a quarrel between us if you live.

King

    I embrace it.   200

Williams

    How shall I know thee again?

King

    Give me any gage of thine, and I will wear it in my
bonnet; then if ever thou dar'st acknowledge it, I will
make it my quarrel.

Williams

    Here's my glove; give me another of thine.   205

King

    There.

Williams

    This will I also wear in my cap; if ever thou come to
me and say, after to-morrow, 'This is my glove', by
this hand I will take thee a box on the ear.

King

    If ever I live to see it, I will challenge it.   210

Williams

    Thou dar'st as well be hang'd.

King

    Well, I will do it, though I take thee in the King's
company.

215–16. *we have French . . . reckon:* if you could count you'd realize that we've got more than enough French enemies to cope with, without fighting amongst ourselves.

217. *lay:* bet. *crowns* refers both to the coin and to the crown of the head: the French can offer odds of twenty to one that they will win because they have twenty times as many heads (men). But the king is exaggerating.

221. *clipper:* one who cut bits off coins; such criminals were punished for treason. But in this battle it is not treason *to cut French crowns* (heads), and the king himself will do it.

222–76. Now that he is left entirely on his own, the king expresses his true feelings about the attitude of the soldiers, especially of Williams, who in lines 130–42 talked about the king having to carry all the responsibility for the war, for the deaths of his men, for the way they die, and for their subsequent fate in the after-life. Henry seems at first pettishly hurt that his men want to blame him for everything, and shows a sensitivity to criticism that we do not see anywhere else in the play; as a result he seems particularly human and natural in this soliloquy.

222–4. He is speaking as one of the common soldiers: 'Let's blame the king for everything,' they say, 'even for the worries of our wives.' The wives are *careful* (anxious, full of care) because their men are in danger.

225–8. *O hard condition . . . wringing:* 'it's a hard life for a king, being exposed to the criticism of every idiot who hasn't the sense to understand anybody's problems but his own.'

Twin-born with greatness means that this hard predicament and greatness go together like twins: any man born into a high position has to put up with it.

228. *wringing:* belly-ache.

229. *neglect:* 'learn to live without'.

231. *ceremony:* the pomp that accompanies a king, the outward signs of respect which men show towards a king. *general:* public.

232–50. Now he addresses ceremony personified (*thou idol Ceremony*) and asks what use it is, implying that although it is the only advantage a king has over ordinary men it is a feeble compensation for all the responsibility a king has to carry.

233. *that suffer'st:* the idol Ceremony (i.e. the king with whom it is identified) suffers more grief than those who worship it (i.e. the king's subjects).

235. *rents . . . comings-in:* advantages.

236. *show me but:* just show me.

237. *thy soul of adoration:* the true value of the respect paid to you.

238. *Art thou . . . form:* 'is there anything more to you than high position and outward display of authority?'

243–50. Being king cannot protect him against illness, and the hypocritical praise of flatterers cannot put out the fires of fever any more than the king with all his power and authority can order his people to be healthy. In short, ceremony is nothing but a *proud dream.*

Williams

Keep thy word. Fare thee well.

Bates

Be friends, you English fools, be friends; we have French 215
quarrels enow, if you could tell how to reckon.

King

Indeed, the French may lay twenty French crowns to
one they will beat us, for they bear them on their
shoulders; but it is no English treason to cut French
crowns, and to-morrow the King himself will be a 220
clipper.

[Exeunt SOLDIERS]

Upon the King! Let us our lives, our souls,
Our debts, our careful wives,
Our children, and our sins, lay on the King!
We must bear all. O hard condition, 225
Twin-born with greatness, subject to the breath
Of every fool, whose sense no more can feel
But his own wringing! What infinite heart's ease
Must kings neglect that private men enjoy!
And what have kings that privates have not too, 230
Save ceremony – save general ceremony?
And what art thou, thou idol Ceremony?
What kind of god art thou, that suffer'st more
Of mortal griefs than do thy worshippers?
What are thy rents? What are thy comings-in? 235
O Ceremony, show me but thy worth!
What is thy soul of adoration?
Art thou aught else but place, degree, and form,
Creating awe and fear in other men?
Wherein thou art less happy being fear'd 240
Than they in fearing.
What drink'st thou oft, instead of homage sweet,
But poison'd flattery? O, be sick, great greatness,
And bid thy ceremony give thee cure!
Thinks thou the fiery fever will go out 245

246. *titles blown from adulation:* the exaggerated compliments of flatterers.

247. *flexure:* bowing as a gesture of respect to a superior.

251–76. The thought of ceremony as a dream which troubles the king's sleep evokes this envious and vivid picture of the working man and his carefree existence (is it a true picture?), as though Henry would happily give up his titles and privileges in return for one really sound night's sleep. There is added point in this when we remember that at this very moment he is wide awake, busy and anxious, while lesser men are sound asleep.

251. *I am a king that find thee:* 'I am a king myself, and I know from my own experience how unreal you are.'

251–5. He refers here to the coronation ceremony: the *balm* is the holy oil used to consecrate a new monarch, and the *sceptre, ball* etc. are richly-jewelled golden symbols of sovereignty.

intertissued: interwoven.

farced: long-winded and exaggerated (literally 'stuffed'), and refers to the lengthy titles given to the king on ceremonial occasions.

260–1. The *wretched slave* is any ordinary working man, not a slave in the strict sense but a lowly subject of the king, with a *vacant mind* in contrast with the king's constant anxiety.

262. The working man has to struggle to earn his living, and enjoys no luxuries: his diet is mainly *distressful bread*, which is indigestible and not very nutritious.

263. *horrid:* terrifying.

264. *lackey:* the lowest grade of servant, here equivalent to the *slave* in line 260.

265–7. *Phoebus* and *Hyperion* are both personifications of the sun, being different names for mythical sun-gods, and *Elysium* is an ancient Greek name for heaven. The working man gets up and goes to bed with the sun all the year round, but Shakespeare imagines him helping the sun-god on to the horse which will pull the sun across the sky.

272–2. *but for ceremony . . . king:* the worker leads such a happy life, working all day and sleeping peacefully all night, that he would be superior to the king and better off, were it not for the *ceremony* that sets the king on top.

273–6. *The slave . . . advantages:* the worker enjoys and benefits from the country's well-being, but his simple mind doesn't understand how much sleep the king loses in his anxiety to maintain that well-being, although it is the worker who in fact benefits most.

wots: knows.

advantages is used as a verb here, with *hours* as its subject.

277. *jealous of your absence:* worried about what might have happened to you.

With titles blown from adulation?
Will it give place to flexure and low bending?
Canst thou, when thou command'st the beggar's knee,
Command the health of it? No, thou proud dream,
That play'st so subtly with a king's repose. 250
I am a king that find thee; and I know
'Tis not the balm, the sceptre, and the ball,
The sword, the mace, the crown imperial,
The intertissued robe of gold and pearl,
The farced title running fore the king, 255
The throne he sits on, nor the tide of pomp
That beats upon the high shore of this world—
No, not all these, thrice gorgeous ceremony,
Not all these, laid in bed majestical,
Can sleep so soundly as the wretched slave 260
Who, with a body fill'd and vacant mind,
Gets him to rest, cramm'd with distressful bread;
Never sees horrid night, the child of hell;
But, like a lackey, from the rise to set
Sweats in the eye of Phoebus, and all night 265
Sleeps in Elysium; next day, after dawn,
Doth rise and help Hyperion to his horse;
And follows so the ever-running year
With profitable labour, to his grave.
And but for ceremony, such a wretch, 270
Winding up days with toil and nights with sleep,
Had the fore-hand and vantage of a king.
The slave, a member of the country's peace,
Enjoys it; but in gross brain little wots
What watch the king keeps to maintain the peace 275
Whose hours the peasant best advantages.

[Enter ERPINGHAM*]*

Erpingham
My lord, your nobles, jealous of your absence,
Seek through your camp to find you.
King
                              Good old knight,

281–97. Now, as the dreaded day dawns, Henry makes his last appeal for God's help.

281. *steel:* make them strong and brave.

282–4. *Take from them . . . them:* 'take away from them the ability to count, so that the vastly superior numbers of the enemy won't destroy their courage.'

285–6. His father, Henry IV, usurped the throne by driving his cousin, Richard II, off it. The king asks God not to choose today as the day of punishment for his father's offence.

286. *compassing:* obtaining.

287–94. He has tried to make amends in various ways: he has had Richard's body moved from its obscure grave at King's Langley to a glorious one in Westminster Abbey; he has wept penitently over it (he and Richard had in fact been good friends); he has given employment to five hundred poor people by paying them to pray for forgiveness; and he has set up two chapels for monks to sing prayers for Richard's soul.

289. *forced drops of blood.* Richard was murdered in prison.

293. *sad:* very serious, grave. He is referring to monks who are utterly dedicated to their religion.

294. *still:* continually.

295–7. 'My penitential works are worthless since they come after those old sins (which nothing can wipe out)'.

298–300. His humble prayer is interrupted, and now he must face his responsibility. Notice how beautifully the last line expresses his acceptance of this. *stay for me:* this suggests that he feels that everything now depends on him, just as a moment ago everything seemed to depend on God. After what has been said in this scene, we know how heavy he feels the responsibility to be.

Collect them all together at my tent;
I'll be before thee.

Erpingham

                    I shall do't, my lord.   280

                    [Exit]

King

O God of battles, steel my soldiers' hearts,
Possess them not with fear! Take from them now
The sense of reck'ning, if th' opposed numbers
Pluck their hearts from them! Not to-day, O Lord,
O, not to-day, think not upon the fault   285
My father made in compassing the crown!
I Richard's body have interred new,
And on it have bestowed more contrite tears
Than from it issued forced drops of blood;
Five hundred poor I have in yearly pay,   290
Who twice a day their wither'd hands hold up
Toward heaven, to pardon blood; and I have built
Two chantries, where the sad and solemn priests
Sing still for Richard's soul. More will I do;
Though all that I can do is nothing worth,   295
Since that my penitence comes after all,
Imploring pardon.

                    [Enter GLOUCESTER]

Gloucester
My liege!

King
          My brother Gloucester's voice? Ay;
I know thy errand, I will go with thee;
The day, my friends, and all things, stay for me.   300

                    [Exeunt]

SCENE II

2. *Montez à cheval:* Mount your horses.

4–6. The Dauphin and Orleans are playing with the idea of the four elements (see the note on the first line of the play). When the Dauphin says 'Away! Over water and earth –' he is presumably still thinking of the magnificence of his horse, as he was in Act III, Scene vii. Orleans replies to the effect that such a horse in such a battle would surely fly up with the purer elements of air and fire, and the Dauphin goes further yet (*ciel* means 'sky' or 'heaven').

8. *present service:* immediate action.

9. *make incision:* cut into the horses' skin with spurs.

11. *dout them with superfluous courage:* 'extinguish the English with the excess of blood pouring from our horses' sides.' It was thought that courage lived in the blood.

12–13. Rambures assumes that the English will weep, and makes a joke of it: 'Don't drench them with blood,' he says, 'We want to be able to see their real tears.' The same arrogant over-confidence is shown by the Constable and then Grandpré; it reminds us of the way the French nobles boasted in Act III, Scene vii, and makes the audience even more anxious to see them soundly thrashed in battle.

14. *embattl'd:* drawn up in lines, ready for battle.

17. *your fair show shall suck away their souls:* the splendour of your appearance will ruin what little spirit they have left.

18. *shales and husks:* empty, lifeless shells.

Scene II

The French camp

[Enter the DAUPHIN, ORLEANS, RAMBURES, *and* OTHERS*]*

Orleans
The sun doth gild our armour; up, my lords!
Dauphin
Montez à cheval! My horse! Varlet, laquais! Ha!
Orleans
O brave spirit!
Dauphin
Via! Les eaux et la terre—
Orleans
Rien puis? L'air et le feu.   5
Dauphin
Ciel! cousin Orleans.

[Enter CONSTABLE*]*

Now, my Lord Constable!
Constable
Hark how our steeds for present service neigh!
Dauphin
Mount them, and make incision in their hides,
That their hot blood may spin in English eyes,   10
And dout them with superfluous courage, ha!
Rambures
What, will you have them weep our horses' blood?
How shall we then behold their natural tears?

[Enter a MESSENGER*]*

Messenger
The English are embattl'd, you French peers.
Constable
To horse, you gallant Princes! straight to horse!   15
Do but behold yon poor and starved band,
And your fair show shall suck away their souls,
Leaving them but the shales and husks of men.

21. *curtle-axe:* a cutlass or short sword.

22. *gallants:* young adventurers.

25–32. The Constable reckons there are enough servants and peasants hanging about the battlefield to beat the English; the real soldiers could just stand and watch – except that of course their honour obliged them to lead the fight.
'gainst all exceptions: beyond any doubt.

enow: enough.

hilding: originally a useless horse.

30. *this mountain's basis by:* this nearby hill.

31. *Took stand for idle speculation:* took our position to watch without interfering.

32. *What's to say?:* 'what is there to be said?' *or* 'there's no need to say anything; let's just go and do the little that has to be done.'

35. *The tucket sonance . . .:* battle call and signal to mount.

36. *dare the field:* paralyse the enemy army (a term from duck-shooting).

37. *couch down in fear:* another shooting term, used of a creature that lies down in terror.

39–40. *Yond island carrions . . . field:* those English skeletons have come out on to the battlefield, and a pretty miserable sight they are, as though they have lost all hope of saving their bony carcases.

41. *curtains:* flags and banners.

42. *passing:* extremely. The winds of France shake the ragged English flags contemptuously.

43. *Mars:* the Roman god of war, but Grandpré means that the will to fight is *bankrupt* (almost entirely absent) in the English army.

44. *And faintly . . . peeps.* The spirit of war is now a typical English soldier, peeping through his armoured helmet, but instead of glaring aggressively at his enemy he peeps *faintly*.

45. *The horsemen . . . candlesticks.* Candlesticks were sometimes shaped like horsemen holding a *stave* (or spear) on which the candle was impaled.

46–50. The *jades* are horses: the word is used particularly of old, wornout horses, and these lines vividly depict the unhealthy lethargic appearance of these English horses: the ropes of gum hanging from their eyes, the sagging heads and drooping flesh, and the half-chewed grass fouling their mouths. The *gimmal'd bit* is the hinged metal bar that is inserted in the horse's mouth and attached to the reins so that the rider can pull the horse's head to control it.

51. *executors:* people who look after a man's property when he dies. Here the crows will 'look after' the English bodies; already they know they are going to have a feast, and are just hovering over the English, waiting.

There is not work enough for all our hands;
Scarce blood enough in all their sickly veins   20
To give each naked curtle-axe a stain
That our French gallants shall to-day draw out,
And sheathe for lack of sport. Let us but blow on
    them,
The vapour of our valour will o'erturn them.
'Tis positive 'gainst all exceptions, lords,   25
That our superfluous lackeys and our peasants—
Who in unnecessary action swarm
About our squares of battle – were enow
To purge this field of such a hilding foe;
Though we upon this mountain's basis by   30
Took stand for idle speculation—
But that our honours must not. What's to say?
A very little little let us do,
And all is done. Then let the trumpets sound
The tucket sonance and the note to mount;   35
For our approach shall so much dare the field
That England shall couch down in fear and yield.

[Enter GRANDPRÉ]

Grandpré
Why do you stay so long, my lords of France?
Yond island carrions, desperate of their bones,
Ill-favouredly become the morning field;   40
Their ragged curtains poorly are let loose,
And our air shakes them passing scornfully;
Big Mars seems bankrupt in their beggar'd host,
And faintly through a rusty beaver peeps.
The horsemen sit like fixed candlesticks   45
With torch-staves in their hand; and their poor jades
Lob down their heads, dropping the hides and hips,
The gum down-roping from their pale-dead eyes,
And in their pale dull mouths the gimmal'd bit
Lies foul with chaw'd grass, still and motionless;   50
And their executors, the knavish crows,
Fly o'er them, all impatient for their hour.

53–5. *Description . . . itself:* description cannot find suitable words to paint a true likeness (*demonstrate the life*) of such an army (*battle*) since it shows itself so deficient (*lifeless*) in life, (playing on different contemporary meanings of *life*).

56. *stay for:* wait for.

57–9. A typically frivolous and bumptious suggestion by the Dauphin; he feels it's not fair to fight such a feeble enemy, and suggests feeding and clothing them first; but he doesn't mean anyone to take him seriously, and nobody does. Later on we shall look back on this arrogance with pleasure (see Act IV, Scene v).

60. *guidon:* his own personal banner, to be carried into battle ahead of him by one of his squires. But he can't wait for it, he is too impatient, so he takes the banner from a trumpeter and uses that instead.

63. *outwear:* waste.

SCENE III

2. *their battle:* the French forces.

4. *five to one:* this would make the English about twelve thousand.

6. *God bye you:* our modern 'goodbye' comes from 'God be with ye', which became shortened to 'God bye' and at times the 'you' was added again.

10. *kinsman:* Westmoreland, who had married Salisbury's daughter.

Description cannot suit itself in words
To demonstrate the life of such a battle
In life so lifeless as it shows itself.   55

Constable

They have said their prayers and they stay for death.

Dauphin

Shall we go send them dinners and fresh suits,
And give their fasting horses provender,
And after fight with them?

Constable

I stay but for my guidon. To the field!   60
I will the banner from a trumpet take,
And use it for my haste. Come, come, away!
The sun is high, and we outwear the day.

[Exeunt]

Scene III

The English camp

[Enter GLOUCESTER, BEDFORD, EXETER, ERPINGHAM,
with all his HOST; SALISBURY *and* WESTMORELAND*]*

Gloucester

Where is the King?

Bedford

The King himself is rode to view their battle.

Westmoreland

Of fighting men they have full three-score thousand.

Exeter

There's five to one; besides, they all are fresh.

Salisbury

God's arm strike with us! 'tis a fearful odds.   5
God bye you, Princes all; I'll to my charge.
If we no more meet till we meet in heaven,
Then joyfully, my noble Lord of Bedford,
My dear Lord Gloucester, and my good Lord Exeter,
And my kind kinsman – warriors all, adieu!   10

12–14. *Fight valiantly . . . valour:* fight bravely today and yet it is an insult to say such a thing, because you are made of true valour itself.

15–16. Compare these lines with comments the French nobles make behind the Dauphin's back in Act III, Scene vii.

16–18. Westmoreland is probably referring to the English soldiers left behind to defend the kingdom against the Scots (see Act I, Scene ii, lines 136–9).

18. *What's he that wishes so?* 'Who is it expressing such a wish?'

20–1. *we are enow . . . loss:* there are quite enough of us for the country to lose. The smaller the number, the better for England if they lose, and the better for them if they win.

24–33. The king says he doesn't care about money and such material things, and his people can milk him as much as they like, but he does value honour and will not tolerate having to share the honour of victory with a single man more.

30. *coz:* cousin.

33. *the best hope I have:* my hopes of victory.

35. *stomach:* inclination.
37. *crowns for convoy:* money for his travel. Everything possible will be done to enable such a man to escape safely from the battlefield; instead of wishing for more men, like Westmoreland, he wants fewer, if any of his men are not fully enthusiastic.

Bedford
    Farewell, good Salisbury; and good luck go with thee!
Exeter
    Farewell, kind lord. Fight valiantly to-day;
    And yet I do thee wrong to mind thee of it,
    For thou art fram'd of the firm truth of valour.

[Exit SALISBURY*]*

Bedford
    He is as full of valour as of kindness;   15
    Princely in both.

[Enter the KING*]*

Westmoreland
               O that we now had here
    But one ten thousand of those men in England
    That do no work to-day!
King
                    What's he that wishes so?
    My cousin Westmoreland? No, my fair cousin;
    If we are mark'd to die, we are enow   20
    To do our country loss; and if to live,
    The fewer men, the greater share of honour.
    God's will! I pray thee, wish not one man more.
    By Jove, I am not covetous for gold,
    Nor care I who doth feed upon my cost;   25
    It yearns me not if men my garments wear;
    Such outward things dwell not in my desires.
    But if it be a sin to covet honour,
    I am the most offending soul alive.
    No, faith, my coz, wish not a man from England.   30
    God's peace! I would not lose so great an honour
    As one man more methinks would share from me
    For the best hope I have. O, do not wish one more!
    Rather proclaim it, Westmoreland, through my host,
    That he which hath no stomach to this fight,   35
    Let him depart; his passport shall be made,
    And crowns for convoy put into his purse;
    We would not die in that man's company

39. *That fears . . . us:* who is afraid that keeping company with me might lead to his death.

40. *Crispian.* Two brothers, Crispinus (Crispin) and Crispianus, were martyred in a.d. 287. Having been shoemakers, they became the patron saints of shoemakers.

41–51. There is some marvellous psychology in this speech. Having persuaded his hearers not to wish for more men, because the greater the odds against them the more sensational will be their triumph if they win, he now describes in glowing detail something that must be close to a soldier's heart: the dream of returning home and telling a crowd of admirers all about the great battle, showing his scars and remembering his deeds ***with advantages*** (with a little exaggeration here and there, the stories will 'improve' with time).

42. *stand a tip-toe:* draw himself up in pride.

45. *vigil:* the night before the feast day, traditionally kept as a vigil.

62. *vile:* low-class.

63. *this day shall gentle his condition:* he will be raised to the rank of gentleman as a result of fighting with the king today. In fact, as in line 60, they are now all brothers: another telling and shrewd appeal to human nature. (See also the note on Act III, Scene i, lines 29–30.)

66. *hold their manhoods cheap:* they'll have to keep quiet about their own puny achievements while they are in the presence of anyone who fought with the king on St Crispin's day.

68. *bestow yourself:* take up your battle position.

69. *bravely in their battles set:* drawn up in impressive array.

70. *expedience:* speed.

That fears his fellowship to die with us.
This day is call'd the feast of Crispian.   40
He that outlives this day, and comes safe home,
Will stand a tip-toe when this day is nam'd,
And rouse him at the name of Crispian.
He that shall live this day, and see old age,
Will yearly on the vigil feast his neighbours,   45
And say 'To-morrow is Saint Crispian'.
Then will he strip his sleeve and show his scars,
And say 'These wounds I had on Crispian's day'.
Old men forget; yet all shall be forgot,
But he'll remember, with advantages,   50
What feats he did that day. Then shall our names,
Familiar in his mouth as household words—
Harry the King, Bedford and Exeter,
Warwick and Talbot, Salisbury and Gloucester—
Be in their flowing cups freshly remember'd.   55
This story shall the good man teach his son;
And Crispin Crispian shall ne'er go by,
From this day to the ending of the world,
But we in it shall be remembered—
We few, we happy few, we band of brothers;   60
For he to-day that sheds his blood with me
Shall be my brother; be he ne'er so vile,
This day shall gentle his condition;
And gentlemen in England now-a-bed
Shall think themselves accurs'd they were not here,   65
And hold their manhoods cheap whiles any speaks
That fought with us upon Saint Crispin's day.

[Re-enter SALISBURY*]*

Salisbury
My sovereign lord, bestow yourself with speed:
The French are bravely in their battles set,
And will with all expedience charge on us.   70
King
All things are ready, if our minds be so.

72–7. The effectiveness of the king's speech (lines 18–67) is shown in the change in Westmoreland's attitude: before, he wished for more men, but now he wishes that he and the king alone could fight the battle; he has *unwish'd* the rest of the army (wished they were not there to help).

77. *Which likes me better:* which pleases me more.

80. *compound:* settle.

82. *gulf:* whirlpool: a metaphor for the disaster that the English are being swept inescapably into, in which they will shortly be *englutted* (swallowed up).

84. *mind:* remind.

85–8. *that their souls . . . fester:* so that their souls may pass peacefully into heaven, though their bodies lie on the battlefield to rot.

91. *achieve:* capture.

92. The king quite naturally becomes impatient with these repeated French offers to accept his ransom, and particularly with the infuriating arrogance and over-confidence of the French message brought by Montjoy. He uses the lion-hunter story to illustrate the folly of optimistic assumptions, such as Montjoy's in lines 85–8.

95–6. *A many of our bodies . . . graves:* no doubt many of us will survive this battle and eventually die in our own country.

97. He hopes the gravestones of such survivors will have a brass plate on them to commemorate their contribution to this day's battle.

98–107. Those who do die in the battle will leave their bodies to fester in the sun and pollute the French atmosphere with foul smells, doing a second injury to France, like a bullet that ricochets off one person and goes on to kill another.

Westmoreland

    Perish the man whose mind is backward now!

King

    Thou dost not wish more help from England, coz?

Westmoreland

    God's will, my liege! would you and I alone,

    Without more help, could fight this royal battle!   75

King

    Why, now thou hast unwish'd five thousand men;

    Which likes me better than to wish us one.

    You know your places. God be with you all!

[Tucket. Enter MONTJOY]

Montjoy

    Once more I come to know of thee, King Harry,

    If for thy ransom thou wilt now compound,   80

    Before thy most assured overthrow;

    For certainly thou art so near the gulf

    Thou needs must be englutted. Besides, in mercy,

    The Constable desires thee thou wilt mind

    Thy followers of repentance, that their souls   85

    May make a peaceful and a sweet retire

    From off these fields, where, wretches, their poor bodies

    Must lie and fester.

King

                Who hath sent thee now?

Montjoy

    The Constable of France.

King

    I pray thee bear my former answer back: 90

    Bid them achieve me, and then sell my bones.

    Good God! why should they mock poor fellows thus?

    The man that once did sell the lion's skin

    While the beast liv'd was kill'd with hunting him.

    A many of our bodies shall no doubt   95

    Find native graves; upon the which, I trust,

    Shall witness live in brass of this day's work.

    And those that leave their valiant bones in France,

107. *Killing in relapse of mortality:* killing by fatal rebound (ricochet).

109. *We are but warriors for the working-day.* We are just soldiers with a job of work to do and are dressed accordingly.

110. *gilt:* gold, literally, but he means all the finery of clothes and armour. *besmirch'd:* made filthy.

111. *in the painful field:* over difficult and tiring country.

112–13. The finery is so spoilt that there isn't even *a piece of feather* left in the whole army, a fact which he makes fun of by saying that without feathers they can't fly (i.e. run away like cowards).

114. *slovenry:* slovenliness, not caring about appearances.

115. *in the trim:* well-dressed, in good fettle. 'We may look a complete shambles on the surface, but by God there's nothing wrong with our spirit.'

116–18. By nightfall the English soldiers will either be in *fresher robes* (angel's robes, in other words they will be dead) or they will have won the battle and will be able to strip the *gay new coats* from the French dead and captured. Henry is commenting ironically on the French vanity in dressing themselves up for battle; he implies that the clothes one wears are unimportant at a time like this.

119. *And turn them out of service.* Soldiers usually wore the uniform of the lords who employed them, a distinctive livery which was stripped off them if they were dismissed. The English soldiers will 'dismiss' the Frenchmen in two ways: by killing them and by removing their livery.

120–1. *my ransom . . . levied:* it will be easy to raise money if they win because they will be able to sell their prisoners. But of course he won't need a ransom then. He is still making fun of Montjoy: he has no intention of even considering being ransomed, but will either win the battle or die in the attempt. And the same is true of all his men.

123. *They:* the French leaders.

124–5. He intends to fight to the death. By the time the French capture his bones there won't be any flesh left on them.

128. *I fear . . . ransom.* On the surface this is a joke at Mountjoy's expense, 'in spite of what you say I'm afraid you'll be back again'. It is also a striking piece of dramatic irony: in spite of his threat Montjoy does appear before the king again, in very different circumstances (Scene vii).

Dying like men, though buried in your dunghills,
They shall be fam'd; for there the sun shall greet
   them   100
And draw their honours reeking up to heaven,
Leaving their earthly parts to choke your clime,
The smell whereof shall breed a plague in France.
Mark then abounding valour in our English,
That, being dead, like to the bullet's grazing   105
Break out into a second course of mischief,
Killing in relapse of mortality.
Let me speak proudly: tell the Constable
We are but warriors for the working-day;
Our gayness and our gilt are all besmirch'd   110
With rainy marching in the painful field;
There's not a piece of feather in our host—
Good argument, I hope, we will not fly—
And time hath worn us into slovenry.
But, by the mass, our hearts are in the trim;   115
And my poor soldiers tell me yet ere night
They'll be in fresher robes, or they will pluck
The gay new coats o'er the French soldiers' heads
And turn them out of service. If they do this—
As, if God please, they shall – my ransom then   120
Will soon be levied. Herald, save thou thy labour;
Come thou no more for ransom, gentle herald;
They shall have none, I swear, but these my joints;
Which if they have, as I will leave 'em them,
Shall yield them little, tell the Constable.   125

Montjoy

I shall, King Harry. And so fare thee well:
Thou never shalt hear herald any more.

[Exit]

King

I fear thou wilt once more come again for a ransom.

[Enter the DUKE OF YORK*]*

130. *vaward:* vanguard, the first line of attack.

132. As usual, the king dedicates his deeds to God; the very last thing he does or says before leading his men into battle. At once the noise of battle begins.

SCENE IV

Stage Direction. *Excursions* are movements of troops to and fro across the stage, first English, then French soldiers, fighting each other hand-to-hand and driving each other back. In one of these skirmishes a Frenchman falls and lies low until those he was fighting with and against have moved on, whereupon Pistol creeps out of some convenient hiding-place to seize the opportunity of taking a prisoner. He draws his sword and points it at the Frenchman, who cowers away in terror, still on the ground with Pistol towering above him.
2–3. *Je pense . . . qualité:* I think you are a gentleman of noble rank.

4. *Cality! Calen o custure me:* Pistol knows very little French and thinks the French Soldier's word *qualité* is part of a popular song in Irish.

7. Pistol, having asked the Frenchman his name and received the answer *O Seigneur Dieu!* (O Lord God), thinks the name must be Signieur Dew.
8. *Perpend:* consider carefully.
9. *fox:* sword, so called because some swordmakers marked their swords with a fox as their trademark.
11. *Egregious:* extraordinary.

12. *ayez petié de moi:* have pity on me.

13. Pistol misunderstands the *moi* ('me') as *moy*, an English measure of about a bushel: perhaps he thinks the Frenchman is offering him a bushel of wheat as a ransom.
14. *rim:* diaphragm.

York
> My lord, most humbly on my knee I beg
> The leading of the vaward.   130
King
> Take it, brave York. Now, soldiers, march away;
> And how thou pleasest, God, dispose the day!

> *[Exeunt]*

Scene IV

The field of battle

[Alarum. Excursions. Enter FRENCH SOLDIER, PISTOL,
and BOY]

Pistol
> Yield, cur!
French Soldier
> Je pense que vous êtes le gentilhomme de bonne
> qualité.
Pistol
> Cality! Calen o custure me! Art thou a gentleman?
> What is thy name? Discuss.   5
French Soldier
> O Seigneur Dieu!
Pistol
> O, Signieur Dew should be a gentleman.
> Perpend my words, O Signieur Dew, and mark:
> O Signieur Dew, thou diest on point of fox,
> Except, O Signieur, thou do give to me   10
> Egregious ransom.
French Soldier
> O, prennez miséricorde; ayez pitié de moi!
Pistol
> Moy shall not serve; I will have forty moys;
> Or I will fetch thy rim out at thy throat
> In drops of crimson blood.   15

16. *Est-il . . . bras?* Is it possible to escape the strength of your arm?

17. *Bras* ('arm') sounds like *brass* to Pistol.

18. *luxurious:* lustful, over-sexed. Goats were famed for this quality, and perhaps Pistol thinks Frenchmen should be similarly described.

20. *pardonnez-moi:* pardon me.

24. The Boy now shows a good command of French in addition to his other excellent qualities, and acts as interpreter for the rest of the scene.

27. *firk:* whip, thrash.
ferret: worry like a ferret worrying a rabbit. (Ferrets are half-tamed animals like weasels which are used to hunt rabbits by driving them from their burrows but Pistol chooses the word mainly for the sake of alliteration.)

35. *permafoy:* an English pronunciation of 'par ma foi' (French for 'by my faith').

French Soldier

Est-il impossible d'échapper la force de ton bras?

Pistol

Brass, cur?

Thou damned and luxurious mountain-goat,

Offer'st me brass?

French Soldier

O, pardonnez-moi!   20

Pistol

Say'st thou me so? Is that a ton of moys?

Come hither, boy; ask me this slave in French

What is his name.

Boy

Ecoutez: comment êtes-vous appelé?

French Soldier

Monsieur le Fer.   25

Boy

He says his name is Master Fer.

Pistol

Master Fer! I'll fer him, and firk him, and ferret him

– discuss the same in French unto him.

Boy

I do not know the French for fer, and ferret, and firk.

Pistol

Bid him prepare; for I will cut his throat.   30

French Soldier

Que dit-il, monsieur?

Boy

Il me commande à vous dire que vous faites vous prêt;

car ce soldat ici est disposé tout à cette heure de couper

votre gorge.

Pistol

Owy, cuppele gorge, permafoy!   35

Peasant, unless thou give me crowns, brave crowns;

Or mangled shalt thou be by this my sword.

French Soldier

O, je vous supplie, pour l'amour de Dieu, me pardonner!

48–51. The Boy does Pistol a good turn here, making him sound very impressive indeed: 'Although it is against his principles to pardon any prisoner, nevertheless on account of the crowns you have promised him he will make an exception in this case.'

59. *as he thinks:* the Boy seems to be enjoying helping Pistol to put on his great act, but he can't resist making this delightfully subtle dig. The Frenchman actually said he thought Pistol *the most brave* etc., but in translating it into *as he thinks*, with stress on *he*, the Boy makes it clear that he himself does not think so.

63. *Suivez-vous . . . capitaine:* follow the great captain. Another pleasant touch of irony, especially when the Boy goes on to say that only Pistol's voice is great.

Je suis gentilhomme de bonne maison. Gardez ma vie,
et je vous donnerai deux cents écus.   40

Pistol

What are his words?

Boy

He prays you to save his life; he is a gentleman of a
good house, and for his ransom he will give you two
hundred crowns.

Pistol

Tell him my fury shall abate, and I   45
The crowns will take.

French Soldier

Petit monsieur, que dit-il?

Boy

Encore qu'il est contre son jurement de pardonner
aucun prisonnier, néanmoins, pour les écus que vous
l'avez promis, il est content à vous donner la liberté,   50
le franchisement.

French Soldier

Sur mes genoux je vous donne mille remercîmens; et
je m'estime heureux que je suis tombé entre les mains
d'un chevalier, je pense, le plus brave, vaillant, et très
distingué seigneur d'Angleterre.   55

Pistol

Expound unto me, boy.

Boy

He gives you, upon his knees, a thousand thanks; and
he esteems himself happy that he hath fall'n into the
hands of one – as he thinks – the most brave, valorous,
and thrice-worthy signieur of England.   60

Pistol

As I suck blood, I will some mercy show.
Follow me.

[Exit]

Boy

Suivez-vous le grand capitaine. *[Exit French Soldier]* I did
never know so full a voice issue from so empty

67–8. roaring devil . . . dagger. He likens Pistol to the Devil who was beaten with wooden daggers and driven roaring round the stage in the old morality plays. These plays were simple allegorical stories in which actors personified various vices and virtues. He was so feeble that anyone could *pare* (cut) his claws without danger. Pistol is the same: full of noise but quite harmless.

70. durst: dared. This is the first time we have heard of Nym's execution; evidently he and Bardolph took their filching a bit too far, whereas Pistol has kept out of trouble through sheer cowardice.

70–3. The *luggage* is the baggage and stores of the whole army, dumped in one place and guarded by *lackeys* (camp-followers and servants who did not fight). But at the moment there are only some boys to guard it, so *the French might have a good prey* of them: they could easily overcome the boys and loot the stores. The *he in if he knew of it refers to the enemy collectively.*

SCENE V

1. diable: devil. This is one of the play's most satisfying moment the French nobles, after all their bragging in the earlier scenes, now enter beaten, dejected, cursing, and bewildered.

2. 'The day is lost, all is lost.'

5. plumes: the feathers in their helmets, usually a symbol of pride, but now drooping in shame.

Stage Direction. The *alarum* is probably a trumpet call to retreat, and there may be some men running in confusion across the stage, prompting the Dauphin's agonized cry in the next line.

6. méchante: evil, spiteful.

8. perdurable: everlasting. The shame of this defeat will hang over them for ever, so they may as well commit suicide.

8–9. The two lines remind us gratifyingly of how much the English have been underestimated, and of how heavy is the fall of the proud.

a heart; but the saying is true – the empty vessel makes 65
the greatest sound. Bardolph and Nym had ten times
more valour than this roaring devil i' th' old play, that
every one may pare his nails with a wooden dagger;
and they are both hang'd; and so would this be, if he
durst steal anything adventurously. I must stay with 70
the lackeys, with the luggage of our camp. The French
might have a good prey of us, if he knew of it; for
there is none to guard it but boys.

[Exit]

Scene V

_____

Another part of the field of battle

[Enter CONSTABLE, ORLEANS, BOURBON, DAUPHIN,
and RAMBURES]

Constable
    O diable!
Orleans
    O Seigneur! le jour est perdu, tout est perdu!
Dauphin
    Mort Dieu, ma vie! all is confounded, all!
    Reproach and everlasting shame
    Sits mocking in our plumes. 5

[A short alarum]

    O méchante fortune! Do not run away.
Constable
    Why, all our ranks are broke.
Dauphin
    O perdurable shame! Let's stab ourselves.
    Be these the wretches that we play'd at dice for?
Orleans
    Is this the king we sent to for his ransom? 10

11–17. Bourbon tries to lead a last desperate effort, hoping that at least he will die honourably. The word *pander* is derived from Pandarus, the uncle of Cressida, who acted as go-between in her love affair with Troilus, and is used for one who encourages or assists any low forms of satisfaction. Bourbon means that anyone who will not follow him back into the battle has no sense of shame and honour, and is fit only to be a *base pander*.

16. *no gentler:* no better, no nobler, no more worthy of the privilege of loving *his fairest daughter* than a dog is.

17. *contaminated:* raped.

18–24. Note the repetition of *Disorder* and *order:* the French didn't bother to plan their tactics for the battle, relying entirely on their superior numbers and fitness; when things went wrong for them they had no organization for regrouping their forces and trying again. Even now, confused, ashamed, and morally thrashed as they are, there are still enough of them to *smother up the English in our throngs*, if only they could get themselves sorted out. Their real weakness is lack of leadership. Bourbon seems to be acting on his own, almost hysterically at that, and no-one rushes to back him up. In contrast, there is no mistaking the clear leadership and consequently firm organization on the English side.

18. *spoil'd:* ruined.

friend: befriend, help.

24. Bourbon would rather die quickly than suffer a lifetime of shame.

SCENE VI

2. *But all's not done . . . field:* but we haven't finished yet – the French haven't run away in complete rout.

8. *Larding:* enriching with the blood pouring from his wounds. The blood is supposed to make the earth rich in fertility as well as colour.

Bourbon
    Shame, and eternal shame, nothing but shame!
    Let us die in honour: once more back again;
    And he that will not follow Bourbon now,
    Let him go hence and, with his cap in hand
    Like a base pander, hold the chamber-door   15
    Whilst by a slave, no gentler than my dog,
    His fairest daughter is contaminated.
Constable
    Disorder, that hath spoil'd us, friend us now!
    Let us on heaps go offer up our lives.
Orleans
    We are enow yet living in the field   20
    To smother up the English in our throngs,
    If any order might be thought upon.
Bourbon
    The devil take order now! I'll to the throng.
    Let life be short, else shame will be too long.

[Exeunt]

Scene VI

Another part of the field

[Alarum. Enter the KING *and his* TRAIN, *with*
PRISONERS; EXETER *and* OTHERS]

King
    Well have we done, thrice-valiant countrymen;
    But all's not done – yet keep the French the field.
Exeter
    The Duke of York commends him to your Majesty.
King
    Lives he, good uncle? Thrice within this hour
    I saw him down; thrice up again, and fighting;   5
    From helmet to the spur all blood he was.
Exeter
    In which array, brave soldier, doth he lie
    Larding the plain; and by his bloody side,

9. *Yoke-fellow . . . wounds:* companion in battle, sharing his honourable wounds.

11. *haggled over:* mutilated with many fierce sword cuts.

12. *where in gore he lay insteeped:* where he lay soaked in blood.

14. *yawn:* the wounds are like red mouths opening wide as if yawning.

15. *Tarry:* wait. York wants to continue to keep Suffolk company, even in death.

19. *We kept together in our chivalry.* This line suggests that York and Suffolk fought side by side throughout the battle, inspiring each other and helping each other out of difficulties.

21. *raught me his hand:* reached out to me with his hand.

26–7. The kiss may seem slightly abnormal and macabre to us, but Exeter is deeply moved by it: it reminds him of the bridegroom kissing his bride as a token of faithfulness. York married death in the form of the already dead Suffolk, and the **testament** (contract) was sealed with blood. *espous'd:* 'married.'

28–32. *The pretty and sweet manner . . . tears:* 'it was done so beautifully that I was moved to tears; I tried to stop myself from weeping, but I wasn't man enough and the female in me took over.' Even in Shakespeare's time men were not supposed to cry; to do so was and still is thought effeminate.

33–4. *For, hearing this . . . issue too:* for your story makes my eyes misty, and I shall have to put up with it (*compound:* come to terms) or I shall burst into tears too.

35–8. The French, it seems, have followed Bourbon's lead and started a new attack. There are many French prisoners on the stage at this moment, perhaps more of them than of Englishmen guarding them; they grow excited and restless at the prospect of being freed by their countrymen, while their English guards are torn between staying with them and going to help fight off the new attack. The king makes the only decision possible, a cruel one that to us would be against all the rules of war and of humanity, but a decision that has to be made if he is to avoid losing the advantage his troops have already gained. The scene shows Henry's self-control, his ability to snap his mind from the grief of York's death back to more urgent matters. Above all, as we have noted before, he is unmistakably the leader, whereas the French seem to have no clear leader. True, Bourbon has whipped up some enthusiasm, but we shall soon see the direction in which he leads it.

Yoke-fellow to his honour-owing wounds,
The noble Earl of Suffolk also lies.   10
Suffolk first died; and York, all haggled over,
Comes to him, where in gore he lay insteeped,
And takes him by the beard, kisses the gashes
That bloodily did yawn upon his face,
He cries aloud 'Tarry, my cousin Suffolk.   15
My soul shall thine keep company to heaven;
Tarry, sweet soul, for mine, then fly abreast;
As in this glorious and well-foughten field
We kept together in our chivalry'.
Upon these words I came and cheer'd him up;   20
He smil'd me in the face, raught me his hand,
And, with a feeble grip, says 'Dear my lord,
Commend my service to my sovereign'.
So did he turn, and over Suffolk's neck
He threw his wounded arm and kiss'd his lips;   25
And so, espous'd to death, with blood he seal'd
A testament of noble-ending love.
The pretty and sweet manner of it forc'd
Those waters from me which I would have stopp'd;
But I had not so much of man in me,   30
And all my mother came into mine eyes
And gave me up to tears.

King
                    I blame you not;
For, hearing this, I must perforce compound
With mistful eyes, or they will issue too.

[Alarum]

But hark! what new alarum is this same?   35
The French have reinforc'd their scatter'd men.
Then every soldier kill his prisoners;
Give the word through.

[Exeunt]

SCENE VII

1–10. This is the result of the attack led by Bourbon: the French have taken advantage of the fact that the English tents and stores are guarded only by boys, and have looted them and killed the boys. Now we remember the Boy's remark at the end of Act IV, Scene iv, and it seems a ghastly premonition. Both Fluellen and Gower express horror, but Gower is mistaken in thinking that this outrage was the cause of the king's order to kill the prisoners: we saw at the end of the previous scene that it was the renewal of the French attack that caused it, not the fact that they attacked the tents.

2. *arrant:* thorough, downright.

11–13. *porn* and ***Pig:*** Fluellen's way of saying 'born' and 'big.'

15–18. Fluellen is trying to say, in his odd way, that all these words mean the same as 'big,' with minor variations. He fails to see that poor old Gower has merely been misled by his pronunciation, and sees fit to give the Englishman a lesson in English!

21–50. Fluellen constructs an elaborate and gloriously illogical comparison between Alexander the Great and King Henry. He wants to show that their lives follow the same pattern, so that Henry will seem as good as, if not better than, Alexander; but the argument that both men were born in towns that had rivers and that both rivers had salmon in them is not very convincing, to put it mildly.

22. *'orld:* world.

27. *it is out of my prains:* 'I can't remember.'

Scene VII

Another part of the field

[*Enter* FLUELLEN *and* GOWER]

Fluellen

Kill the poys and the luggage! 'Tis expressly against
the law of arms; 'tis as arrant a piece of knavery, mark
you now, as can be offert; in your conscience, now, is
it not?

Gower

'Tis certain there's not a boy left alive; and the cowardly   5
rascals that ran from the battle ha' done this slaughter;
besides, they have burned and carried away all that
was in the King's tent; wherefore the King most
worthily hath caus'd every soldier to cut his prisoner's
throat. O, 'tis a gallant King!   10

Fluellen

Ay, he was porn at Monmouth, Captain Gower. What
call you the town's name where Alexander the
Pig was born?

Gower

Alexander the Great.

Fluellen

Why, I pray you, is not 'pig' great? The pig, or the   15
great, or the mighty, or the huge, or the magnanimous,
are all one reckonings, save the phrase is a little
variations.

Gower

I think Alexander the Great was born in Macedon; his
father was called Philip of Macedon, as I take it.   20

Fluellen

I think it is in Macedon where Alexander is porn. I
tell you, Captain, if you look in the maps of the 'orld,
I warrant you sall find, in the comparisons between
Macedon and Monmouth, that the situations, look
you, is both alike. There is a river in Macedon; and   25
there is also moreover a river at Monmouth; it is
call'd Wye at Monmouth, but it is out of my prains

31–2. *is come after it indifferent well:* resembles it quite closely. *figures:* parallels, resemblances, points of comparison.

34. *cholers:* angry moods.

36. *intoxicates in his prains:* drunk.

40–7. Fluellen is not at all pleased when Gower points out the dissimilarity between Alexander and Henry, because Gower has anticipated and partly spoilt the climax of Fluellen's comparison: both men had deadly quarrels with their best friends, but whereas Alexander was drunk at the time Henry was utterly sober – *in his right wits and his good judgments* – and his action in dismissing Falstaff was wise. Thus Henry may be seen to have gone one better than Alexander, and to be even greater than that great man. So reasons Fluellen.

46. *great belly doublet.* The doublet was a kind of vest which originally had double thickness, hence the name. In between the two thicknesses there was some padding; a doublet with a lot of padding was a 'great belly' doublet. Falstaff was very fat, and looked as though he was wearing one of these.

46. *gipes:* gibes (taunting, mocking jokes).

52–6. Henry has often shown little respect for the French, and has made scornful jokes about their fighting ability (as in Act III, Scene vi, lines 145–9), but now to scorn is added anger and the sort of contemptuous hatred we usually feel for vermin: *they do offend our sight.* Before, he challenged their right to certain lands and titles; now he wants to rid the earth of them completely. His anger is understandable: they will not fight properly, nor will they give in, and when they do attack they attack the defenceless boys.

what is the name of the other river; but 'tis all one, 'tis alike as my fingers is to my fingers, and there is salmons in both. If you mark Alexander's life well, 30 Harry of Monmouth's life is come after it indifferent well; for there is figures in all things. Alexander – God knows, and you know – in his rages, and his furies, and his wraths, and his cholers, and his moods, and his displeasures, and his indignations, and also being 35 a little intoxicates in his prains, did, in his ales and his angers, look you, kill his best friend, Cleitus.

Gower

Our king is not like him in that: he never kill'd any of his friends.

Fluellen

It is not well done, mark you now, to take the tales 40 out of my mouth ere it is made and finished. I speak but in the figures and comparisons of it; as Alexander kill'd his friend Cleitus, being in his ales and his cups, so also Harry Monmouth, being in his right wits and his good judgments, turn'd away the fat knight with 45 the great belly doublet; he was full of jests, and gipes, and knaveries, and mocks; I have forgot his name.

Gower

Sir John Falstaff.

Fluellen

That is he. I'll tell you there is good men porn at Monmouth.   50

Gower

Here comes his Majesty.

[*Alarum. Enter the* KING, WARWICK, GLOUCESTER, EXETER, *and* OTHERS, *with* PRISONERS. *Flourish*]

King

I was not angry since I came to France
Until this instant. Take a trumpet, herald;
Ride thou unto the horsemen on yond hill;
If they will fight with us, bid them come down   55

56. *void:* empty, leave the field, evacuate their troops.

58. *skirr:* scurry, run. The word suggests hurried, frightened movement, like the beating of a frightened bird's wings.

59. Assyrian warriors had a reputation for skill with the sling.

63–7. Montjoy's last words were ***Thou never shalt hear herald any more*** (Scene iii); now he must feel very foolish, and the king can't resist the temptation to remind him and to make fun of him.

fin'd means 'staked': he agreed to pay with his bones (i.e. his life) if he lost the battle.

68. *charitable licence:* kind permission.

70. *book:* record the names and count the numbers.

73. *mercenary:* a professional soldier, fighting for money rather than for duty or patriotism, and considered vulgar and low-class. Montjoy means that the corpses of the nobles and the ordinary soldiers are mixed up in such confusion that one cannot tell which is which.

76. ***Fret fetlock deep in gore:*** struggle ankle deep in blood. The *fetlock* is part of a horse's leg: the picture of blood flooding the field to this depth is another of the immense hyperboles with which Shakespeare conveys to us some of the dramatic vision that cannot be physically presented on the stage. (Compare Act IV, Scene vi, lines 11–14.)

77. *Yerk:* kick out sharply in violent jerks. The horses themselves are wounded, and in their agony they lash out with their feet, which being *armed* with iron shoes are very dangerous, or would be to any living person within range.

82. *peer:* appear.

83. ***The day is yours***. This seems to be the official French declaration of surrender; until this moment the English could not be quite certain that the French were not preparing for yet another attack, and we can imagine shouts of jubilation.

Or void the field; they do offend our sight.
If they'll do neither, we will come to them
And make them skirr away as swift as stones
Enforced from the old Assyrian slings;
Besides, we'll cut the throats of those we have,   60
And not a man of them that we shall take
Shall taste our mercy. Go and tell them so.

[Enter MONTJOY]

Exeter
Here comes the herald of the French, my liege.
Gloucester
His eyes are humbler than they us'd to be.
King
How now! What means this, herald? know'st thou   65
    not
That I have fin'd these bones of mine for ransom?
    Com'st thou again for ransom?
Montjoy
                   No, great King;
I come to thee for charitable licence,
That we may wander o'er this bloody field
To book our dead, and then to bury them;   70
To sort our nobles from our common men;
For many of our princes – woe the while!—
Lie drown'd and soak'd in mercenary blood;
So do our vulgar drench their peasant limbs
In blood of princes; and their wounded steeds   75
Fret fetlock deep in gore, and with wild rage
Yerk out their armed heels at their dead masters,
Killing them twice. O, give us leave, great King,
To view the field in safety, and dispose
Of their dead bodies!
King
              I tell thee truly, herald,   80
I know not if the day be ours or no;
For yet a many of your horsemen peer
And gallop o'er the field.
Montjoy
             The day is yours.

84. As usual, Henry promptly gives the credit to God.

87–8. The naming of the battle is quite a formal business, not unlike our modern manner of naming a ship.

89–111. In the general rejoicing and relief that follows the pronouncement of victory and the naming of the battle, the king relaxes for a few moments of informal chat with Fluellen, who happens to be near him. Fluellen seems especially proud at this moment to claim the king as a fellow-Welshman, in fact he positively glows with pleasure at the thought of Henry, like a true patriot of Wales, wearing a leek on St David's Day (the custom already mentioned in the note on Act IV, Scene i, lines 54–5). Note that for this relaxed interlude and right up to the exit of Fluellen at line 162 the speech also relaxes from verse to prose.

89. *grandfather:* Fluellen probably means Edward III, who was Henry's great-grandfather.

95–7. Another apparent slip by Fluellen: the tradition of wearing a leek on St David's Day is usually thought to date from an English victory over the Saxons in a.d. 540; there is no historical record of this *service in a garden where leeks did grow* during the Battle of Crécy, which must be the battle Fluellen is referring to in line 92.

Monmouth caps. A certain kind of cap originally made at Monmouth in Wales.

105–6. *God pless it:* God bless it (the Welsh blood in Henry).

109–11. *I need not be asham'd . . . honest man.* A good example of Fluellen's well-meaning bluntness: he won't feel ashamed of being Henry's fellow-countryman as long as Henry remains honest – a remarkable thing to say to a king who has just pulled off one of the greatest military triumphs of all time!

King

Praised be God, and not our strength, for it!

What is this castle call'd that stands hard by?　　85

Montjoy

They call it Agincourt.

King

Then call we this the field of Agincourt,

Fought on the day of Crispin Crispianus.

Fluellen

Your grandfather of famous memory, an't please your
Majesty, and your great-uncle Edward the Plack Prince　90
of Wales, as I have read in the chronicles, fought a
most prave pattle here in France.

King

They did, Fluellen.

Fluellen

Your Majesty says very true; if your Majesties is
remember'd of it, the Welshmen did good service in　95
a garden where leeks did grow, wearing leeks in their
Monmouth caps; which your Majesty know to this
hour is an honourable badge of the service; and I do
believe your Majesty takes no scorn to wear the leek
upon Saint Tavy's day.　　100

King

I wear it for a memorable honour;

For I am Welsh, you know, good countryman.

Fluellen

All the water in Wye cannot wash your Majesty's Welsh
plood out of your pody, I can tell you that Got pless
it and preserve it as long as it pleases his Grace and　105
his Majesty too!

King

Thanks, good my countryman.

Fluellen

By Jeshu, I am your Majesty's countryman, I care not
who know it; I will confess it to all the 'orld: I need
not be asham'd of your Majesty, praised be Got,　110

112. *him:* Montjoy, who has been standing around all this time waiting for an answer. During this conversation with Fluellen, which is a sort of unwinding process after the tension of battle, the king may be stripping off his helmet and part of his armour. Now he can return to business.

114. *On both our parts:* on both sides. *yonder fellow:* this is Williams, who has just appeared on the stage, wearing prominently in his cap the glove the king had given him as a *gage* (challenge) after their quarrel during the previous night. The glove enables the king to recognize Williams, but Williams doesn't recognize the king as his opponent in the argument, because the king is not wearing Williams's glove. However, the audience may be able to see him holding it while he talks to Williams, though of course he does not let Williams see it.

128. *craven:* self-confessed coward.

else: otherwise.

an't please your Majesty is equivalent to a modern phrase such as 'if your Majesty doesn't mind my saying so.'

129. *in my conscience:* 'I really think so.'

130–1. *It may be . . . degree:* 'perhaps his opponent is a nobleman, above answering challenges from men of this chap's class.' This explains why the king is not wearing the glove as he promised he would: if he did, Williams would never dare to challenge it, but would hide his own glove and nothing would happen.

132–3. The Devil is thought to be a gentleman: he holds the highest rank in hell. *Lucifer* and *Belzebub* are other notables in hell.

134–8. *if he be perjur'd . . . la:* if he doesn't keep his vow then I really think he's as thorough and shameless a rogue as ever walked on God's earth. Fluellen loves superlatives, and all this must add considerably to the king's embarrassment.

so long as your Majesty is an honest man.

[Enter WILLIAMS]

King

God keep me so! Our heralds go with him:
Bring me just notice of the numbers dead
On both our parts. Call yonder fellow hither.

[Exeunt HERALDS *with* MONTJOY]

Exeter

Soldier, you must come to the King.   115

King

Soldier, why wear'st thou that glove in thy cap?

Williams

An't please your Majesty, 'tis the gage of one that I
should fight withal, if he be alive.

King

An Englishman?

Williams

An't please your Majesty, a rascal that swagger'd with 120
me last night; who, if 'a live and ever dare to challenge
this glove, I have sworn to take him a box o' th' ear;
or if I can see my glove in his cap – which he swore,
as he was a soldier, he would wear if alive – I will strike
it out soundly.   125

King

What think you, Captain Fluellen, is it fit this soldier
keep his oath?

Fluellen

He is a craven and a villain else, an't please your
Majesty, in my conscience.

King

It may be his enemy is a gentleman of great sort, quite 130
from the answer of his degree.

Fluellen

Though he be as good a gentleman as the Devil is, as
Lucifer and Belzebub himself, it is necessary, look your
Grace, that he keep his vow and his oath; if he

139. *sirrah:* a term of address used to inferiors and subordinates.

145. *literatured in the wars:* well-read in the books of war.

146. The king sends Williams off to fetch Gower merely as a way of getting rid of him so that he can develop his own plan for confronting him with his identity.

148. *favour:* Williams's glove.
149–50. History records that Henry was nearly killed by Alençon, but recovered well enough to kill Alençon and two of his followers. It is clear that he actually fought, and did not merely direct operations. But of course the story about plucking the glove from Alençon's helmet is a fiction invented to put Fluellen on his mettle.
153. *an:* if.

154–8. The Alençon story has had its desired effect. Fluellen is breathing fire, positively longing for someone to challenge the glove and start a fight.

be perjur'd, see you now, his reputation is as arrant 135
a villain and a Jacksauce as ever his black shoe trod
upon God's ground and his earth, in my conscience,
la.

King

Then keep thy vow, sirrah, when thou meet'st the
fellow. 140

Williams

So I will, my liege, as I live.

King

Who serv'st thou under?

Williams

Under Captain Gower, my liege.

Fluellen

Gower is a good captain, and is good knowledge and
literatured in the wars. 145

King

Call him hither to me, soldier.

Williams

I will, my liege.

[Exit]

King

Here, Fluellen; wear thou this favour for me, and stick
it in thy cap; when Alençon and myself were down
together, I pluck'd this glove from his helm. If any 150
man challenge this, he is a friend to Alençon and an
enemy to our person; if thou encounter any such,
apprehend him, an thou dost me love.

Fluellen

Your Grace does me as great honours as can be desir'd
in the hearts of his subjects. I would fain see the man 155
that has but two legs that shall find himself aggrief'd
at this glove, that is all; but I would fain see it once,
an please God of his grace that I might see.

King

Know'st thou Gower?

161. The king quite deliberately sends Fluellen to find Gower so that he and Williams are certain to meet.

163–76. The king shows anxiety to prevent trouble. Williams has the sort of *blunt bearing* that suggests *he will keep his word* and challenge Fluellen boldly as soon as he sees the glove; while Fluellen is very quick-tempered and violent; When *touch'd with choler* (anger) he is as *hot as gunpowder*. These two might kill each other within seconds once they started quarrelling.

SCENE VIII

1–5. Both Williams and Fluellen assumed that the king is about to bestow some great honour on Gower, and that that is why he has sent for him.

Fluellen
He is my dear friend, an please you.   160
King
Pray thee, go seek him, and bring him to my tent.
Fluellen
I will fetch him.

[Exit]

King
My Lord of Warwick and my brother Gloucester,
Follow Fluellen closely at the heels;
The glove which I have given him for a favour   165
May haply purchase him a box o' th' ear.
It is the soldier's: I, by bargain, should
Wear it myself. Follow, good cousin Warwick;
If that the soldier strike him, as I judge
By his blunt bearing he will keep his word,   170
Some sudden mischief may arise of it;
For I do know Fluellen valiant,
And touch'd with choler, hot as gunpowder,
And quickly will return an injury;
Follow, and see there be no harm between them.   175
Go you with me, uncle of Exeter.

[Exeunt]

Scene VIII

Before King Henry's pavilion

[Enter GOWER and WILLIAMS]

Williams
I warrant it is to knight you, Captain.

[Enter FLUELLEN]

Fluellen
God's will and his pleasure, Captain, I beseech you
now, come apace to the King: there is more good

6–7. Williams bridles at once when he sees the glove, but Fluellen replies sarcastically, daring him to commit himself to a proper challenge. Williams promptly obliges.

9. *'Sblood:* 'God's blood' in short, a violent oath.
universal world: Fluellen's exaggerated phrase for the whole of the world. Note the anticlimax.

12. *Do you think I'll be forsworn?* 'do you think I'll break my pledge?'

14. *into plows:* in blows. He is going to punish Williams's treason by thrashing him personally. They stand glaring threateningly at each other, a few blows are exchanged in a preliminary way, but Gower is in the way, and anyway Warwick and Gloucester intervene before the fight really works up.
16. *a lie in thy throat:* a deliberate lie. (A lie in the teeth was less serious.)

21. *contagious:* poisonous.
22. *as you shall desire in a summer's day:* as it's possible to imagine.

toward you peradventure than is in your knowledge
to dream of. 5

Williams

Sir, know you this glove?

Fluellen

Know the glove? I know the glove is a glove.

Williams

I know this; and thus I challenge it.

[Strikes him]

Fluellen

'Sblood, an arrant traitor as any's in the universal world,
or in France, or in England! 10

Gower

How now, sir! you villain!

Williams

Do you think I'll be forsworn?

Fluellen

Stand away, Captain Gower; I will give treason his
payment into plows, I warrant you.

Williams

I am no traitor. 15

Fluellen

That's a lie in thy throat. I charge you in his Majesty's
name, apprehend him: he's a friend of the Duke
Alençon's.

[Enter WARWICK and GLOUCESTER]

Warwick

How now! how now! what's the matter?

Fluellen

My Lord of Warwick, here is – praised be God for it! 20
– a most contagious treason come to light, look you,
as you shall desire in a summer's day. Here is his
Majesty.

[Enter the KING and EXETER]

28. *the fellow of it:* the other one of the pair.

29. *change:* exchange.

33. *saving:* without disrespect to.

35–6. *is pear me . . . avouchment:* bear witness on my behalf and will confirm.

39. *thy glove:* the glove Williams is wearing in his cap, which is really the king's. Now it is the King's turn to produce the other glove of the pair, startling poor Williams into dismayed silence – but only for a few moments.

42. *let his neck answer for it:* let him hang.

44. *make me satisfaction:* compensate me.

49. *witness:* let the night, etc., serve as evidence.

King

How now! what's the matter?

Fluellen

My liege, here is a villain and a traitor, that, look your 25
Grace, has struck the glove which your Majesty is take
out of the helmet of Alençon.

Williams

My liege, this was my glove: here is the fellow of it;
and he that I gave it to in change promis'd to wear it
in his cap; I promis'd to strike him if he did; I met 30
this man with my glove in his cap, and I have been
as good as my word.

Fluellen

Your Majesty hear now, saving your Majesty's
manhood, what an arrant, rascally, beggarly, lousy
knave it is; I hope your Majesty is pear me testimony 35
and witness, and will avouchment, that this is the
glove of Alençon that your Majesty is give me; in your
conscience, now.

King

Give me thy glove, soldier; look, here is the fellow
of it.

'Twas I, indeed, thou promised'st to strike, 40
And thou hast given me most bitter terms.

Fluellen

An please your Majesty, let his neck answer for it, if
there is any martial law in the world.

King

How canst thou make me satisfaction?

Williams

All offences, my lord, come from the heart: never came 45
any from mine that might offend your Majesty.

King

It was ourself thou didst abuse.

Williams

Your Majesty came not like yourself: you appear'd to
me but as a common man; witness the night, your

51. *under that shape:* in the disguise of a common man. Williams doesn't mince words when he asks for the king's forgiveness; he says straight out what he thinks, and it is of course perfectly good sense: 'If you go about disguised as a common man you must expect people to treat you as a common man, and it's your own fault if you don't get the respect you're used to.'

52–3. *for had you been . . . offence:* 'for if you really had been a common man there would have been nothing offensive in my behaviour.'

56–9. Far from taking offence at Williams's outspoken defence of his mistake, the king readily recognizes the truth of what he says and his courage in saying it, and rewards him generously. He shows, in fact, the same sense of justice as that which enables him to punish old friends when they deserve it.

60. Fluellen's anger is still visible: once having started a fight with Williams he is not going to give it up easily. But on this instruction from the king he changes his tone, and offers Williams money. *mettle:* spirit, courage.

61. The *belly* was thought to be the part of the body in which courage was generated.

63. *prabbles:* squabbles.

65. *I will none of your money:* 'I don't want your rotten money' would be a modern equivalent.

66–9. Fluellen's essentially generous nature seems to have re-asserted itself.

Stage Direction. Henry takes the paper from the herald and reads from it.

72. *of good sort:* of high rank.

garments, your lowliness; and what your Highness 50
suffer'd under that shape I beseech you take it for your
own fault, and not mine; for had you been as I took
you for, I made no offence; therefore, I beseech your
Highness pardon me.

King

Here, uncle Exeter, fill this glove with crowns, 55
And give it to this fellow. Keep it, fellow;
And wear it for an honour in thy cap
Till I do challenge it. Give him the crowns;
And, Captain, you must needs be friends with him.

Fluellen

By this day and this light, the fellow has mettle enough 60
in his pelly: hold, there is twelve pence for you; and
I pray you to serve God, and keep you out of prawls,
and prabbles, and quarrels, and dissensions, and, I
warrant you, it is the petter for you.

Williams

I will none of your money. 65

Fluellen

It is with a good will; I can tell you it will serve you
to mend your shoes. Come, wherefore should you be
so pashful? your shoes is not so good, 'tis a good silling,
I warrant you, or I will change it.

[Enter an ENGLISH HERALD]

King

Now, herald, are the dead number'd? 70

Herald

Here is the number of the slaughter'd French.

[Gives a paper]

King

What prisoners of good sort are taken, uncle?

Exeter

Charles Duke of Orleans, nephew to the King;
John Duke of Bourbon, and Lord Bouciqualt;

83. *dubb'd knights:* had their knighthoods conferred on them.

85. *mercenaries:* ordinary, paid soldiers, as opposed to the nobles, knights, and gentlemen.

102. *None else of name:* nobody else of noble rank.

103–5. The king himself and all those around him are awed into silence by these extraordinary numbers. It is natural for them to feel that only God could have performed such a miracle, an idea which the king himself puts into words.

105. *Ascribe we all:* we give all the credit.

105–9. It is possible that such extraordinary results have been achieved before when one side has ambushed the other, or played some other military trick, but this was *plain shock and even play of battle;* both sides met face to face in the ordinary way. (See the note at the end of the scene.)

Of other lords and barons, knights and squires, 75
Full fifteen hundred, besides common men.

King

This note doth tell me of ten thousand French
That in the field lie slain; of princes, in this number,
And nobles bearing banners, there lie dead
One hundred twenty-six; added to these, 80
Of knights, esquires, and gallant gentlemen,
Eight thousand and four hundred; of the which
Five hundred were but yesterday dubb'd knights.
So that, in these ten thousand they have lost,
There are but sixteen hundred mercenaries; 85
The rest are princes, barons, lords, knights, squires,
And gentlemen of blood and quality.
The names of those their nobles that lie dead:
Charles Delabreth, High Constable of France;
Jaques of Chatillon, Admiral of France; 90
The master of the cross-bows, Lord Rambures;
Great Master of France, the brave Sir Guichard Dolphin;
John Duke of Alençon; Antony Duke of Brabant,
The brother to the Duke of Burgundy;
And Edward Duke of Bar. Of lusty earls, 95
Grandpré and Roussi, Fauconbridge and Folx,
Beaumont and Marie, Vaudemont and Lestrake.
Here was a royal fellowship of death!
Where is the number of our English dead?

[HERALD *presents another paper*]

Edward the Duke of York, the Earl of Suffolk, 100
Sir Richard Kikely, Davy Gam, Esquire;
None else of name; and of all other men
But five and twenty. O God, thy arm was here!
And not to us, but to thy arm alone,
Ascribe we all. When, without stratagem, 105
But in plain shock and even play of battle,
Was ever known so great and little loss
On one part and on th' other? Take it, God,

111. *And be it . . . host:* proclaim to the whole army that it will be a crime punishable by death . . .

120. *Non nobis:* part of the Latin hymn which means 'Not to us, O Lord but to thee be the glory given.' *Te Deum* is another song in praise of God.

The scene ends in a mood of thanksgiving to God: no man is to boast of the English triumph, for it was not the work of men but of God. The numbers involved make the victory seem something of a miracle: the French outnumber the English by five to one (60,000 to 12,000), yet the French losses are 10,000 compared with a mere 29 on the English side. This is difficult to believe, and indeed historians nowadays put the losses at about 7,000 to 500 respectively, but even so it is clear that Henry completely out-generalled his enemies; the English archers fired with such deadly discipline and accuracy that the charging French cavalry were thrown into confusion, and in ground made muddy by recent heavy rain were unable to manoeuvre freely, their heavy armour hindering them more than protecting them.

However, Shakespeare is apparently less concerned with tactical explanations than with suggesting that God intervened. Before the battle Salisbury, hearing that the odds are five to one, exclaims *God's arm strike with us!,* and Henry, when he reads the details of the losses after the battle, says *O God, thy arm was here!* God has fought for England, and we are left with the feeling that God has chosen this young king for special protection.

For it is none but thine.

Exeter

      'Tis wonderful!

King

Come, go we in procession to the village;   110
And be it death proclaimed through our host
To boast of this or take that praise from God
Which is his only.

Fluellen

Is it not lawful, an please your Majesty, to tell how
many is kill'd?   115

King

Yes, Captain; but with this acknowledgment,
That God fought for us.

Fluellen

Yes, my conscience, he did us great good.

King

Do we all holy rites:
Let there be sung 'Non nobis' and 'Te Deum';   120
The dead with charity enclos'd in clay—
And then to Calais; and to England then;
Where ne'er from France arriv'd more happy men.

[Exeunt]

ACT FIVE

PROLOGUE

1. *Vouchsafe:* permit. *the story* is the historical account of King Henry's life, which the better educated members of the audience would probably have read for themselves.

3–6. *to admit . . . presented:* to forgive the way we cut down the time, the numbers involved and the proper sequence of events, things we can't show fully on the stage.

6. *Now we bear the King:* now the king moves in our imagination.

9. *Athwart:* across.

10. *Pales in . . . boys:* there is a huge crowd of men, women, and children waiting on the beach to cheer the king home, and as they stand there they look like a sort of fence (of palings) which *pales in the flood* (fences the sea in).

11. *out-voice:* they are noisier than the sea.

12. *whiffler:* a man who went ahead of a procession to clear the way for it; like a modern motorbike outrider. The Chorus is suggesting that even the sea has become Henry's servant, roaring and booming to announce his coming.

17–22. It would have been quite normal for the conquering hero to march through London in a triumphant procession, having his dented helmet and bent sword carried prominently for all to see, so that they would be impressed by his heroism. Henry, though pressed, refuses to do this, insisting as he has done since the battle that the glory must be given to God and not to himself. *full trophy, signal and ostent:* all tokens, signs and outward displays he dedicates to God.

23. Line 15 mentions the speed with which the imagination can work. As so often when Shakespeare's mind is at full stretch *quick* carries both its meanings at once, 'speedy' and 'living'. The image of the forge of thought is an excellent one.

25. *in best sort:* dressed in all their finery.

27. *plebeians:* common people. Social classes in ancient Rome were sharply defined, 'plebs' on the lower side and 'patricians', including senators, on the upper. The picture of the Roman crowd welcoming Caesar home from his triumphs provides a simile for Henry's return.

ACT FIVE
Prologue

[Enter CHORUS]

Chorus
    Vouchsafe to those that have not read the story
    That I may prompt them; and of such as have,
    I humbly pray them to admit th' excuse
    Of time, of numbers, and due course of things,
    Which cannot in their huge and proper life   5
    Be here presented. Now we bear the King
    Toward Calais. Grant him there. There seen,
    Heave him away upon your winged thoughts
    Athwart the sea. Behold, the English beach
    Pales in the flood with men, with wives, and boys,   10
    Whose shouts and claps out-voice the deep-mouth'd sea,
    Which, like a mighty whiffler, fore the King
    Seems to prepare his way. So let him land,
    And solemnly see him set on to London.
    So swift a pace hath thought that even now   15
    You may imagine him upon Blackheath;
    Where that his lords desire him to have borne
    His bruised helmet and his bended sword
    Before him through the city. He forbids it,
    Being free from vainness and self-glorious pride;   20
    Giving full trophy, signal, and ostent,
    Quite from himself to God. But now behold
    In the quick forge and working-house of thought,
    How London doth pour out her citizens!
    The mayor and all his brethren in best sort—   25
    Like to the senators of th' antique Rome,
    With the plebeians swarming at their heels—

29–34. Shakespeare takes this opportunity for a topical reference and a deft compliment to Queen Elizabeth (*our gracious Empress*). When he wrote this play an expedition had left London under the Earl of Essex (*the General*) to quell a rebellion in Ireland, and news was expected every day of its success. (This enables us to know that the play, or at least this Prologue, was written between late 1598 and September 1599.) Essex was of course *lower* than King Henry, but the success expected of him would be as popular as Henry's and would bring the people out of London to greet him in the same way.

likelihood: 'similarity'. The Essex scene would be a similar demonstration of the people's love and patriotism: *a lower but loving likelihood*.

32. *broached:* spitted. The picture is of Essex brandishing a sword on which the rebels are impaled.

36–7. The French are still lamenting their defeat and licking their wounds, so there is no need for the English to return to France.

38. *The Emperor:* Sigismund, of the Holy Roman Empire, who came to negotiate on behalf of France.

39–41. *omit . . . France:* the Chorus asks us to jump in imagination over everything else that may have happened until Henry's return to France (actually some years later).

42–3. *and myself have play'd . . . past:* and I have played the part of the interval by telling you all the intervening history and reminding you that it is now in the past.

44. *brook abridgement:* be tolerant of this cutting short.

SCENE I

This scene provides a last taste of the comic ingredient of the play, and winds up the Pistol/Fluellen quarrel just as the next scene winds up the king's efforts to obtain the French throne for himself.

4. *ass:* as.

5. *scald:* literally, affected with a skin disease known as scall (scurvy), but Fluellen is using it to mean worthless – just as *lousy* means literally full of lice but is used colloquially to mean 'no good.' It is of course quite possible that Pistol literally was ridden with disease and lice.

9. *yesterday*. Evidently it is now the day after St David's Day, the day on which the Welsh traditionally wore a leak as a national emblem. Pistol ridiculed the emblem by asking Fluellen to eat it, as though it were nothing but a vegetable.

Go forth and fetch their conqu'ring Caesar in;
As, by a lower but loving likelihood,
Were now the General of our gracious Empress—   30
As in good time he may – from Ireland coming,
Bringing rebellion broached on his sword,
How many would the peaceful city quit
To welcome him! Much more, and much more cause,
Did they this Harry. Now in London place him—   35
As yet the lamentation of the French
Invites the King of England's stay at home;
The Emperor's coming in behalf of France
To order peace between them; and omit
All the occurrences, whatever chanc'd,   40
Till Harry's back-return again to France.
There must we bring him; and myself have play'd
The interim, by rememb'ring you 'tis past.
Then brook abridgment; and your eyes advance,
After your thoughts, straight back again to France.

[Exit]

Scene I

France.The English camp

[Enter FLUELLEN *and* GOWER*]*

Gower

Nay, that's right; but why wear you your leek
   to-day?
Saint Davy's day is past.

Fluellen

There is occasions and causes why and wherefore in
all things. I will tell you, ass my friend, Captain Gower:
the rascally, scald, beggarly, lousy, pragging knave,   5
Pistol – which you and yourself and all the world
know to be no petter than a fellow, look you now,
of no merits – he is come to me, and prings me pread
and salt yesterday, look you, and bid me eat

10–11. *breed no contention:* start an argument.

14. Turkey-cocks strut importantly with their chests thrust out and their heads back, which helps us to visualize Pistol's manner.

16. *scurvy:* infected with a disease which causes the skin to go dry and flaky (similar to *scald* in line 5).

18. *bedlam:* mad. The word comes from Bethlehem, the name of a lunatic asylum in London. A *Troyan* (or Trojan) was an inhabitant of Troy, but the term was used colloquially for a person of dissolute character.
19. *fold up Parca's fatal web:* kill you. Parca is a Pistolian mistake for the three Parcae (Fates) who respectively spun, measured and cut the thread of life.
20. *qualmish:* squeamish. The smell of leeks makes him sick.
21–6. Pistol tries to turn away from the offending leek, but Fluellen forces it under his nose.

27. *Cadwallader.* A famous king who defended Wales against the Saxons in the seventh century. *goats* are also associated with Wales.
28. *There is one goat for you.* Fluellen hits Pistol with a stick as he says this, as though he were a goat butting him with his horns.

31. *when God's will is.* Fluellen agrees that he will die, but naturally, not at the hands of Pistol.
32–3. Fluellen means that he wants Pistol to live, and is therefore providing the *victuals* (food) to keep him alive. The *sauce* is the blow he gives him: it is sharp, and helps the food down.
34–5. A *mountain-squire* is one who owns worthless mountain land; the term therefore is contemptuous. Fluellen will make Pistol *a squire of low degree* (he will bring him to his knees and reduce him to nothing). Shakespeare's audience would have recognized *a squire of low degree* as a reference to the title of a popular medieval romance.
35–6. *fall to:* get on with it, start eating.

my leek; it was in a place where I could not breed no   10
contention with him; but I will be so bold as to wear
it in my cap till I see him once again, and then I will
tell him a little piece of my desires.

[Enter PISTOL]

Gower

Why, here he comes, swelling like a turkey-cock.

Fluellen

'Tis no matter for his swellings nor his turkey-cocks.   15
God pless you, Aunchient Pistol! you scurvy, lousy
knave, God pless you!

Pistol

Ha! art thou bedlam? Dost thou thirst, base Troyan,
To have me fold up Parca's fatal web?
Hence! I am qualmish at the smell of leek.   20

Fluellen

I peseech you heartily, scurvy, lousy knave, at my
desires, and my requests, and my petitions, to eat, look
you, this leek; because, look you, you do not love it,
nor your affections, and your appetites, and your diges-
tions, does not agree with it, I would desire you to eat   25
it.

Pistol

Not for Cadwallader and all his goats.

Fluellen

There is one goat for you. *[Strikes him]* Will you be
    so good, scald knave, as eat it?

Pistol

Base Troyan, thou shalt die.   30

Fluellen

You say very true, scald knave – when God's will is.
I will desire you to live in the meantime, and eat your
victuals; come, there is sauce for it. *[Striking him again]*
You call'd me yesterday mountain-squire; but I will
make you to-day a squire of low degree. I pray you fall   35
to; if you can mock a leek, you can eat a leek.

37. *astonish'd:* stunned. Pistol is reeling from Fluellen's blows.

39. *pate:* head.
40. A *green wound* is a fresh, raw wound: evidently Pistol's head is bleeding from Fluellen's blows. *coxcomb:* bloody head. Eating the leek is good for his head because it will save it from further blows.

46–8. Fluellen raises his *cudgel* (stick) to give Pistol some more encouragement, but Pistol implores him to *quiet* it, i.e. keep it still.

49. *Much good do you:* much good may it do you.

54. *groat.* a coin then worth 1½ pence. Pistol is insulted to be offered such a gift: at least he pretends to be above such pettiness.

59. But now he decides he could do with the money after all. *in earnest of revenge*: an excuse for taking it: he will keep it, he says, as a kind of reminder to get his revenge.

Gower
Enough, Captain, you have astonish'd him.
Fluellen
I say I will make him eat some part of my leek, or I
will peat his pate four days. Bite, I pray you, it is good
for your green wound and your ploody coxcomb.   40
Pistol
Must I bite?
Fluellen
Yes, certainly, and out of doubt, and out of question
too, and ambiguities.
Pistol
By this leek, I will most horribly revenge – I eat and
eat, I swear—   45
Fluellen
Eat, I pray you; will you have some more sauce to your
leek? There is not enough leek to swear by.
Pistol
Quiet thy cudgel: thou dost see I eat.
Fluellen
Much good do you, scald knave, heartily. Nay, pray
you throw none away; the skin is good for your broken 50
coxcomb. When you take occasions to see leeks here-
after, I pray you mock at 'em; that is all.
Pistol
Good.
Fluellen
Ay, leeks is good. Hold you, there is a groat to heal
your pate.   55
Pistol
Me a groat!
Fluellen
Yes, verily and in truth, you shall take it; or I have
another leek in my pocket which you shall eat.
Pistol
I take thy groat in earnest of revenge.

60–2. Pistol will be like a dealer in wood, buying cudgels from Fluellen, i.e. getting nothing from him but a good thrashing.

62. *God bye you:* God be with you.

65–75. Gower sums the argument up with a few crisp comments which put Pistol firmly in his place, coming as they do from one who is a disinterested observer, and which at the same time help us to appreciate Fluellen and his eccentricity better.

66–7. *upon an honourable respect:* for an honourable reason. The custom of wearing a leek was begun, according to Fluellen, when some Welsh soldiers *did good service in a garden where leeks did grow* (Act IV, Scene vii, lines 95–6).

68. *predeceased valour:* the bravery shown by those men in the past. *avouch:* confirm, back up. Gower gives a good summary of Pistol's character: he talks a lot but dares not back his words up with actions.

69–70. *gleeking and galling at:* poking fun at and irritating.

72. *garb:* fashion.

74. *condition:* way to behave. 'Let's hope the Welshman has taught you some good old English manners.'

76. *huswife:* housewife, or more commonly 'hussy,' a woman who changes her mind and feelings out of spite, as Pistol says Dame Fortune does to him. For a moment we may feel almost sorry for Pistol as he stands, cowed, bloody, and forlorn, lamenting the death of his Nell and all his friends.

77. *spital:* hospital.

78. *malady of France:* venereal disease. Caught from Pistol? Or does this confirm our suspicions of Nell in Act II, Scene i?

79. *And there . . . cut off:* 'and my reunion with her won't happen now.'

80. *wax:* grow.

81–2. He brightens again already at the thought of the mischief he will get up to once he is back in London. A *bawd* procured prostitutes for men who wanted them.

84–5. Just the sort of confidence trick Gower talked about in Act III, Scene vi, lines 67–81. So Pistol departs, saddened but apparently no wiser, and certainly not at all reformed; and this is in fact the last we see of him.

Fluellen

If I owe you anything I will pay you in cudgels; you   60
shall be a woodmonger, and buy nothing of me but
cudgels. God bye you, and keep you, and heal your
pate.

[Exit]

Pistol

All hell shall stir for this.

Gower

Go, go: you are a counterfeit cowardly knave. Will   65
you mock at an ancient tradition, begun upon an
honourable respect, and worn as a memorable trophy
of predeceased valour, and dare not avouch in your
deeds any of your words? I have seen you gleeking
and galling at this gentleman twice or thrice. You   70
thought, because he could not speak English in the
native garb, he could not therefore handle an English
cudgel; you find it otherwise, and henceforth let a
Welsh correction teach you a good English condition.
Fare ye well.   75

[Exit]

Pistol

Doth Fortune play the huswife with me now?
News have I that my Nell is dead i' th' spital
Of malady of France;
And there my rendezvous is quite cut off.
Old I do wax; and from my weary limbs   80
Honour is cudgell'd. Well, bawd I'll turn,
And something lean to cutpurse of quick hand.
To England will I steal, and there I'll steal;
And patches will I get unto these cudgell'd scars,
And swear I got them in the Gallia wars.   85

[Exit]

SCENE II

This final scene shows the reconciliation between England and France in the palace at Troyes (in France) in May 1420. From the antics of Fluellen and Pistol in the previous scene, we move now to a state occasion of a formal kind.

1. The meeting has been arranged to bring about peace, and Henry begins by hoping that the meeting itself will be peaceful. He tactfully refers to the king and queen of France as 'brother' and 'sister', and to Katherine as 'cousin'.

3. *fair time of day:* a polite greeting, like 'good-day to you.'

5–7. Burgundy organized the meeting between the two sides.

12–14. The queen hopes the outcome of the meeting will be as happy as she and her husband already feel on meeting Henry face-to-face in this friendly way; their previous meetings, as she goes on to explain, have been hostile.

16. *that met them in their bent:* that got in their way (*bent:* line of sight; cf. bend one's eyes upon).

17. *basilisks:* Originally these were strange mythical creatures, alleged to be hatched by a serpent from a cock's egg, and to be able to kill their enemies by merely looking at them. The name was later transferred to large brass cannons which hurled huge cannon-balls and thus also murdered what they 'looked at.' Here both meanings occur: the *fatal balls* are the cannon-balls and Henry's eyeballs, both of which brought death to the French. The queen makes him sound a terrifying person, and she still seems half afraid of him.

19. *and that this day:* and we hope that this day . . .

21. *To cry amen to that:* to support that wish, to give it our blessing. *amen:* 'so be it.'

Scene II

France. The French King's palace

[Enter at one door, KING HENRY, EXETER, BEDFORD,
GLOUCESTER, WARWICK, WESTMORELAND *and other*
LORDS; *at another, the* FRENCH KING, QUEEN ISABEL,
the PRINCESS KATHERINE, ALICE *and other* LADIES; *the*
DUKE OF BURGUNDY *and his* TRAIN]

King

Peace to this meeting, wherefore we are met!
Unto our brother France, and to our sister,
Health and fair time of day; joy and good wishes
To our most fair and princely cousin Katherine.
And, as a branch and member of this royalty,   5
By whom this great assembly is contriv'd,
We do salute you, Duke of Burgundy.
And, princes French, and peers, health to you all!

French King

Right joyous are we to behold your face,
Most worthy brother England; fairly met!   10
So are you, princes English, every one.

Queen Isabel

So happy be the issue, brother England,
Of this good day and of this gracious meeting
As we are now glad to behold your eyes—
Your eyes, which hitherto have borne in them,   15
Against the French that met them in their bent,
The fatal balls of murdering basilisks;
The venom of such looks, we fairly hope,
Have lost their quality; and that this day
Shall change all griefs and quarrels into love.   20

King

To cry amen to that, thus we appear.

Queen Isabel

You English princes all, I do salute you.

Burgundy

My duty to you both, on equal love,

27. *bur.* Originally this was the wooden rail in a court room at which prisoners stood during their trial, but used here metaphorically for the meeting-place where the dispute is to be settled.

28. *Your mightiness . . . witness:* Your two Majesties know best.

29. *prevail'd:* succeeded.

31. *congreeted:* met together.

31–2. *let it not . . . view:* 'I hope I shan't be thought impolite if I ask straight out in front of all these royal people.'

33. *rub:* difficulty. (See the note on Act II, Scene ii, line 188.)

34–8. Burgundy is really asking a simple question: 'What difficulty is there now to prevent our countries from being at peace?' But Shakespeare transforms it into an imaginative personification of peace as a beautiful and tender woman who has been savagely maltreated and thrown out.

37. *put up:* lift up for all to see.

39. *her husbandry:* the proper management of the land that one would normally find in France in peacetime. Burgundy is continuing the idea that France is a fertile garden, of which Peace is the gardener, but she has been absent so long that all her crops are rotting in heaps, weeds predominate, and everything is overgrown.

40. *it:* its.

42. *even-pleach'd:* with neatly and evenly interlaced branches, as a good hedge should be.

44. *fallow leas:* fields that are bare of crops. These, he says, are overrun with weeds.

45. *darnel, hemlock . . . fumitory:* names of weeds.

46–7. *while . . . savagery:* while the plough that ought to be rooting up the weeds just lies idle and goes rusty. Strictly, the *coulter* is the knife that cuts the earth in front of the ploughshare.

48. *even mead:* smooth meadow. *erst:* previously.

50. *Wanting the scythe:* lacking the scythe, i.e. needing to be cut.

51. *conceives by idleness:* through being left to lie idle, it produces its own crop of weeds.

52. *kecksy:* hemlock, a poisonous weed.

53. *Losing both beauty and utility:* the meadow has become both ugly and useless.

54–67. Burgundy's appeal for peace has so far been based on the terrible wastage of war: the formerly beautiful and productive countryside has become an unsightly wilderness because everyone has been too busy fighting to attend to it properly. Now he goes further: the French people too, especially the children, have grown wild and unnatural.

55. Everything is naturally corrupt, it seems, and left to itself goes wild, whereas cultivation restores order.

57–8. *Have lost . . . country:* have forgotten, or haven't the time to learn, the sciences that our country ought to be expert in.

Great Kings of France and England! That I have
   labour'd
With all my wits, my pains, and strong endeavours,   25
To bring your most imperial Majesties
Unto this bar and royal interview,
Your mightiness on both parts best can witness.
Since then my office hath so far prevail'd
That face to face and royal eye to eye   30
You have congreeted, let it not disgrace me
If I demand, before this royal view,
What rub or what impediment there is
Why that the naked, poor, and mangled Peace,
Dear nurse of arts, plenties, and joyful births,   35
Should not in this best garden of the world,
Our fertile France, put up her lovely visage?
Alas, she hath from France too long been chas'd!
And all her husbandry doth lie on heaps,
Corrupting in it own fertility.   40
Her vine, the merry cheerer of the heart,
Unpruned dies; her hedges even-pleach'd,
Like prisoners wildly overgrown with hair,
Put forth disorder'd twigs; her fallow leas
The darnel, hemlock, and rank fumitory,   45
Doth root upon, while that the coulter rusts
That should deracinate such savagery;
The even mead, that erst brought sweetly forth
The freckled cowslip, burnet, and green clover,
Wanting the scythe, all uncorrected, rank,   50
Conceives by idleness, and nothing teems
But hateful docks, rough thistles, kecksies, burs,
Losing both beauty and utility.
And as our vineyards, fallows, meads, and hedges,
Defective in their natures, grow to wildness;   55
Even so our houses and ourselves and children
Have lost, or do not learn for want of time,
The sciences that should become our country;
But grow, like savages – as soldiers will,

60. 'that do nothing but think about blood.'

61. *diffus'd attire:* untidy clothes.

63–4. The meeting has been arranged to restore the order which has been lacking, and to make France look as beautiful as it used to look. *favour:* appearance.

65. *let:* hindrance.

68. *would:* want. Henry points out bluntly that if the French want peace they must buy it on his terms at his price.

69. *want:* absence.

72–3. *Whose tenours . . . hands:* the general sense and significant details of which are briefly set out in that document which you are holding. The *tenour* of a passage is the general sense or gist of it.

77. *cursorary:* cursory, hasty. The French king has only had a quick glance through Henry's peace conditions.

78. *pleaseth your Grace:* a polite request. We should probably say 'Would your Grace be kind enough to . . . ?'

81–2. *we will suddenly . . . answer:* we will quickly come to a decision and give you our final answer.

83–90. A demonstration of the art of delegation: Henry not only asks his delegates to argue on his behalf, but trusts them with the job of altering the peace terms in any way which might be to his advantage. *And we'll consign thereto* is as good as saying 'And I'll agree to whatever you suggest.'

That nothing do but meditate on blood— 60
To swearing and stern looks, diffus'd attire,
And everything that seems unnatural.
Which to reduce into our former favour
You are assembled; and my speech entreats
That I may know the let why gentle Peace 65
Should not expel these inconveniences
And bless us with her former qualities.

King

If, Duke of Burgundy, you would the peace
Whose want gives growth to th' imperfections
Which you have cited, you must buy that peace 70
With full accord to all our just demands;
Whose tenours and particular effects
You have, enschedul'd briefly, in your hands.

Burgundy

The King hath heard them; to the which as yet
There is no answer made.

King

             Well then, the peace, 75
Which you before so urg'd, lies in his answer.

French King

I have but with a cursorary eye
O'erglanced the articles; pleaseth your Grace
To appoint some of your council presently
To sit with us once more, with better heed
To re-survey them, we will suddenly
Pass our accept and peremptory answer.

King

Brother, we shall. Go, uncle Exeter,
And brother Clarence, and you, brother Gloucester,
Warwick, and Huntingdon, go with the King; 85
And take with you free power to ratify,
Augment, or alter, as your wisdoms best
Shall see advantageable for our dignity,
Any thing in or out of our demands;
And we'll consign thereto. Will you, fair sister, 90
Go with the princes or stay here with us?

92–4. The French Queen may want to leave Henry and Katherine together, to give them a chance to get acquainted. Her excuse for joining in the conference with the other nobles is that 'a woman may perhaps be able to introduce a little common-sense when the men get too fussy over minor details.' Note that *nice* here means precise, scrupulous.

96. *capital:* most important.

99. Henry is now committed to a formal wooing of Katherine, with Alice as a witness. He begins in verse, with some rather forced and conventional ideas, but as soon as Katherine points out that she cannot understand he relaxes into a prose style and an honest, semi-humorous manner that seems much more natural to him. His French (and Katherine's English) contains many errors, which the acting and the fact that many of Shakespeare's audience would know French would make funny.

111. 'What does he say? That I am like the angels?'

112. 'Yes, indeed, that is what he said.'

Queen Isabel
Our gracious brother, I will go with them;
Haply a woman's voice may do some good,
When articles too nicely urg'd be stood on.
King
Yet leave our cousin Katherine here with us;   95
She is our capital demand, compris'd
Within the fore-rank of our articles.
Queen Isabel
She hath good leave.

[*Exeunt all but the* KING, KATHERINE *and* ALICE]

King
Fair Katherine, and most fair,
Will you vouchsafe to teach a soldier terms   100
Such as will enter at a lady's ear,
And plead his love-suit to her gentle heart?
Katherine
Your Majesty shall mock at me; I cannot speak your
England.
King
O fair Katherine, if you will love me soundly with your 105
French heart, I will be glad to hear you confess it
brokenly with your English tongue. Do you like me,
Kate?
Katherine
Pardonnez-moi, I cannot tell vat is like me.
King
An Angel is like you, Kate, and you are like an angel. 110
Katherine
Que dit-il? que je suis semblable à les anges?
Alice
Oui, vraiment, sauf votre grace, ainsi dit-il.
King
I said so, dear Katherine, and I must not blush to affirm
it.

120. *dat is de Princess:* that is what the princess said.

121. *the better English-woman:* better at speaking English than Alice. Alice's translation in line 119 is in less correct English than Katherine's speeches in lines 103 and 109. But Henry's real motive is to speak directly to Katherine, to dispense with Alice, and if possible to get her out of the way altogether.

124. *a plain king:* an unusually ordinary man to be a king, lacking any sort of brilliance; plain-spoken and blunt.

125-7. He says he has no skill with words to put his proposal more convincingly; all he can do is to say straight out what he means. In fact, of course, his plain-speaking is more persuasive for being sincere (and we may remember that earlier he has spoken the most eloquent lines in the play).

128. *I wear out my suit.* A pun on the two meanings of *suit:* the suit of clothes which can be worn out, and his love-suit, which would come to a halt if she asked him to amplify or explain it.

129. *clap hands and a bargain:* a very blunt way of putting it, as though Henry is deliberately being as plain-spoken as he can. Men would shake hands to seal a bargain (e.g. selling farm produce or livestock), but marriage contracts usually have a more elegant method.

134. *measure:* playing on different meanings of *measure:* (1) the sense of rhythm necessary for writing poetry; (2) dancing (he is no good at it); (3) amount (he is reasonably strong).

136-41. Henry was a very athletic young man; vaulting into the saddle in full armour was a considerable feat, as armour was extremely heavy in those days.

139. *leap into a wife:* win a wife and get married. He means 'If I could win you by feats of athletics and fighting, I should have no difficulty; but if I've got to make a show of being lovesick I am lost.'

140. *bound:* take my horse over jumps.

140-1. *lay on:* fight.

141. *jack-an-apes:* a tame monkey that rode on horseback, clinging so tightly that it was never thrown off.

142. *greenly:* in a lovesick fashion.

143-4. *cunning in protestation:* skill in arguing his case.

143. *for urging:* when people try to persuade me. He is referring to his oath, or promise, which he never breaks.

Katherine

O bon Dieu! les langues des hommes sont pleines de 115
tromperies.

King

What says she, fair one? that the tongues of men are
full of deceits?

Alice

Oui, dat de tongues of de mans is be full of deceits –
dat is de Princess. 120

King

The Princess is the better Englishwoman. I'faith, Kate,
my wooing is fit for thy understanding: I am glad thou
canst speak no better English; for if thou couldst, thou
wouldst find me such a plain king that thou wouldst
think I had sold my farm to buy my crown. I know 125
no ways to mince it in love, but directly to say 'I love
you'. Then, if you urge me farther than to say 'Do you
in faith?' I wear out my suit. Give me your answer;
i'faith, do; and so clap hands and a bargain. How say
you, lady? 130

Katherine

Sauf votre honneur, me understand well.

King

Marry, if you would put me to verses or to dance for
your sake, Kate, why you undid me; for the one I have
neither words nor measure, and for the other I have
no strength in measure, yet a reasonable measure in 135
strength. If I could win a lady at leap-frog, or by
vaulting into my saddle with my armour on my back,
under the correction of bragging be it spoken, I should
quickly leap into a wife. Or if I might buffet for my
love, or bound my horse for her favours, I could lay 140
on like a butcher, and sit like a jack-an-apes, never
off. But, before God, Kate, I cannot look greenly, nor
gasp out my eloquence, nor I have no cunning in
protestation; only downright oaths, which I never use
till urg'd, nor never break for urging. If thou canst 145

146–9. He makes himself out to be plain-looking as well as plain-spoken, a touch of modesty which is attractive in itself. *Let thine eye be thy cook:* 'Let your eye work like a cook, working on raw food and turning it into something more palatable.' His appearance needs similar treatment, but it's *not worth sun-burning*.

149. *plain soldier:* the straight, downright talk of soldiers.

150–1. To say 'I shall die if you refuse me' would be untrue and dishonest, the sort of sentimental nonsense Henry refuses to indulge in. He has already said he has no ability for that kind of love-making, but that was modesty again; later, in lines 155–7, he ridicules men who are good at it.

153. *uncoined constancy:* the faithfulness of one who is innocent and inexperienced with women; like metal that has not been moulded and stamped for common coins.

153–5. He could never be unfaithful to her, because he simply lacks the necessary guile.

155–7. *for these fellows . . . out again:* 'for these great talkers who spin off charming verses to win ladies always find reasons for being unfaithful to them when they've had enough of them.'

158. *prater:* one who 'prates,' chatters a lot without saying anything of value. A *ballad* was thought to be a rhyme of little value. In these lines Henry is pointing out the way superficial things lose their charm, but *a good heart* is constant and enduring, like the sun (the moon is proverbially inconstant).

160. *pate:* head (referring here to the hair).

love a fellow of this temper, Kate, whose face is not
worth sun-burning, that never looks in his glass for
love of anything he sees there, let thine eye be thy
cook. I speak to thee plain soldier. If thou canst love
me for this, take me; if not, to say to thee that I shall 150
die is true – but for thy love, by the Lord, no; yet I
love thee too. And while thou liv'st, dear Kate, take
a fellow of plain and uncoined constancy; for he
perforce must do thee right, because he hath not the
gift to woo in other places; for these fellows of infinite 155
tongue, that can rhyme themselves into ladies'
favours, they do always reason themselves out again.
What! a speaker is but a prater: a rhyme is but a
ballad. A good leg will fall; a straight back will stoop;
a black beard will turn white; a curl'd pate will grow 160
bald; a fair face will wither; a full eye will wax hollow.
But a good heart, Kate, is the sun and the moon; or,
rather, the sun, and not the moon – for it shines
bright and never changes, but keeps his course truly.
If thou would have such a one, take me; and take 165
me, take a soldier; take a soldier, take a king. And
what say'st thou, then, to my love? Speak, my fair,
and fairly, I pray thee.

Katherine
Is it possible dat I should love de enemy of France?
King
No, it is not possible you should love the enemy of 170
France, Kate, but in loving me you should love the
friend of France; for I love France so well that I will
not part with a village of it; I will have it all mine.
And, Kate, when France is mine and I am yours, then
yours is France and you are mine. 175
Katherine
I cannot tell vat is dat.
King
No, Kate? I will tell thee in French, which I am sure
will hang upon my tongue like a new-married wife

181–2. *Saint Denis:* the patron saint of France.
be my speed: 'help me!'

184. *so much more French:* 'as much French as that again.' In fact, his French is a fair translation of what he has previously said in English, but it is ungrammatical and he obviously lacks confidence.

186–7. 'Pardon me, but your French is better than my English.'

190. *most truly falsely:* with good ideas and sound feelings but very inaccurate expression.
191. *much at one:* very similar.

196. Her *closet* is her private apartment in the palace, where her *gentlewoman* (Alice, who is still in attendance) would keep her company, help her with her clothes, and generally wait on her.
198. *dispraise:* find fault with. He seems to know how women behave: he can imagine her pretending to dislike him for the very qualities she secretly admires.
200–1. *thou beest:* you are or you become. A *saving faith* is a faith that is so strong that it gets its reward (like the Christian's faith in salvation).
202. *I get thee with scambling:* It will be the result of my rough, pugnacious methods.
204–6. He imagines the two patron saints of France and England collaborating (by means of Kate and himself) to produce a fine young soldier, who would achieve the much-cherished ambition of all Christian kings, namely to recapture Constantinople from the 'infidel'.
208. *flower-de-luce:* the fleur-de-lys, or lily, the emblem of France.

about her husband's neck, hardly to be shook off. Je
quand sur le possession de France, et quand vous avez 180
le possession de moi – let me see, what then? Saint
Denis be my speed! – donc votre est France et vous
êtes mienne. It is as easy for me, Kate, to conquer the
kingdom as to speak so much more French: I shall
never move thee in French, unless it be to laugh at 185
me.

Katherine

Sauf votre honneur, le Français que vous parlez, il est
meilleur que l'Anglais lequel je parle.

King

No, faith, is't not, Kate; but thy speaking of my tongue,
and I thine, most truly falsely, must needs be granted 190
to be much at one. But, Kate, dost thou understand
thus much English – Canst thou love me?

Katherine

I cannot tell.

King

Can any of your neighbours tell, Kate? I'll ask them.
Come, I know thou lovest me; and at night, when you 195
come into your closet, you'll question this gentlewoman about me; and I know, Kate, you will to her
dispraise those parts in me that you love with your
heart. But, good Kate, mock me mercifully; the rather,
gentle Princess, because I love thee cruelly. If ever thou 200
beest mine, Kate, as I have a saving faith within me
tells me thou shalt, I get thee with scambling, and
thou must therefore needs prove a good soldier-breeder.
Shall not thou and I, between Saint Denis and Saint
George, compound a boy, half French, half English, 205
that shall go to Constantinople and take the Turk by
the beard? Shall we not? What say'st thou, my fair
flower-de-luce?

Katherine

I do not know dat.

211. *endeavour for:* try to achieve your part.

212. *moiety:* half; his half of the bargain.

214–15. *la plus belle . . . déesse*: my Katherine, most beautiful girl in the world, my most dear and divine goddess.

216–17. 'Your Majesty has enough false French to deceive the wisest girl in France.' She is referring to his last speech in French, and its fluent flattery.

218–22. He can't be sure she loves him, but he feels a sort of excitement of the blood which tells him she does, in spite of the *untempering effect* (unattractiveness) of his face.

222. *beshrew:* a curse. We might say 'Blast my father's ambition.' When Henry was conceived, his father was a bitter opponent of King Richard II; his hard features reflect the hard thoughts which were in his father's heart at that moment.

226–31. Old age, which is usually the destroyer of beauty, can do no harm to him because he is already as ugly as it is possible to be – his appearance can only improve with *wear*. Here, *wear* has two meanings: (1) use (as with clothes) and (2) possession.

233. *avouch:* declare. Evidently Katherine is blushing in confusion as a result of his forwardness; he wants her to be confident and admit that she loves him.

239–41. *who, though I speak it . . . fellows:* 'who though I criticize him (myself) to his face, may not be among the best of kings, you will find him to be among the best of good fellows'.
241. *broken music:* music arranged for a group of instruments.

King

No: 'tis hereafter to know, but now to promise; do but 210
now promise, Kate, you will endeavour for your French
part of such a boy; and for my English moiety take
the word of a king and a bachelor. How answer you,
la plus belle Katherine du monde, mon très chèr et
divin déesse? 215

Katherine

Your Majestee ave fausse French enough to deceive de
most sage damoiseile dat is en France.

King

Now, fie upon my false French! By mine honour, in
true English, I love thee, Kate; by which honour I dare
not swear thou lovest me; yet my blood begins to 220
flatter me that thou dost, notwithstanding the poor
and untempering effect of my visage. Now beshrew
my father's ambition! He was thinking of civil wars
when he got me; therefore was I created with a stubborn outside, with an aspect of iron, that when I come 225
to woo ladies I fright them. But, in faith, Kate, the
elder I wax, the better I shall appear: my comfort is,
that old age, that ill layer-up of beauty, can do no
more spoil upon my face; thou hast me, if thou hast
me, at the worst; and thou shalt wear me, if thou wear 230
me, better and better. And therefore tell me, most fair
Katherine, will you have me? Put off your maiden
blushes; avouch the thoughts of your heart with the
looks of an empress; take me by the hand and say
'Harry of England, I am thine'. Which word thou shalt 235
no sooner bless mine ear withal but I will tell thee
aloud 'England is thine, Ireland is thine, France is
thine, and Henry Plantagenet is thine'; who, though
I speak it before his face, if he be not fellow with the
best king, thou shalt find the best king of good 240
fellows. Come, your answer in broken music – for
thy voice is music and thy English broken; therefore,
Queen of all, Katherine, break thy mind to me

245. 'I shall have to see what my father wants.'

246–7. *it shall please him:* the emphatic *shall* almost implies a threat; 'If he doesn't agree he'll have to reckon with me!'

249–54. Henry's attempt to kiss her hand shocks her. She protests that she is a mere servant to him, and he would lower his dignity by such a humble action.

256–7. 'It is not the custom in France for ladies to be kissed before they are married.'

266. *nice customs curtsey to great kings:* fussy traditions bend before the wishes of great kings. As he goes on to explain, his and Kate's positions give them a certain freedom from the rules that govern lesser people.

in broken English, wilt thou have me?

Katherine

Dat is as it shall please de roi mon père. 245

King

Nay, it will please him well, Kate – it shall please him, Kate.

Katherine

Den it sall also content me.

King

Upon that I kiss your hand, and I call you my queen.

Katherine

Laissez, mon seigneur, laissez, laissez! Ma foi, je ne 250
veux point que vous abaissiez votre grandeur en baisant
la main d'une, notre seigneur, indigne serviteur;
excusez-moi, je vous supplies, mon trés puissant
seigneur.

King

Then I will kiss your lips, Kate. 255

Katherine

Les dames et demoiselles pour être baisées devant
leur noces, il n'est pas la coutume de France.

King

Madam my interpreter, what says she?

Alice

Dat it is not be de fashion pour le ladies of France – I
cannot tell vat is baiser en Anglish. 260

King

To kiss.

Alice

Your Majestee entendre bettre que moi.

King

It is not a fashion for the maids in France to kiss before
they are married, would she say?

Alice

Oui, vraiment. 265

King

O Kate, nice customs curtsy to great kings. Dear Kate,

267. *list:* limits, from the old word for the fence enclosing the field in which tilting tournaments were held.

269. *the liberty that follows our places:* the freedom allowed to people in our position.

269–70. *stops the mouth of all find-faults:* silences criticism. *as I will do yours:* he neatly turns the metaphor to account, and 'stops' *her* mouth by kissing her.

273–5. *there is more eloquence . . . council.* He suggests that her charms are more likely to persuade him to be generous to France than all the eloquence of the French politicians.

278–9. A touch of gentle sarcasm from Burgundy: he and the other lords have caught Henry and Katherine embracing.

282. *apt:* ready to learn.

283–7. A repetition of the *plain king* idea which Henry developed earlier (lines 122–66); he has *neither the voice nor the heart of flattery* (neither the skill with words nor the inclination to charm her with flattery), and consequently feels he has failed to rouse any tender feelings in her.

288–95. Burgundy seizes the opportunity to make an elaborate bawdy joke out of the idea of conjuring up the spirit of love in Kate, a joke which depends on the double-meanings of certain words. The *circle is* the 'magic circle' which conjurors make in order to perform their magic, but also the female sex organ. *blind:* sightless (the *naked blind boy* is Cupid, the god of love), but also lustful, so full of passion as to be unaware of everything else. Katherine, being still a blushing virgin, can hardly be blamed for not allowing such conjuring.

you and I cannot be confin'd within the weak list of a country's fashion; we are the makers of manners, Kate; and the liberty that follows our places stops the mouth of all find-faults – as I will do yours for 270 upholding the nice fashion of your country in denying me a kiss; therefore, patiently and yielding. [*Kissing her*] You have witchcraft in your lips, Kate: there is more eloquence in a sugar touch of them than in the tongues of the French council; and they should sooner 275 persuade Henry of England than a general petition of monarchs. Here comes your father.

[Enter the FRENCH POWER *and the* ENGLISH LORDS*]*

Burgundy
God save your Majesty! My royal cousin,
Teach you our princess English?

King
I would have her learn, my fair cousin, how perfectly 280
I love her; and that is good English.

Burgundy
Is she not apt?

King
Our tongue is rough, coz, and my condition is not smooth; so that, having neither the voice nor the heart of flattery about me, I cannot so conjure up the spirit 285 of love in her that he will appear in his true likeness.

Burgundy
Pardon the frankness of my mirth, if I answer you for that. If you would conjure in her, you must make a circle; if conjure up love in her in his true likeness, he 290 must appear naked and blind. Can you blame her, then, being a maid yet ros'd over with the virgin crimson of modesty, if she deny the appearance of a naked blind boy in her naked seeing self? It were, my lord, a hard condition for a maid to consign to. 295

296. *wink:* close their eyes.

300–1. *to consent winking:* to agree with her eyes shut (i.e. so that she will not see what she does in submitting to my love).

304–5. *Bartholomew-tide* is in late summer, when flies become drowsy and easier to catch. According to Burgundy, girls that have been *well-summer'd and warm kept* (well looked after and brought up in comfort) are the same.

308. *This moral . . . summer:* your argument will force me to wait until the end of a hot summer, i.e., you are imposing restrictions on me.

312–14. Henry seems to feel now that his bawdy banter with Burgundy has gone on long enough; he turns to the rest of the French court and tells them that they have to thank the blindness of his love for Katherine for the fact that he is accepting her instead of many of their French cities (echoing the comment he made about the persuasiveness of her charms, lines 273–5).

315. *perspectively:* a perspective was a special lens which produced an optical illusion when you looked through it. The French king suggests that when Henry looks at the cities he sees Katherine: she and they are similar in being still intact.

320–1. *so the maiden cities . . . her:* provided she brings these virgin cities with her as a wedding gift. It sounds as though he is going to have the French cities after all: the shrewdly practical streak in Henry is still in evidence.

King

Yet they do wink and yield, as love is blind and enforces.

Burgundy

They are then excus'd, my lord, when they see not what they do.

King

Then, good my lord, teach your cousin to consent 300 winking.

Burgundy

I will wink on her to consent, my lord, if you will teach her to know my meaning; for maids well summer'd and warm kept are like flies at Bartholomewtide, blind, though they have their eyes; 305 and then they will endure handling, which before would not abide looking on.

King

This moral ties me over to time and a hot summer; and so I shall catch the fly, your cousin, in the latter end, and she must be blind too. 310

Burgundy

As love is, my lord, before it loves.

King

It is so; and you may, some of you, thank love for my blindness, who cannot see many a fair French city for one fair French maid that stands in my way.

French King

Yes, my lord, you see them perspectively, the cities 315 turned into a maid; for they are all girdled with maiden walls that war hath never enter'd.

King

Shall Kate be my wife?

French King

So please you.

King

I am content, so the maiden cities you talk of may 320 wait on her; so the maid that stood in the way for my

325–7. The French king has accepted all the conditions which have been firmly put to him.

330. *for matter of grant:* in matters concerned with titles. The French king is hesitating to agree to the request to name Henry formally as the heir to the French throne.

332–5. The French and Latin both mean 'Our very dear son Henry, king of England and heir of France.'

336–7. 'But I have not refused so strongly that, if you press me, I shall not give in.'

343. *whose very shores look pale:* he fancifully imagines the white cliffs which face each other across the English Channel to be the faces of England and France, looking *pale with envy*.

345. *this dear conjunction:* the solemn union between Henry and Katherine.

346. *neighbourhood:* friendliness.

wish shall show me the way to my will.

French King

We have consented to all terms of reason.

King

Is't so, my lords of England?

Westmoreland

The king hath granted every article: 325
His daughter first; and then in sequel all,
According to their firm proposed natures.

Exeter

Only he hath not yet subscribed this:
Where your Majesty demands that the King of France,
having any occasion to write for matter of grant, shall 330
name your Highness in this form and with this addition, in French, Notre très cher fils Henri, Roi
d'Angleterre, Héritier de France; and thus in Latin,
Praeclarissimus filius noster Henricus, Rex Angliae et
Haeres Franciae. 335

French King

Nor this I have not, brother, so denied
But your request shall make me let it pass.

King

I pray you, then, in love and dear alliance,
Let that one article rank with the rest;
And thereupon give me your daughter. 340

French King

Take her, fair son, and from her blood raise up
Issue to me; that the contending kingdoms
Of France and England, whose very shores look pale
With envy of each other's happiness,
May cease their hatred; and this dear conjunction 345
Plant neighbourhood and Christian-like accord
In their sweet bosoms, that never war advance
His bleeding sword 'twixt England and fair France.

Lords

Amen!

352–61. The Queen expresses the hope in everyone's mind that the marriage will unite the two kingdoms in lasting and trusting friendship.

355. *spousal:* marriage.
356. *ill office:* malicious interference.
fell: fierce, destructive.

358. *paction:* agreement.

359. *incorporate league:* joining together as one body (continuing the metaphor of the two kingdoms uniting in 'marriage').

365. *for surety of our leagues:* as a guarantee of our union. The French peers will be required to swear their allegiance to Henry.

Stage Direction. *Sennet:* a trumpet fanfare played as the procession leaves the stage.

FINAL CHORUS

This epilogue is in the form of a Shakespearian sonnet: three groups of four lines rhyming alternately, followed by a rhyming couplet.
369. *Our bending author:* Shakespeare may be on the stage to take a bow. He may even have taken the part of the Chorus and spoken these lines in person.
371. *Mangling by starts:* distorting by chopping the story about.
372. *Small time.* Henry died at the age of thirty-five.
374. *the world's best garden:* France. *achieved:* won.

King

> Now, welcome, Kate; and bear me witness all, 350
> That here I kiss her as my sovereign queen.

[Flourish]

Queen Isabel

> God, the best maker of all marriages,
> Combine your hearts in one, your realms in one!
> As man and wife, being two, are one in love,
> So be there 'twixt your kingdoms such a spousal 355
> That never may ill office or fell jealousy,
> Which troubles oft the bed of blessed marriage,
> Thrust in between the paction of these kingdoms,
> To make divorce of their incorporate league;
> That English may as French, French Englishmen, 360
> Receive each other. God speak this Amen!

All

> Amen!

King

> Prepare we for our marriage; on which day,
> My Lord of Burgundy, we'll take your oath,
> And all the peers', for surety of our leagues. 365
> Then shall I swear to Kate, and you to me,
> And may our oaths well kept and prosp'rous be!

[Sennet. Exeunt. Enter CHORUS]

Chorus

> Thus far, with rough and all-unable pen,
> Our bending author hath pursu'd the story,
> In little room confining mighty men, 370
> Mangling by starts the full course of their glory.
> Small time, but, in that small, most greatly lived
> This star of England. Fortune made his sword;
> By which the world's best garden he achieved,
> And of it left his son imperial lord. 375

376. *infant bands:* baby clothes.

376–9. The Chorus reminds the audience that Henry's son became king in infancy and that his rule was so mismanaged by others that in the end all his father's great gains in France were lost again. Shakespeare's three plays about Henry VI had already been produced before his *Henry V*. The word *oft* probably applies to *Henry VI Part I* which is known to have been an exceptionally popular play in Shakespeare's time.

380–1. *and, for their sake . . . take:* for the sake of the people and events presented in the other plays, and enjoyed by you, accept this one in the same spirit.

Henry the Sixth, in infant bands crown'd king
Of France and England, did this king succeed;
Whose state so many had the managing
That they lost France and made his England bleed;
Which oft our stage hath shown; and, for their
    sake,   380
In your fair minds let this acceptance take.

[Exit]

SUMMING UP

After reading or seeing a play which depends so much for its appeal on our willingness to accept that these remarkable events really happened, we not unnaturally want to know how much of it is historically true. It is a fair question. Shakespeare's history plays, although transformed into living drama by the power of his imagination, are in fact reasonably faithful to the sources available to him. Modern historians point out distortions – that Henry's raid on France in 1415 was really a strategic error which he was lucky to survive, that the siege of Harfleur was a prolonged disaster in which disease as well as enemy action killed a huge part of his army, and that the trek to Calais which followed was a piece of irresponsible bravado which he got away with more because of the sheer folly of the French at Agincourt than because of any special guile or bravery on the English side. And of course the numbers involved and lost in the battle don't stand up to modern examination (see the note at the end of Act IV, Scene viii). But our modern knowledge was not available to Shakespeare. The story came to him partly through popular legend, partly through the chronicles of such men as Edward Hall (written in about 1548) and Raphael Holinshed (about 1578), and partly through popular plays about the past which appeared from time to time. These sources were more or less imaginative, lacking the accuracy and precise documentation which modern scholarship demands, and were rather one-sided in their adulation of King Henry. Nevertheless, this was the Henry Shakespeare's audience expected to see, the heroking of their legends, and no doubt they had no difficulty in swallowing the whole story.

What about our reaction today? Even if we are bound to be more sceptical, and can hardly help feeling that the king is idealized and his achievements exaggerated, we can still find him a credible human being on the stage. It is worth paying some attention to the skill with which Shakespeare establishes the character of his hero. From the beginning of the play, some time before the king makes his first appearance, we are led to expect a man of impressive power: the imagery of the first Prologue, in which he is likened to Mars, the god of war, and of Canterbury's suggestion in Act I, Scene i that his strength of will is comparable to the physical strength of Hercules, prepares us for the grave, cool, somewhat frightening personality we meet in the second scene. Now at once we see in his handling of the debate a convincing demonstration of the qualities earlier attributed to him: he is in complete command, he will be the one to make the decision, but he listens to the advice of more experienced statesmen, shows understanding of the problems – the Scottish menace, for example, which his advisers seem to have forgotten – and, having considered all aspects of the question, announces his decision firmly: *Now are we well resolv'd.*

The authority of his presence is matched by the control of his own feelings, especially when he replies to the Dauphin's mocking gift of tennis-balls:

> *We are glad the Dauphin is so pleasant with us;*
> *His present and your pains we thank you for.*
> *When we have match'd our rackets to these balls,*
> *We will in France, by God's grace, play a set*
> *Shall strike his father's crown into the hazard.*
>
> (Act I, Scene ii, lines 259–63)

From the ironic diplomacy of its opening, the speech soars to towering climaxes of rage and scorn, but his mind is in control throughout, expressing passion with wit and appropriateness.

Comparison with the French king is unavoidable. In Act II, Scene iv, the trembling efforts of King Charles to control his court and reach a decision make us more aware, by contrast, of the virtues of his English counterpart. Charles dithers and procrastinates. Whereas his nobles clearly expect little of him, and show him scant respect, there is never any question in anyone's mind as to who is boss in the English court.

There may be some difficulty in understanding how such a strong leader can have developed from the wild and irresponsible young prince, Hal, whom Shakespeare presents in the two parts of *Henry IV*, and the playwright is sometimes accused of inconsistency here. The matter is partly explained by Ely's *The strawberry grows underneath the nettle* speech in Act I, Scene i, but it is possible to see the three plays as a logical unit if one accepts what Tillyard calls the 'ironic detachment' of Hal's tone and behaviour in *Henry IV*. In simple terms this means that Hal is never fully committed to the low life of Falstaff and his companions, but indulges in it partly as an escape from the sombre responsibilities of his official position, and partly as a means of acquiring the knowledge of ordinary men which will be valuable when he becomes king. Even when he seems most actively one of the Falstaff gang, he is merely toying with them, above them in intellect and character, testing them out and commenting on their behaviour in ways which they fail to understand. His duty as heir to the throne is never far from his mind. Certainly the playful side of his personality is not much in evidence in *Henry V*, but if we read the earlier plays in this way we can see Prince Hal and King Henry as basically the same man; the change is forced on him by his new responsibility; it is not the sudden reformation suggested by Canterbury.

The miraculous conversion which seems to Canterbury to have occurred is in fact a manifestation of the remarkable self-control already referred to. From the moment of his father's death Henry is able to sacrifice his personal feelings to his public duty: Falstaff is rejected (at the end of *Henry IV, Part II*), Scroop and Bardolph are executed, and during the night before Agincourt, when the desperateness of the situation and the argument with Williams have made him so conscious of the burdens of leadership that a lesser man would offer himself for ransom, he manages to pull himself together so well that he appears positively cheerful in his inspiring speech in the morning.

A quality for which Canterbury gives him full credit is his religious devotion. His expedition to France has to have God's blessing; his last words before the great battle are:

> *And how thou pleasest, God, dispose the day!*
> (Act IV, Scene iii, line 132)

and when he hears the full details of French and English losses his cry of *O God, thy arm was here!* comes from his heart. He will not allow anyone to take any credit for the victory, he will not even allow himself a triumphal return to London, *being free from vainness and self-glorious pride*, and determined that God shall have all the glory. This modesty makes us, the onlookers, more willing to give him credit for his contribution. We may accept that God came to the aid of the English, but there is something Christ-like about the young king himself:

> *Upon his royal face there is no note*
> *How dread an army hath enrounded him;*
> *Nor doth he dedicate one jot of colour*
> *Unto the weary and all-watched night;*
> *But freshly looks, and over-bears attaint*
> *With cheerful semblance and sweet majesty;*
> *That every wretch, pining and pale before,*
> *Beholding him, plucks comfort from his looks;*
> *A largess universal, like the sun,*
> *His liberal eye doth give to every one,*
> *Thawing cold fear, that mean and gentle all*
> *Behold, as may unworthiness define,*
> *A little touch of Harry in the night.*
> (Act IV, Prologue, lines 35–47)

There is nothing remote about Henry's leadership, even if it is almost divine; in fact he has the quality we may call 'the common touch,' the ability to come down to the level of those beneath him. We see it most clearly in his dealings with Fluellen and Williams. Henry disguises himself because he wants to be at one with his men, to remove the barrier between himself and them. Although the attempt ends in a quarrel, he subsequently handles the affair with the sort of humour, fairness, and respect for Williams' plain speaking that make men feel he is one of them. Indeed, he clearly feels himself to be one of them:

> *We few, we happy few, we band of brothers;*
> *For he today that sheds his blood with me*
> *Shall be my brother; be he ne'er so vile,*
> *This day shall gentle his condition.*
>
> (Act IV, Scene iii, lines 60–3)

He knows just how to touch their deepest feelings.

At this point in the play our understanding of the man has deepened somewhat. We have seen new aspects of his inner feelings, just as in the wooing of Katherine in the final Act we see another side of him. It has been said that he is a 'flat' character, that he doesn't develop during the course of the play, that there is no inner conflict to make him interesting. In the Introduction I have suggested that this is because Shakespeare was not trying to write a play of character, but was rather using the form of a chronicle play as a vehicle for expressing some of his own convictions. Nevertheless, he does explore different facets of Henry's character, including some of his weaknesses, and there are conflicts which have to be resolved. The difference between Henry and the tragic heroes is that Henry resolves his conflicts successfully.

What are his weaknesses? In the quarrel with Williams and the subsequent soliloquy he seems rather sensitive to criticism, and there is an element of vanity in his desire to be well-thought of. His threats to the citizens of Harfleur smack of an almost callous enjoyment of horror – *What is it then to me . . . ?* he says. But the fact is that these threats have the effect of actually preventing bloodshed: Harfleur surrenders, and he is able to give the order to *use mercy to them all*. A better founded criticism is that he is ruthless: former friends are dismissed or executed, the order to kill the French prisoners is given without hesitation; we might have expected a more humane person to waver a little. However, I have mentioned above the self-control which Henry displays in such situations. It is also clear that he has an unusually strong sense of justice, the essence of which is that the law is the same for all. Furthermore, he knows that discipline is essential in wartime. Notice the emphasis on the lack of order in the French ranks at Agincourt. It was necessary in peacetime too in those days: the assassination plot is a hint of the chaos which could destroy the country and which Henry's firmness helped to transform.

However, even if there are minor faults in Henry's makeup, the total effect we receive from the play is an impression of near-perfection. The signs of weakness enable us to like him much more; we could barely forgive him if he were able to carry off the burdens of kingship without misgivings, without some sort of longing to reduce himself to the level of:

> *the wretched slave*
> *Who, with a body fill'd and vacant mind,*
> *Gets him to rest, cramm'd with distressful bread;*
>
> (Act IV, Scene i, lines 260–2)

Here we are seeing through the surface of the man into his deepest feelings. If we were not given this glimpse we could not so fully appreciate the self-control which enables the 'surface' man to be such an inspiring leader.

The order and control which Henry displays in his own personality are reflected in the country as a whole.

We have already noticed the discipline in the army and the swift justice meted out to offenders. Apart from this, there is a general impression throughout the play that this England under King Harry is a well-organized kingdom, based on trust, mutual respect, and sound common-sense. Compare the tone in which the English nobles address their king and each other with the Constable's scorn of the Dauphin; the chivalry and courage of Williams with the quaking Frenchman whom Pistol, of all people, is able to take prisoner; or the way the English approach the battle, aware of the *fearful odds* but grimly determined, with the rank overconfidence and presumptuous boasting of the French. There are frequent references to the superiority of the English fighting man, who *in health* is worth three Frenchmen; the triumph of the Black Prince at Crécy is described rapturously by Canterbury and ruefully by the French King. At Agincourt history repeats itself; now the English prove themselves better than five times as many French.

The French certainly make a poor showing in this play. There are unsatisfactory elements on the English side: there is sin and vice and corruption, and petty squabbling like the Welsh-Irish feud exemplified by Fluellen and Macmorris; but they are under control. The four captains all do their duty wholeheartedly; Fluellen, for all his peculiarities and quarrelsomeness, is the epitome of valour and devotion to the cause. We feel that all the people of the country, comprising many varied elements, are a successful working unit, like their army in the field. To force this fact more clearly on our attention, Shakespeare uses the French as a contrast: they lack harmony and order, and consequently they are unsuccessful. At Southampton Henry can say

> *We carry not a heart with us from hence*
> *That grows not in a fair consent with ours;*
> *Nor leave not one behind that doth not wish*
> *Success and conquest to attend on us.*
>
> (Act II, Scene ii, lines 21–4)

Ironically, the men he says it to are the very conspirators who are plotting to kill him, but even they are glad when they are prevented, so that in spite of the conspiracy we are left with a strong sense of a completely united people.

The moral framework of the play then is a simple one: the French and English are 'bad' and 'good' or almost, and God intervenes to exalt the one at the expense of the other. Bardolph, Nym, and the conspirators are executed for disobedience and treachery; Pistol is beaten up for mocking national pride as symbolized by Fluellen's leek. War, too, although a very complex subject when one tries to work out the rights and wrongs of it, is given fairly simple treatment. The king himself dwells repeatedly on the horrors of it, and he makes every effort to avoid them; moreover he has to be fully convinced of the justice of his cause before he embarks on it. But once that point has been cleared up the horror of war is accepted simply as something that has to be suffered in order to achieve justice.

We may feel that military expediency does not justify cruelty, but we must beware of judging fifteenth century practice by twentieth century standards. War does have its attractions: nothing else in literature appeals so strongly to our sense of heroism and adventure, and I wonder whether the whole body of war poetry contains anything more inspiring than Henry's St Crispin's Day speech.

> O, do not wish one more!
> Rather proclaim it, Westmoreland, through my host,
> That he which hath no stomach to this fight,
> Let him depart: his passport shall be made,
> And crowns for convoy put into his purse;
> We would not die in that man's company
> That fears his fellowship to die with us.
>
> (Act IV, Scene iii, lines 33–9)

It is a magnificently simple and direct expression of fortitude and comradeship in the face of danger.

There is comedy in war too. Anyone who has lived through a war knows the value of a sense of humour: it relieves tension, keeps up the spirits, and draws people together. An example of this occurs in the first nineteen lines of Act IV, Scene i, where both the king and Erpingham show ability to see the funny side of their unhappy situation. Shakespeare often uses this tension-relieving quality of humour, or comic relief, as it is usually called, as part of his dramatic technique: after the horrifying threats to Harfleur we have the frivolity of Katherine's English lesson; scenes of intense negotiation are followed by the antics of Pistol.

In the note at the beginning of the Prologue to Act I, I have suggested some special functions that the Chorus fulfils in this play, and we can now go on to discuss why Shakespeare made so much more use of the Chorus in *Henry V* than he did in other plays. Usually a dramatist shows us what he wants us to know; here the Chorus tells us. Would anything be lost if the Prologues were all cut? For one thing, the Chorus adds imaginative ingredients which could not be included dramatically without severe loss of economy – the size and scope of the preparations for war, for example, or *the little touch of Harry in the night*. For another, the Chorus supplies links in the chain of narrative. The play lacks the usual Shakespearian plot, which moves from character to action to result, the result affecting character and thus developing further action. Shakespeare appears to be aiming at something different here: wanting to show King Henry in as brilliant a light as possible, he extracts from his life a series of great moments, and imaginatively binds them together around the central triumph of Agincourt – rather like a succession of separate pictures on a central theme. The Chorus helps with the binding process, and maintains the momentum of the story, giving it a forward movement which is quite exciting:

Now all the youth of England are on fire

leads us into Act II, and later:

> *Follow, follow!*
> *Grapple your minds to sternage of this navy*
> *And leave your England as dead midnight still,*

draws us across the Channel for the siege of Harfleur.

But while an important function of the Prologues is to give information, more memorable are those brilliant descriptive passages which enable us to see and hear and feel experiences as almost physical sensations. The Prologue to Act III creates so vivid an impression of the fleet sailing across the Channel that we do not need to be urged to imagine that we

> *stand upon the rivage and behold*
> *A city on th' inconstant billows dancing.*

The Prologue to Act IV, similarly, asks us to imagine the night before Agincourt, and then enables us to feel the stillness which exaggerates the sounds, to see the fires and the shadowy faces of the men peering into them, to experience the tension in the air:

> *Now entertain conjecture of a time*
> *When creeping murmur and the poring dark*
> *Fills the wide vessels of the universe.*
> *From camp to camp, through the foul womb of night,*
> *The hum of either army stilly sounds,*
> *That the fix'd sentinels almost receive*
> *The secret whispers of each other's watch.*
> *Fire answers fire, and through their paly flames*
> *Each battle sees the other's umber'd face;*
> *Steed threatens steed, in high and boastful neighs*
> *Piercing the night's dull ear; and from the tents*
> *The armourers accomplishing the knights,*
> *With busy hammers closing rivets up,*
> *Give dreadful note of preparation.*
> *The country cocks do crow, the clocks do toll,*
> *And the third hour of drowsy morning name.*

An important point to note here is Shakespeare's mastery of rhythmic variety. These two Prologues provide a good example: the excitement and gaiety of the Prologue to Act III is achieved by a lively, bouncing rhythm which contrasts sharply with the measured, dream-like movement and soft consonants of the more sombre Prologue to Act IV. The king's speech before Harfleur is full of optimistic vigour:

> *Now set the teeth and stretch the nostril wide;*
> *Hold hard the breath, and bend up every spirit*
> *To his full height. On, on, you noblest English,*
>
> (Act III, Scene i, lines 15–17)

while his Crispin's Day oration, which because of the situation is more resigned, more thoughtful, more closely reasoned, is rhythmically slower and smoother, stressing longer, fuller vowels:

> *This story shall the good man teach his son;*
> *And Crispin Crispian shall ne'er go by,*
> *From this day to the ending of the world,*
> *But we in it shall be remembered.*
>
> (Act IV, Scene iii, lines 56–9)

Other examples of the way verse rhythms suggest mood or character can be found throughout the play: in the fussy pedantry of Canterbury, the impressively threatening tone of Exeter in his role of Ambassador, the timidity and indecisiveness of the French King, the arrogance of the Dauphin, the empty bombast of Pistol.

The prose passages demonstrate varieties of a different kind. Here Shakespeare seems to be amusing himself by playing about with different dialects and languages; there is a good deal of implied comment on the problems of communication, and much of the humour derives from such problems; Katherine's attempts to learn English, for example, or the ludicrous jargon of Pistol and Nym. We even have an Englishman, an Irishman, a Scotsman and a Welshman brought together as the four captains. But peculiarities of speech are no obstacle to sincerity of purpose: whereas Pistol and Nym get their just reward, Fluellen is praised for his valour – *though it appear a little out of fashion*. Henry admires plain-speaking, and rewards both Williams and Montjoy for their bluntness. He himself speaks to Katherine *plain soldier*, and makes it clear that he has little time for *these fellows of infinite tongue, that can rhyme themselves into ladies' favours*; love surmounts the language barrier in the end.

The language of the play, then, is as rich in variety as the characters themselves. All the strata of English life are paraded for our admiration, amusement, or scorn, from the majestic king, his noble advisers and church dignitaries, through captains and soldiers to camp-followers, from the brilliantly accomplished to the inarticulate.

THEME INDEX

Henry V, in common with other Shakespeare plays, does more than tell a story; it provokes thought about issues of philosophy and morals relevant to the central plot. These issues may be raised in the dialogue, or illustrated in different ways by the behaviour of characters in different situations and at different levels in the social scale, giving the play a kind of psychological unity which reinforces the unity of the action. For example, the retribution which Henry exacts for the Dauphin's mockery is supported by that which Fluellen exacts for Pistol's.

Some of the more obvious of such themes are listed below, with references to parts of the play which illustrate them best. References to prominent characteristics of some of the leading personalities are also given.

Order, discipline and justice
I ii 3–6, 96, 174–213, II ii 166–81, III vi 51–5, IV v 18–22, V i 65–74, V ii 34–67.

War
Horror: I ii 281–8, II iv 97–109, III iii 5–41.
Honour and glory: II Prologue 1–11, IV iii 16–67.
Dishonour of failure: III v 27–35, IV v 1–17.
Moral responsibility: I ii 289–96, II iv 99–110, III iii 42–3, IV i 111–86 and 226–32.

National Pride
English: I ii 100–21, III i 16–34, III vi 140–6, IV viii 100–9.
French: III v 4–24, III vii 77–82.
Welsh: IV vii 95–111, V i 1–39.

Humour
Of language: Nym II i 4–9. Pistol II i 28–78, IV iv 1–62.
Hostess II i 113–16, II iii 31–6. The four captains III ii

68–133. Katherine III iv, V ii 216–17.
Of cowardice: II i 58–66 and 95–8, III ii 1–37, V i 21–63.

Characters
King Henry
His 'conversion': I i 24–37 and 53–69, II iv 29–40 and 134–9.
His religious devotion: I ii 289–93, IV, i 285–300, IV viii 111–21.
His accomplishments: I i 38–52.
His leadership and example: II Prologue 5–6, III i 1–34, IV Prologue 28–47, IV iii 18–67.
His humanity: I ii 18–28, III iii 51–4, IV viii 55–9.
His ruthless sense of justice: II ii 79–81 and 166–81, III vi 100–128.
His wit: I ii 259–66, IV i 35–63, IV vii 65–7, V ii 169–75 and 263–77.
The Dauphin
His quarrelsomeness: II iv 14–23 and 41–2, III vii 49–74.
His boasting and over-confidence: II iv 14–23, 41–8 and 69–73, III vii 31–40 and 77–105.
His misjudgment of Henry: I ii 246–58 and 266–72, II iv 24–42 and 127–39.
Henry's view of him: II iv 111–19.
Fluellen
His insistence on traditional discipline: III vi 39–56, IV i 65–81, IV vii 1–4.
His loyalty: IV vii 108–11, IV viii 9–43.
His pride in being Welsh: IV vii 90–110, V i 1–35.
His contentiousness: III ii 92–138, IV vii 21–49.
Pistol
His pretentiousness and cowardice: II i 27–109, III ii 21–4 and 32–5, IV iv, V i 14–64.
His villainy: II i 108–9, II iii 44–53, III ii 37–51, III vi 19–57.
His punishment: V i.

FURTHER READING

For a more detailed commentary on the text, background and sources of *Henry V* consult J. H. Walter's edition in the Arden series and A. R. Humphreys' in the New Penguin series, although the one which probably achieves the most helpful combination of scholarly annotation and imaginative interpretation is G. C. Moore Smith's Warwick Shakespeare edition (Blackie). Some critics have found *Henry V* a far from satisfactory play, and of these perhaps the most pungent is Hazlitt, the famous 19th Century writer, whose essay on *Henry V* is contained in his *Elizabethan Literature and Characters of Shakespeare*, and the most illuminating Mark van Doren, who, in *Shakespeare* (Allen & Unwin), describes Henry as 'a hearty undergraduate with enormous initials on his chest'. More enthusiastic surveys are given by M. M. Reese in *The Cease of Majesty* (Arnold) and J. Middleton Murry in *Shakespeare* (Cape). Anyone who wants to read for himself the written sources from which Shakespeare obtained his historical material and some of his dramatic ideas will find them clearly set out with helpful comments in *Narrative and Dramatic Sources of Shakespeare, Volume IV*, edited by G. Bullough (Routledge and Kegan Paul). *Twentieth Century Interpretations of 'Henry V'*, edited by Ronald Berman (Prentice-Hall), is a useful collection of the comments of various writers, including some of the above. As for the historical king himself, *Henry V* by Harold F. Hutchison (Eyre and Spottiswoode) is a pleasantly readable biography which frankly sets to rights some of the historical inaccuracies of Shakespeare's play.

Shakespeare:
Words and Phrases

adapted from the Collins English Dictionary

abate 1 VERB to abate here means to lessen or diminish ❏ *There lives within the very flame of love/ A kind of wick or snuff that will abate it* (*Hamlet 4.7*) 2 VERB to abate here means to shorten ❏ *Abate thy hours* (*A Midsummer Night's Dream 3.2*) 3 VERB to abate here means to deprive ❏ *She hath abated me of half my train* (*King Lear 2.4*)

abjure VERB to abjure means to renounce or give up ❏ *this rough magic I here abjure* (*Tempest 5.1*)

abroad ADV abroad means elsewhere or everywhere ❏ *You have heard of the news abroad* (*King Lear 2.1*)

abrogate VERB to abrogate means to put an end to ❏ *so it shall praise you to abrogate scurrility* (*Love's Labours Lost 4.2*)

abuse 1 NOUN abuse in this context means deception or fraud ❏ *What should this mean? Are all the rest come back?/ Or is it some abuse, and no such thing?* (*Hamlet 4.7*) 2 NOUN an abuse in this context means insult or offence ❏ *I will be deaf to pleading and excuses/ Nor tears nor prayers shall purchase our abuses* (*Romeo and Juliet 3.1*) 3 NOUN an abuse in this context means using something improperly ❏ *we'll digest/ Th'abuse*

of distance (*Henry II Chorus*) 4 NOUN an abuse in this context means doing something which is corrupt or dishonest ❏ *Come, bring them away: if these be good people in a commonweal that do nothing but their abuses in common houses, I know no law: bring them away.* (*Measure for Measure 2.1*)

abuser NOUN the abuser here is someone who betrays, a betrayer ❏ *I ... do attach thee/ For an abuser of the world* (*Othello 1.2*)

accent NOUN accent here means language ❏ *In states unborn, and accents yet unknown* (*Julius Caesar 3.1*)

accident NOUN an accident in this context is an event or something that happened ❏ *think no more of this night's accidents* (*A Midsummer Night's Dream 4.1*)

accommodate VERB to accommodate in this context means to equip or to give someone the equipment to do something ❏ *The safer sense will ne'er accommodate/ His master thus.* (*King Lear 4.6*)

according ADJ according means sympathetic or ready to agree ❏ *within the scope of choice/ Lies*

my consent and fair according voice
(*Romeo and Juliet* 1.2)

account NOUN account often means
judgement (by God) or reckoning
❑ *No reckoning made, but sent to my
account/ With all my imperfections on
my head* (*Hamlet* 1.5)

accountant ADJ accountant here
means answerable or accountable
❑ *his offence is… /Accountant to the
law* (*Measure for Measure* 2.4)

ace NOUN ace here means one or first
referring to the lowest score on a dice
❑ *No die, but an ace, for him; for he is
but one./ Less than an ace, man; for he
is dead; he is nothing.* (*A Midsummer
Night's Dream* 5.1)

acquit VERB here acquit means to be
rid of or free of. It is related to the
verb quit ❑ *I am glad I am so acquit
of this tinderbox* (*The Merry Wives of
Windsor* 1.3)

afeard ADJ afeard means afraid or
frightened ❑ *Nothing afeard of what
thyself didst make* (*Macbeth* 1.3)

affiance NOUN affiance means
confidence or trust ❑ *O how hast
thou with jealousy infected/ The
sweetness of affiance* (*Henry V* 2.2)

affinity NOUN in this context, affinity
means important connections, or
relationships with important people
❑ *The Moor replies/ That he you hurt
is of great fame in Cyprus,/ And great
affinity* (*Othello* 3.1)

agnize VERB to agnize is an old
word that means that you recognize
or acknowledge something ❑ *I do
agnize/ A natural and prompt alacrity
I find in hardness* (*Othello* 1.3)

ague NOUN an ague is a fever in
which the patient has hot and cold

shivers one after the other ❑ *This
is some monster of the isle with four
legs, who hath got … an ague* (*The
Tempest* 2.2)

alarm, alarum NOUN an alarm or
alarum is a call to arms or a signal for
soldiers to prepare to fight ❑ *Whence
cometh this alarum and the noise?*
(*Henry VI part I* 1.4)

Albion NOUN Albion is another
word for England ❑ *but I will sell my
dukedom,/ To buy a slobbery and a
dirty farm In that nook-shotten isle of
Albion* (*Henry V* 3.5)

all of all PHRASE all of all means
everything, or the sum of all things
❑ *The very all of all* (*Love's Labours
Lost* 5.1)

amend VERB amend in this context
means to get better or to heal ❑ *at
his touch… They presently amend*
(*Macbeth* 4.3)

anchor VERB if you anchor on
something you concentrate on it or
fix on it ❑ *My invention … Anchors
on Isabel* (*Measure for Measure* 2.4)

anon ADV anon was a common word
for soon ❑ *You shall see anon how the
murderer gets the love of Gonzago's
wife* (*Hamlet* 3.2)

antic 1 ADJ antic here means weird
or strange ❑ *I'll charm the air to give
a sound/ While you perform your antic
round* (*Macbeth* 4.1) 2 NOUN in
this context antic means a clown or
a strange, unattractive creature ❑ *If
black, why nature, drawing an antic,/
Made a foul blot* (*Much Ado About
Nothing* 3.1)

apace ADV apace was a common word
for quickly ❑ *Come apace* (*As You
Like It* 3.3)

apparel NOUN apparel means clothes or clothing ❑ *one suit of apparel* (*Hamlet 3.2*)

appliance NOUN appliance here means cure ❑ *Diseases desperate grown/ By desperate appliance are relieved* (*Hamlet 4.3*)

argument NOUN argument here means a topic of conversation or the subject ❑ *Why 'tis the rarest argument of wonder that hath shot out in our latter times* (*All's Well That Ends Well 2.3*)

arrant ADJ arrant means absolute, complete. It strengthens the meaning of a noun ❑ *Fortune, that arrant whore* (*King Lear 2.4*)

arras NOUN an arras is a tapestry, a large cloth with a picture sewn on it using coloured thread ❑ *Behind the arras I'll convey myself/ To hear the process* (*Hamlet 3.3*)

art 1 NOUN art in this context means knowledge ❑ *Their malady convinces/ The great essay of art* (*Macbeth 4.3*) 2 NOUN art can also mean skill as it does here ❑ *He ... gave you such a masterly report/ For art and exercise in your defence* (*Hamlet 4.7*) 3 NOUN art here means magic ❑ *Now I want/ Spirits to enforce, art to enchant* (*The Tempest 5 Epilogue*)

assay 1 NOUN an assay was an attempt, a try ❑ *Make assay./ Bow, stubborn knees* (*Hamlet 3.3*) 2 NOUN assay can also mean a test or a trial ❑ *he hath made assay of her virtue* (*Measure for Measure 3.1*)

attend (on/upon) VERB attend on means to wait for or to expect ❑ *Tarry I here, I but attend on death* (*Two Gentlemen of Verona 3.1*)

auditor NOUN an auditor was a member of an audience or someone who listens ❑ *I'll be an auditor* (*A Midsummer Night's Dream 3.1*)

aught NOUN aught was a common word which meant anything ❑ *if my love thou holdest at aught* (*Hamlet 4.3*)

aunt 1 NOUN an aunt was another word for an old woman and also means someone who talks a lot or a gossip ❑ *The wisest aunt telling the saddest tale* (*A Midsummer Night's Dream 2.1*) 2 NOUN aunt could also mean a mistress or a prostitute ❑ *the thrush and the jay/ Are summer songs for me and my aunts/ While we lie tumbling in the hay* (*The Winter's Tale 4.3*)

avaunt EXCLAM avaunt was a common word which meant go away ❑ *Avaunt, you curs!* (*King Lear 3.6*)

aye ADV here aye means always or ever ❑ *Whose state and honour I for aye allow* (*Richard II 5.2*)

baffle VERB baffle meant to be disgraced in public or humiliated ❑ *I am disgraced, impeached, and baffled here* (*Richard II 1.1*)

bald ADJ bald means trivial or silly ❑ *I knew 'twould be a bald conclusion* (*The Comedy of Errors 2.2*)

ban NOUN a ban was a curse or an evil spell ❑ *Sometimes with lunatic bans... Enforce their charity* (*King Lear 2.3*)

barren ADJ barren meant empty or hollow ❑ *now I let go your hand, I am barren.* (*Twelfth Night 1.3*)

base ADJ base is an adjective that means unworthy or dishonourable ❑ *civet is of a baser birth than tar* (*As You Like It 3.2*)

273

base 1 ADJ base can also mean of low social standing or someone who was not part of the ruling class ❑ *Why brand they us with 'base'?* (*King Lear 1.2*) 2 ADJ here base means poor quality ❑ *Base cousin,/ Darest thou break first?* (*Two Noble Kinsmen 3.3*)

bawdy NOUN bawdy means obscene or rude ❑ *Bloody, bawdy villain!* (*Hamlet 2.2*)

bear in hand PHRASE bear in hand means taken advantage of or fooled ❑ *This I made good to you In our last conference, passed in probation with you/ How you were borne in hand* (*Macbeth 3.1*)

beard VERB to beard someone was to oppose or confront them ❑ *Com'st thou to beard me in Denmark?* (*Hamlet 2.2*)

beard, in one's PHRASE if you say something in someone's beard you say it to their face ❑ *I will verify as much in his beard* (*Henry V 3.2*)

beaver NOUN a beaver was a visor on a battle helmet ❑ *O yes, my lord, he wore his beaver up* (*Hamlet 1.2*)

become VERB if something becomes you it suits you or is appropriate to you ❑ *Nothing in his life became him like the leaving it* (*Macbeth 1.4*)

bed, brought to PHRASE to be brought to bed means to give birth ❑ *His wife but yesternight was brought to bed* (*Titus Andronicus 4.2*)

bedabbled ADJ if something is bedabbled it is sprinkled ❑ *Bedabbled with the dew, and torn with briers* (*A Midsummer Night's Dream 3.2*)

Bedlam NOUN Bedlam was a word used for Bethlehem Hospital which was a place the insane were sent to ❑ *The country give me proof and precedent/ Of Bedlam beggars* (*King Lear 2.3*)

bed-swerver NOUN a bed-swerver was someone who was unfaithful in marriage, an adulterer ❑ *she's/ A bed-swerver* (*Winter's Tale 2.1*)

befall 1 VERB to befall is to happen, occur or take place ❑ *In this same interlude it doth befall/ That I present a wall* (*A Midsummer Night's Dream 5.1*) 2 VERB to befall can also mean to happen to someone or something ❑ *fair befall thee and thy noble house* (*Richard III 1.3*)

behoof NOUN behoof was an advantage or benefit ❑ *All our surgeons/ Convent in their behoof* (*Two Noble Kinsmen 1.4*)

beldam NOUN a beldam was a witch or old woman ❑ *Have I not reason, beldams as you are?* (*Macbeth 3.5*)

belike ADV belike meant probably, perhaps or presumably ❑ *belike he likes it not* (*Hamlet 3.2*)

bent 1 NOUN bent means a preference or a direction ❑ *Let me work,/ For I can give his humour true bent,/ And I will bring him to the Capitol* (*Julius Caesar 2.1*) 2 ADJ if you are bent on something you are determined to do it ❑ *for now I am bent to know/ By the worst means the worst.* (*Macbeth 3.4*)

beshrew VERB beshrew meant to curse or wish evil on someone ❑ *much beshrew my manners and my pride/ If Hermia meant to say Lysander lied* (*A Midsummer Night's Dream 2.2*)

betime (s) ADV betime means early ❑ *To business that we love we rise betime* (*Antony and Cleopatra 4.4*)

bevy NOUN bevy meant type or sort, it was also used to mean company ❑ *many more of the same bevy* (*Hamlet 5.2*)

blazon VERB to blazon something meant to display or show it ❑ *that thy skill be more to blazon it* (*Romeo and Juliet 2.6*)

blind ADJ if you are blind when you do something you are reckless or do not care about the consequences ❑ *are you yet to your own souls so blind/ That two you will war with God by murdering me* (*Richard III 1.4*)

bombast NOUN bombast was wool stuffing (used in a cushion for example) and so it came to mean padded out or long-winded. Here it means someone who talks a lot about nothing in particular ❑ *How now my sweet creature of bombast* (*Henry IV part 1 2.4*)

bond 1 NOUN a bond is a contract or legal deed ❑ *Well, then, your bond, and let me see* (*Merchant of Venice 1.3*) 2 NOUN bond could also mean duty or commitment ❑ *I love your majesty/ According to my bond* (*King Lear 1.1*)

bottom NOUN here bottom means essence, main point or intent ❑ *Now I see/ The bottom of your purpose* (*All's Well That Ends Well 3.7*)

bounteously ADV bounteously means plentifully, abundantly ❑ *I prithee, and I'll pay thee bounteously* (*Twelfth Night 1.2*)

brace 1 NOUN a brace is a couple or two ❑ *Have lost a brace of kinsmen* (*Romeo and Juliet 5.3*) 2 NOUN if you are in a brace position it means you are ready ❑ *For that it stands not in such warlike brace* (*Othello 1.3*)

brand VERB to mark permanently like the markings on cattle ❑ *the wheeled seat/ Of fortunate Caesar ... branded his baseness that ensued* (*Anthony and Cleopatra 4.14*)

brave ADJ brave meant fine, excellent or splendid ❑ *O brave new world/ That has such people in't* (*The Tempest 5.1*)

brine NOUN brine is sea-water ❑ *He shall drink nought brine, for I'll not show him/ Where the quick freshes are* (*The Tempest 3.2*)

brow NOUN brow in this context means appearance ❑ *doth hourly grow/ Out of his brows* (*Hamlet 3.3*)

burden 1 NOUN the burden here is a chorus ❑ *I would sing my song without a burden* (*As You Like It 3.2*) 2 NOUN burden means load or weight (this is the current meaning) ❑ *the scarfs and the bannerets about thee did manifoldly dissuade me from believing thee a vessel of too great a burden* (*All's Well that Ends Well 2.3*)

buttons, in one's PHRASE this is a phrase that means clear, easy to see ❑ *Tis in his buttons he will carry't* (*The Merry Wives of Windsor 3.2*)

cable NOUN cable here means scope or reach ❑ *The law ... Will give her cable* (*Othello 1.2*)

cadent ADJ if something is cadent it is falling or dropping ❑ *With cadent tears fret channels in her cheeks* (*King Lear 1.4*)

canker VERB to canker is to decay, become corrupt ❑ *And, as with age his body uglier grows,/So his mind cankers* (*The Tempest 4.1*)

canon, from the PHRASE from the canon is an expression meaning out of order, improper ❑ *Twas from the canon* (*Coriolanus 3.1*)

cap-a-pie ADV cap-a-pie means from head to foot, completely ❑ *I am courtier cap-a-pie* (*The Winter's Tale 4.4*)

carbonadoed ADJ if something is carbonadoed it is cut or scored (scratched) with a knife ❑ *it is your carbonadoed* (*All's Well That Ends Well 4.5*)

carouse VERB to carouse is to drink at length, party ❑ *They cast their caps up and carouse together* (*Anthony and Cleopatra 4.12*)

carrack NOUN a carrack was a large old ship, a galleon ❑ *Faith, he tonight hath boarded a land-carrack* (*Othello 1.2*)

cassock NOUN a cassock here means a military cloak, long coat ❑ *half of the which dare not shake the snow from off their cassocks lest they shake themselves to pieces* (*All's Well That Ends Well 4.3*)

catastrophe NOUN catastrophe here means conclusion or end ❑ *pat he comes, like the catastrophe of the old comedy* (*King Lear 1.2*)

cautel NOUN a cautel was a trick or a deceptive act ❑ *Perhaps he loves you now/And now no soil not cautel doth besmirch* (*Hamlet 1.2*)

celerity NOUN celerity was a common word for speed, swiftness ❑ *Hence hath offence his quick celerity/When it is borne in high authority* (*Measure for Measure 4.2*)

chafe NOUN chafe meant anger or temper ❑ *this Herculean Roman does become/The carriage of his chafe* (*Anthony and Cleopatra 1.3*)

chanson NOUN chanson was an old word for a song ❑ *The first row of the pious chanson will show you more* (*Hamlet 2.2*)

chapman NOUN a chapman was a trader or merchant ❑ *Not uttered by base sale of chapman's tongues* (*Love's Labours Lost 2.1*)

chaps, chops NOUN chaps (and chops) was a word for jaws ❑ *Which ne'er shook hands nor bade farewell to him/Till he unseamed him from the nave to th' chops* (*Macbeth 1.2*)

chattels NOUN chattels were your moveable possessions. The word is used in the traditional marriage ceremony ❑ *She is my goods, my chattels* (*The Taming of the Shrew 3.3*)

chide VERB if you are chided by someone you are told off or reprimanded ❑ *Now I but chide, but I should use thee worse* (*A Midsummer Night's Dream 3.2*)

chinks NOUN chinks was a word for cash or money ❑ *he that can lay hold of her/Shall have the chinks* (*Romeo and Juliet 1.5*)

choleric ADJ if something was called choleric it meant that they were quick to get angry ❑ *therewithal unruly waywardness that infirm and choleric years bring with them* (*King Lear 1.1*)

chuff NOUN a chuff was a miser,

someone who clings to his or her money ❑ *ye fat chuffs* (*Henry IV part I 2.2*)

cipher NOUN cipher here means nothing ❑ *Mine were the very cipher of a function* (*Measure for Measure 2.2*)

circummured ADJ circummured means that something is surrounded with a wall ❑ *He hath a garden circummured with brick* (*Measure for Measure 4.1*)

civet NOUN a civet is a type of scent or perfume ❑ *Give me an ounce of civet* (*King Lear 4.6*)

clamorous ADJ clamorous means noisy or boisterous ❑ *Be clamorous and leap all civil bounds* (*Twelfth Night 1.4*)

clangour, clangor NOUN clangour is a word that means ringing (the sound that bells make) ❑ *Like to a dismal clangour heard from far* (*Henry VI part III 2.3*)

cleave VERB if you cleave to something you stick to it or are faithful to it ❑ *Thy thoughts I cleave to* (*The Tempest 4.1*)

clock and clock, 'twixt PHRASE from hour to hour, without stopping or continuously ❑ *To weep 'twixt clock and clock* (*Cymbeline 3.4*)

close ADJ here close means hidden ❑ *Stand close; this is the same Athenian* (*A Midsummer Night's Dream 3.2*)

cloud NOUN a cloud on your face means that you have a troubled, unhappy expression ❑ *He has cloud in's face* (*Anthony and Cleopatra 3.2*)

cloy VERB if you cloy an appetite you satisfy it ❑ *Other women cloy/The appetites they feed* (*Anthony and Cleopatra 2.2*)

cock-a-hoop, set PHRASE if you set cock-a-hoop you become free of everything ❑ *You will set cock-a-hoop* (*Romeo and Juliet 1.5*)

colours NOUN colours is a word used to describe battle-flags or banners. Sometimes we still say that we nail our colours to the mast if we are stating which team or side of an argument we support ❑ *the approbation of those that weep this lamentable divorce under her colours* (*Cymbeline 1.5*)

combustion NOUN combustion was a word meaning disorder or chaos ❑ *prophesying ... Of dire combustion and confused events* (*Macbeth 2.3*)

comely ADJ If you are or something is comely you or it is lovely, beautiful, graceful ❑ *O, what a world is this, when what is comely/Envenoms him that bears it!* (*As You Like It 2.3*)

commend VERB if you commend yourself to someone you send greetings to them ❑ *Commend me to my brother* (*Measure for Measure 1.4*)

compact NOUN a compact is an agreement or a contract ❑ *what compact mean you to have with us?* (*Julius Caesar 3.1*)

compass 1 NOUN here compass means range or scope ❑ *you would sound me from my lowest note to the top of my compass* (*Hamlet 3.2*) 2 VERB to compass here means to achieve, bring about or make happen ❑ *How now shall this be compassed?/ Canst thou bring me to the party?* (*Tempest 3.2*)

comptible ADJ comptible is an old word meaning sensitive ❑ *I am very comptible, even to the least sinister usage.* (*Twelfth Night 1.5*)

confederacy NOUN a confederacy is a group of people usually joined together to commit a crime. It is another word for a conspiracy ❑ *Lo, she is one of this confederacy!* (*A Midsummer Night's Dream 3.2*)

confound VERB if you confound something you confuse it or mix it up; it also means to stop or prevent ❑ *A million fail, confounding oath on oath.* (*A Midsummer Night's Dream 3.2*)

contagion NOUN contagion is an old word for disease or poison ❑ *hell itself breathes out/ Contagion to this world* (*Hamlet 3.2*)

contumely NOUN contumely is an old word for an insult ❑ *the proud man's contumely* (*Hamlet 3.1*)

counterfeit 1 VERB if you counterfeit something you copy or imitate it ❑ *Meantime your cheeks do counterfeit our roses* (*Henry VI part I 2.4*) 2 VERB in this context counterfeit means to pretend or make believe ❑ *I will counterfeit the bewitchment of some popular man* (*Coriolanus*)

coz NOUN coz was a shortened form of the word cousin ❑ *sweet my coz, be merry* (*As You Like It 1.2*)

cozenage NOUN cozenage is an old word meaning cheating or a deception ❑ *Thrown out his angle for my proper life,/ And with such coz'nage* (*Hamlet 5.2*)

crave VERB crave used to mean to beg or request ❑ *I crave your pardon* (*The Comedy of Errors 1.2*)

crotchet NOUN crotchets are strange ideas or whims ❑ *thou hast some strange crotchets in thy head now* (*The Merry Wives of Windsor 2.1*)

cuckold NOUN a cuckold is a man whose wife has been unfaithful to him ❑ *As there is no true cuckold but calamity* (*Twelfth Night 1.5*)

cuffs, go to PHRASE this phrase meant to fight ❑ *the player went to cuffs in the question* (*Hamlet 2.2*)

cup VERB in this context cup is a verb which means to pour drink or fill glasses with alcohol ❑ *cup us til the world go round* (*Anthony and Cleopatra 2.7*)

cur NOUN cur is an insult meaning dog and is also used to mean coward ❑ *Out, dog! out, cur! Thou drivest me past the bounds/ Of maiden's patience* (*A Midsummer Night's Dream 3.2*)

curiously ADV in this context curiously means carefully or skilfully ❑ *The sleeves curiously cut* (*The Taming of the Shrew 4.3*)

curry VERB curry means to flatter or to praise someone more than they are worth ❑ *I would curry with Master Shallow that no man could better command his servants* (*Henry IV part II 5.1*)

custom NOUN custom is a habit or a usual practice ❑ *Hath not old custom made this life more sweet/ Than that of painted pomp?* (*As You Like It 2.1*)

cutpurse NOUN a cutpurse is an old word for a thief. Men used to carry their money in small bags (purse) that hung from their belts; thieves would cut the purse from the belt and steal their money ❑ *A cutpurse of the empire and the rule* (*Hamlet 3.4*)

dainty ADJ dainty used to mean splendid, fine ❑ *Why, that's my dainty Ariel!* (*Tempest 5.1*)

dally VERB if you dally with something you play with it or tease it ❑ *They that dally nicely with words may quickly make them wanton* (*Twelfth Night 3.1*)

damask COLOUR damask is a light-red or pink colour ❑ *Twas just the difference/Betwixt the constant red and mingled damask* (*As You Like It 3.5*)

dare 1 VERB dare means to challenge or, confront ❑ *He goes before me, and still dares me on* (*A Midsummer Night's Dream 3.3*) 2 VERB dare in this context means to present, deliver or inflict ❑ *all that fortune, death, and danger dare* (*Hamlet 4.4*)

darkly ADV darkly was used in this context to mean secretly or cunningly ❑ *I will go darkly to work with her* (*Measure for Measure 5.1*)

daw NOUN a daw was a slang term for idiot or fool (after the bird jackdaw which was famous for its stupidity) ❑ *Yea, just so much as you may take upon a knife's point and choke a daw withal* (*Much Ado About Nothing 3.1*)

debile ADJ debile meant weak or feeble ❑ *And debile minister great power* (*All's Well That Ends Well 2.3*)

deboshed ADJ deboshed was another way of saying corrupted or debauched ❑ *Men so disordered, deboshed and bold* (*King Lear 1.4*)

decoct VERB to decoct was to heat up, warm something ❑ *Can sodden water,/A drench for sur-reained jades*

... Decoct their cold blood to such valiant heat? (*Henry V 3.5*)

deep-revolving ADJ deep-revolving here uses the idea that you turn something over in your mind when you are thinking hard about it and so means deep-thinking, meditating ❑ *The deep-revolving Buckingham/No more shall be the neighbour to my counsels* (*Richard III 4.2*)

defect NOUN defect here means shortcoming or something that is not right ❑ *Being unprepared/Our will became the servant to defect* (*Macbeth 2.1*)

degree 1 NOUN degree here means rank, standing or station ❑ *Should a like language use to all degrees,/And mannerly distinguishment leave out/Betwixt the prince and beggar* (*The Winter's Tale 2.1*) 2 NOUN in this context, degree means extent or measure ❑ *her offence/Must be of such unnatural degree* (*King Lear 1.1*)

deify VERB if you deify something or someone you worship it or them as a God ❑ *all.. deifying the name of Rosalind* (*As You Like It 3.2*)

delated ADJ delated here means detailed ❑ *the scope/Of these delated articles* (*Hamlet 1.2*)

delicate ADJ if something was described as delicate it meant it was of fine quality or valuable ❑ *thou wast a spirit too delicate* (*The Tempest 1.2*)

demise VERB in this context demise means to transmit, give or convey ❑ *what state ... Canst thou demise to any child of mine?* (*Richard III 4.4*)

deplore VERB to deplore means to express with grief or sorrow ❑ *Never more/ Will I my master's tears to you deplore* (*Twelfth Night 3.1*)

depose VERB if you depose someone you make them take an oath, or swear something to be true ❑ *Depose him in the justice of his cause* (*Richard II 1.3*)

depositary NOUN a depositary is a trustee ❑ *Made you ... my depositary* (*King Lear 2.4*)

derive 1 VERB to derive means to comes from or to descend (it usually applies to people) ❑ *No part of it is mine,/ This shame derives itself from unknown loins.* (*Much Ado About Nothing 4.1*) 2 VERB if you derive something from someone you inherit it ❑ *Treason is not inherited ...Or, if we derive it from our friends/ What's that to me?* (*As You Like It 1.3*)

descry VERB to see or catch sight of ❑ *The news is true, my lord. He is descried* (*Anthony and Cleopatra 3.7*)

desert 1 NOUN desert means worth or merit ❑ *That dost in vile misproson shackle up/ My love and her desert* (*All's Well That Ends Well 2.3*) 2 ADJ desert is used here to mean lonely or isolated ❑ *if that love or gold/ Can in this desert place buy entertainment* (*As You LIke It 2.4*)

design 1 VERB to design means to indicate or point out ❑ *we shall see/ Justice design the victor's chivalry* (*Richard II 1.1*) 2 NOUN a design is a plan, an intention or an undertaking ❑ *hinder not the honour of his design* (*All's Well That Ends Well 3.6*)

designment NOUN a designment was a plan or undertaking ❑ *The desperate tempest hath so bang'd the Turks,/ That their designment halts* (*Othello 2.1*)

despite VERB despite here means to spite or attempt to thwart a plan ❑ *Only to despite them I will endeavour anything* (*Much Ado About Nothing 2.2*)

device NOUN a device is a plan, plot or trick ❑ *Excellent, I smell a device* (*Twelfth Night 2.3*)

disable VERB to disable here means to devalue or make little of ❑ *he disabled my judgement* (*As You Like It 5.4*)

discandy VERB here discandy means to melt away or dissolve ❑ *The hearts ... do discandy , melt their sweets* (*Anthony and Cleopatra 4.12*)

disciple VERB to disciple is to teach or train ❑ *He ...was/ Discipled of the bravest* (*All's Well That Ends Well 1.2*)

discommend VERB if you discommend something you criticize it ❑ *my dialect which you discommend so much* (*King Lear 2.2*)

discourse NOUN discourse means conversation, talk or chat ❑ *which part of it I'll waste/ With such discourse as I not doubt shall make it/ Go quick away* (*The Tempest 5.1*)

discover VERB discover used to mean to reveal or show ❑ *the Prince discovered to Claudio that he loved my niece* (*Much Ado About Nothing 1.2*)

disliken VERB disguise, make unlike ❑ *disliken/ The truth of your own seeming* (*The Winter's Tale 4.4*)

dismantle VERB to dismantle is to remove or take away ❑ *Commit a thing so monstrous to dismantle/*

So many folds of favour (*King Lear 1.1*)

disponge VERB disponge means to pour out or rain down ❑ *The poisonous damp of night disponge upon me* (*Anthony and Cleopatra 4.9*)

distrain VERB to distrain something is to confiscate it ❑ *My father's goods are all distrained and sold* (*Richard II 2.3*)

divers ADJ divers is an old word for various ❑ *I will give out divers schedules of my beauty* (*Twelfth Night 1.5*)

doff VERB to doff is to get rid of or dispose ❑ *make our women fight/ To doff their dire distresses* (*Macbeth 4.3*)

dog VERB if you dog someone or something you follow them or it closely ❑ *I will rather leave to see Hector than not to dog him* (*Troilus and Cressida 5.1*)

dotage NOUN dotage here means infatuation ❑ *Her dotage now I do begin to pity* (*A Midsummer NIght's Dream 4.1*)

dotard NOUN a dotard was an old fool ❑ *I speak not like a dotard nor a fool* (*Much Ado About Nothing 5.1*)

dote VERB to dote is to love, cherish, care without seeing any fault ❑ *And won her soul; and she, sweet lady, dotes,/ Devoutly dotes, dotes in idolatry* (*A Midsummer Night's Dream 1.1*)

doublet NOUN a doublet was a man's close-fitting jacket with short skirt ❑ *Lord Hamlet, with his doublet all unbraced* (*Hamlet 2.1*)

dowager NOUN a dowager is a widow ❑ *Like to a step-dame or a dowage* (*A Midsummer Night's Dream 1.1*)

dowdy NOUN a dowdy was an ugly woman ❑ *Dido was a dowdy* (*Romeo and Juliet 2.4*)

dower NOUN a dower (or dowery) is the riches or property given by the father of a bride to her husband-to-be ❑ *Thy truth then by they dower* (*King Lear 1.1*)

dram NOUN a dram is a tiny amount ❑ *Why, everything adheres together that no dram of a scruple* (*Twelfth Night 3.4*)

drift NOUN drift is a plan, scheme or intention ❑ *Shall Romeo by my letters know our drift* (*Romeo and Juliet 4.1*)

dropsied ADJ dropsied means pretentious ❑ *Where great additions swell's and virtues none/ It is a dropsied honour* (*All's Well That Ends Well 2.3*)

drudge NOUN a drudge was a slave, servant ❑ *If I be his cuckold, he's my drudge* (*All's Well That Ends Well 1.3*)

dwell VERB to dwell sometimes meant to exist, to be ❑ *I'd rather dwell in my necessity* (*Merchant of Venice 1.3*)

earnest ADJ an earnest was a pledge to pay or a payment in advance ❑ *for an earnest of a greater honour/ He bade me from him call thee Thane of Cawdor* (*Macbeth 1.3*)

ecstasy NOUN madness ❑ *This is the very ecstasy of love* (*Hamlet 2.1*)

edict NOUN law or declaration ❑ *It stands as an edict in destiny.* (*A Midsummer Night's Dream 1.1*)

egall ADJ egall is an old word meaning equal ❑ *companions/Whose souls do bear an egall yoke of love* (*Merchant of Venice 2.4*)

eisel NOUN eisel meant vinegar ❑ *Woo't drink up eisel?* (*Hamlet 5.1*)

eke, eke out VERB eke meant to add to, to increase. Eke out nowadays means to make something last as long as possible – particularly in the sense of making money last a long time ❑ *Still be kind/And eke out our performance with your mind* (*Henry V Chorus*)

elbow, out at PHRASE out at elbow is an old phrase meaning in poor condition – as when your jacket sleeves are worn at the elbow which shows that it is an old jacket ❑ *He cannot, sir. He's out at elbow* (*Measure for Measure 2.1*)

element NOUN elements were thought to be the things from which all things were made. They were: air, earth, water and fire ❑ *Does not our lives consist of the four elements?* (*Twelfth Night 2.3*)

elf VERB to elf was to tangle ❑ *I'll ... elf all my hairs in knots* (*King Lear 2.3*)

embassy NOUN an embassy was a message ❑ *We'll once more hear Orsino's embassy.* (*Twelfth Night 1.5*)

emphasis NOUN emphasis here means a forceful expression or strong statement ❑ *What is he whose grief/Bears such an emphasis* (*Hamlet 5.1*)

empiric NOUN an empiric was an untrained doctor sometimes called a quack ❑ *we must not ... prostitute our past-cure malady/To empirics* (*All's Well That Ends Well 2.1*)

emulate ADJ emulate here means envious ❑ *pricked on by a most emulate pride* (*Hamlet 1.1*)

enchant VERB to enchant meant to put a magic spell on ❑ *Damn'd as thou art, thou hast enchanted her,/For I'll refer me to all things of sense* (*Othello 1.2*)

enclog VERB to enclog was to hinder something or to provide an obstacle to it ❑ *Traitors enscarped to enclog the guitless keel* (*Othello 1.2*)

endure VERB to endure was to allow or to permit ❑ *and will endure/Our setting down before't.* (*Macbeth 5.4*)

enfranchise VERB if you enfranchised something you set it free ❑ *Do this or this;/Take in that kingdom and enfranchise that;/Perform't, or else we damn thee.'* (*Anthony and Cleopatra 1.1*)

engage VERB to engage here means to pledge or to promise ❑ *This to be true I do engage my life* (*As You Like It 5.4*)

engaol VERB to lock up or put in prison ❑ *Within my mouth you have engaoled my tongue* (*Richard II 1.3*)

engine NOUN an engine was a plot, device or a machine ❑ *their promises, enticements, oaths, tokens, and all these engines, of lust, are not the things they go under* (*All's Well That Ends Well 3.5*)

englut VERB if you were engulfed you were swallowed up or eaten whole ❑ *For certainly thou art so near the gulf,/Thou needs must be englutted.* (*Henry V 4.3*)

enjoined ADJ enjoined describes people joined together for the same reason ❑ *Of enjoined penitents/*

There's four or five (*All's Well That Ends Well 3.5*)

entertain 1 VERB to entertain here means to welcome or receive ❑ *Approach, rich Ceres, her to entertain.* (*The Tempest 4.1*) 2 VERB to entertain in this context means to cherish, hold in high regard or to respect ❑ *and I quake,/ Lest thou a feverous life shouldst entertain/ And six or seven winters more respect/ Than a perpetual honour.* (*Measure for Measure 3.1*) 3 VERB to entertain means here to give something consideration ❑ *But entertain it,/ And though you think me poor, I am the man/ Will give thee all the world.* (*Anthony and Cleopatra 2.7*) 4 VERB to entertain here means to treat or handle ❑ *your highness is not entertained with that ceremonious affection as you were wont* (*King Lear 1.4*)

envious ADJ envious meant spiteful or vindictive ❑ *he shall appear to the envious a scholar* (*Measure for Measure 3.2*)

ere PREP ere was a common word for before ❑ *ere this I should ha' fatted all the region kites* (*Hamlet 2.2*)

err VERB to err means to go astray, to make a mistake ❑ *And as he errs, doting on Hermia's eyes* (*A Midsummer Night's Dream 1.1*)

erst ADV erst was a common word for once or before ❑ *that erst brought sweetly forth/ The freckled cowslip* (*Henry V 5.2*)

eschew VERB if you eschew something you deliberately avoid doing it ❑ *What cannot be eschewed must be embraced* (*The Merry Wives of Windsor 5.5*)

escote VERB to escote meant to pay for, support ❑ *How are they escoted?* (*Hamlet 2.2*)

estimable ADJ estimable meant appreciative ❑ *I could not with such estimable wonder over-far believe that* (*Twelfth Night 2.1*)

extenuate VERB extenuate means to lessen ❑ *Which by no means we may extenuate* (*A Midsummer Night's Dream 1.1*)

fain ADV fain was a common word meaning gladly or willingly ❑ *I would fain prove so* (*Hamlet 2.2*)

fall NOUN in a voice or music fall meant going higher and lower ❑ *and so die/ That strain again! it had a dying fall* (*Twelfth Night 1.1*)

false ADJ false was a common word for treacherous ❑ *this is counter, you false Danish dogs!* (*Hamlet 4.5*)

fare VERB fare means to get on or manage ❑ *I fare well* (*The Taming of the Shrew Introduction 2*)

feign VERB to feign was to make up, pretend or fake ❑ *It is the more like to be feigned* (*Twelfth Night 1.5*)

fie EXCLAM fie was an exclamation of disgust ❑ *Fie, that you'll say so!* (*Twelfth Night 1.3*)

figure VERB to figure was to symbolize or look like ❑ *Wings and no eyes, figure unheedy haste* (*A Midsummer Night's Dream 1.1*)

filch VERB if you filch something you steal it ❑ *With cunning hast thou filch'd my daughter's heart* (*A Midsummer Night's Dream 1.1*)

flout VERB to flout something meant to scorn it ❑ *Why will you suffer her to flout me thus?* (*A Midsummer Night's Dream 3.2*)

fond ADJ fond was a common word meaning foolish ❑ *Shall we their fond pageant see?* (*A Midsummer Night's Dream 3.2*)

footing 1 NOUN footing meant landing on shore, arrival, disembarkation ❑ *Whose footing here anticipates our thoughts/A se'nnight's speed.* (*Othello 2.1*) 2 NOUN footing also means support ❑ *there your charity would have lacked footing* (*Winter's Tale 3.3*)

forsooth ADV in truth, certainly, truly ❑ *I had rather, forsooth, go before you like a man* (*The Merry Wives of Windsor 3.2*)

forswear VERB if you forswear you lie, swear falsely or break your word ❑ *he swore a thing to me on Monday night, which he forswore on Tuesday morning* (*Much Ado About Nothing 5.1*)

freshes NOUN a fresh is a fresh water stream ❑ *He shall drink nought but brine, for I'll not show him/ Where the quick freshes are.* (*Tempest 3.2*)

furlong NOUN a furlong is a measure of distance. It is the equivalent on one eight of a mile ❑ *Now would I give a thousand furlongs of sea for an acre of barren ground* (*Tempest 1.1*)

gaberdine NOUN a gaberdine is a cloak ❑ *My best way is to creep under his gaberdine* (*Tempest 2.2*)

gage NOUN a gage was a challenge to duel or fight ❑ *There is my gage, Aumerle, in gage to thine* (*Richard II 4.1*)

gait NOUN your gait is your way of walking or step ❑ *I know her by her gait* (*Tempest 4.1*)

gall VERB to gall is to annoy or irritate ❑ *Let it not gall your patience, good Iago,/ That I extend my manners* (*Othello 2.1*)

gambol NOUN frolic or play ❑ *Hop in his walks, and gambol in his eyes* (*A Midsummer Night's Dream 3.1*)

gaskins NOUN gaskins is an old word for trousers ❑ *or, if both break, your gaskins fall.* (*Twelfth Night 1.5*)

gentle ADJ gentle means noble or well-born ❑ *thrice-gentle Cassio!* (*Othello 3.4*)

glass NOUN a glass was another word for a mirror ❑ *no woman's face remember/ Save from my glass, mine own* (*Tempest 3.1*)

gleek VERB to gleek means to make a joke or jibe ❑ *Nay, I can gleek upon occasion* (*A Midsummer Night's Dream 3.1*)

gust NOUN gust meant taste, desire or enjoyment. We still say that if you do something with gusto you do it with enjoyment or enthusiasm ❑ *the gust he hath in quarrelling* (*Twelfth Night 1.3*)

habit NOUN habit means clothes ❑ *You know me by my habit* (*Henry V 3.6*)

heaviness NOUN heaviness means sadness or grief ❑ *So sorrow's heaviness doth heavier grow/ For debt that bankrupt sleep doth sorrow owe* (*A Midsummer Night's Dream 3.2*)

heavy ADJ if you are heavy you are said to be sad or sorrowful ❑ *Away from light steals home my heavy son* (*Romeo and Juliet 1.1*)

hie VERB to hie meant to hurry ❑ *My husband hies him home* (*All Well That Ends Well 4.4*)

hollowly ADV if you did something hollowly you did it insincerely ❑ *If hollowly invert/ What best is boded me to mischief!* (*Tempest 3.1*)

holy-water, court PHRASE if you court holy water you make empty promises, or make statements which sound good but have no real meaning ❑ *court holy-water in a dry house is better than this rain-water out o'door* (*King Lear 3.2*)

howsoever ADV howsoever was often used instead of however ❑ *But howsoever strange and admirable* (*A Midsummer Night's Dream 5.1*)

humour NOUN your humour was your mood, frame of mind or temperament ❑ *it fits my humour well* (*As You Like It 3.2*)

ill ADJ ill means bad ❑ *I must thank him only,/ Let my remembrance suffer ill report* (*Antony and Cleopatra 2.2*)

indistinct ADJ inseparable or unable to see a difference ❑ *Even till we make the main and the aerial blue/ An indistinct regard.* (*Othello 2.1*)

indulgence NOUN indulgence meant approval ❑ *As you from crimes would pardoned be,/ Let your indulgence set me free* (*The Tempest Epilogue*)

infirmity NOUN infirmity was weakness or fraility ❑ *Be not disturbed with my infirmity* (*The Tempest 4.1*)

intelligence NOUN here intelligence means information ❑ *Pursue her; and for this intelligence/ If I have thanks* (*A Midsummer Night's Dream 1.1*)

inwards NOUN inwards meant someone's internal organs ❑ *the thought whereof/ Doth like a poisonous mineral gnaw my inwards* (*Othello 2.1*)

issue 1 NOUN the issue of a marriage are the children ❑ *To thine and Albany's issues,/ Be this perpetual* (*King Lear 1.1*) 2 NOUN in this context issue means outcome or result ❑ *I am to pray you, not to strain my speech,/ To grosser issues* (*Othello*)

kind NOUN kind here means situation or case ❑ *But in this kind, wanting your father's voice,/ The other must be held the worthier.* (*A Midsummer Night's Dream 1.1*)

knave NOUN a knave was a common word for scoundrel ❑ *How absolute the knave is!* (*Hamlet 5.1*)

league NOUN A distance. A league was the distance a person could walk in one hour ❑ *From Athens is her house remote seven leagues* (*A Midsummer Night's Dream 1.1*)

lief, had as ADJ I had as lief means I should like just as much ❑ *I had as lief the town crier spoke my lines* (*Hamlet 1.2*)

livery NOUN livery was a costume, outfit, uniform usually worn by a servant ❑ *You can endure the livery of a nun* (*A Midsummer Night's Dream 1.1*)

loam NOUN loam is soil containing decayed vegetable matter and therefore good for growing crops and plants ❑ *and let him have some plaster, or some loam, or some rough-cast about him, to signify wall* (*A Midsummer Night's Dream 3.1*)

lusty ADJ lusty meant strong ❑ *and oared/ Himself with his good arms in lusty stroke/ To th' shore* (*The Tempest 2.1*)

maidenhead NOUN maidenhead means chastity or virginity ❑ *What I am, and what I would, are as secret as maidenhead* (*Twelfth Night 1.5*)

mark VERB mark means to note or pay attention to ❑ *Where sighs and groans,/ Are made not marked* (*Macbeth 4.3*)

marvellous ADJ very or extremely ❑ *here's a marvellous convenient place for our rehearsal* (*A Midsummer Night's Dream 3.1*)

meet ADJ right or proper ❑ *tis most meet you should* (*Macbeth 5.1*)

merely ADV completely or entirely ❑ *Love is merely a madness* (*As You Like It 3.2*)

misgraffed ADJ misgraffed is an old word for mismatched or unequal ❑ *Or else misgraffed in respect of years* (*A Midsummer Night's Dream 1.1*)

misprision NOUN a misprision meant an error or mistake ❑ *Misprision in the highest degree!* (*Twelfth Night 1.5*)

mollification NOUN mollification is appeasement or a way of preventing someone getting angry ❑ *I am to hull here a little longer. Some mollification for your giant* (*Twelfth Night 1.5*)

mouth, cold in the PHRASE a well-known saying of the time which meant to be dead ❑ *What, must our mouths be cold?* (*The Tempest 1.1*)

murmur NOUN murmur was another word for rumour or hearsay ❑ *and then 'twas fresh in murmur* (*Twelfth Night 1.2*)

murrain NOUN murrain was another word for plague, pestilence ❑ *A murrain on your monster, and*

the devil take your fingers! (*The Tempest 3.2*)

neaf NOUN neaf meant fist ❑ *Give me your neaf, Monsieur Mustardseed* (*A Midsummer Night's Dream 4.1*)

nice 1 ADJ nice had a number of meanings here it means fussy or particular ❑ *An therefore, goaded with most sharp occasions,/ Which lay nice manners by, I put you to/ The use of your own virtues* (*All's Well That Ends Well 5.1*) 2 ADJ nice here means critical or delicate ❑ *We're good... To set so rich a man/ On the nice hazard of one doubtful hour?* (*Henry IV part 1*) 3 ADJ nice in this context means carefully accurate, fastidious ❑ *O relation/ Too nice and yet too true!* (*Macbeth 4.3*) 4 ADJ trivial, unimportant ❑ *Romeo .. Bid him bethink/ How nice the quarrel was* (*Romeo and Juliet 3.1*)

nonpareil NOUN if you are nonpareil you are without equal, peerless ❑ *though you were crown'd/ The nonpareil of beauty!* (*Twelfth Night 1.5*)

office NOUN office here means business or work ❑ *Speak your office* (*Twelfth Night 1.5*)

outsport VERB outsport meant to overdo ❑ *Let's teach ourselves that honorable stop,/ Not to outsport discretion.* (*Othello 2.2*)

owe VERB owe meant own, possess ❑ *Lend less than thou owest* (*King Lear 1.4*)

paragon 1 VERB to paragon was to surpass or excede ❑ *he hath achieved a maid/ That paragons description and wild fame* (*Othello 2.1*) 2 VERB to paragon could also mean to compare with ❑ *I will give thee* bloody teeth If thou with Caesar paragon again/ My man of men (Anthony and Cleopatra 1.5)

pate NOUN pate is another word for head ❑ Back, slave, or I will break thy pate across (The Comedy of Errors 2.1)

paunch VERB to paunch someone is to stab (usually in the stomach). Paunch is still a common word for a stomach ❑ Batter his skull, or paunch him with a stake (The Tempest 3.2)

peevish ADJ if you are peevish you are irritable or easily angered ❑ Run after that same peevish messenger (Twelfth Night 1.5)

peradventure ADV perhaps or maybe ❑ Peradventure this is not Fortune's work (As You Like It 1.2)

perforce 1 ADV by force or violently ❑ my rights and royalties,/ Plucked from my arms perforce (Richard II 2.3) 2. ADV necessarily ❑ The hearts of men, they must perforce have melted (Richard II 5.2)

personage NOUN personage meant your appearance ❑ Of what personage and years is he? (Twelfth Night 1.5)

pestilence NOUN pestilence was a common word for plague or disease ❑ Methought she purg'd the air of pestilence! (Twelfth Night 1.1)

physic NOUN physic was medicine or a treatment ❑ tis a physic/ That's bitter to sweet end (Measure for Measure 4.6)

place NOUN place means a person's position or rank ❑ Sons, kinsmen, thanes,/ And you whose places are the nearest (Macbeth 1.4)

post NOUN here a post means a messenger ❑ there are twenty weak and wearied posts/ Come from the north (Henry IV part II 2.4)

pox NOUN pox was a word for any disease during which the victim had blisters on the skin. It was also a curse, a swear word ❑ The pox of such antic, lisping, affecting phantasims (Romeo and Juliet 2.4)

prate VERB to prate means to chatter ❑ if thou prate of mountains (Hamlet 5.1)

prattle VERB to prattle is to chatter or talk without purpose ❑ I prattle out of fashion, and I dote In mine own comforts (Othello 2.1)

precept NOUN a precept was an order or command ❑ and my father's precepts I therein do forget. (The Tempest 3.1)

present ADJ present here means immediate ❑ We'll put the matter to the present push (Hamlet 5.1)

prithee EXCLAM prithee is the equivalent of please or may I ask – a polite request ❑ I prithee, and I'll pay thee bounteously (Twelfth Night 1.2)

prodigal NOUN a prodigal is someone who wastes or squanders money ❑ he's a very fool, and a prodigal (Twelfth Night 1.3)

purpose NOUN purpose is used here to mean intention ❑ understand my purposes aright (King Lear 1.4)

quaff VERB quaff was a common word which meant to drink heavily or take a big drink ❑ That quaffing and drinking will undo you (Twelfth Night 1.3)

quaint 1 ADJ clever, ingenious ❑ *with a quaint device* (*The Tempest 3.3*) 2 ADJ cunning ❑ *I'll… tell quaint lies* (*Merchant of Venice 3.4*) 3 ADJ pretty, attractive ❑ *The clamorous owl, that nightly hoots and wonders/At our quaint spirit* (*A Midsummer Night's Dream 2.2*)

quoth VERB an old word which means say ❑ *'Tis dinner time.' quoth I* (*The Comedy of Errors 2.1*)

rack NOUN a rack described clouds or a cloud formation ❑ *And, like this insubstantial pageant faded,/ Leave not a rack behind* (*The Tempest 4.1*)

rail VERB to rant or swear at. It is still used occasionally today ❑ *Why do I rail on thee* (*Richard II 5.5*)

rate NOUN rate meant estimate, opinion ❑ *My son is lost, and, in my rate, she too* (*The Tempest 2.1*)

recreant NOUN recreant is an old word which means coward ❑ *Come, recreant, come, thou child* (*A Midsummer Night's Dream 3.2*)

remembrance NOUN remembrance is used here to mean memory or recollection ❑ *our remembrances of days foregone* (*All's Well That Ends Well 1.3*)

resolute ADJ firm or not going to change your mind ❑ *You are resolute, then?* (*Twelfth Night 1.5*)

revels NOUN revels means celebrations or a party ❑ *Our revels now are ended* (*The Tempest 4.1*)

rough-cast NOUN a mixture of lime and gravel (sometimes shells too) for use on an outer wall ❑ *and let him have some plaster, or some loam, or some rough-cast about him, to signify wall* (*A Midsummer Night's Dream 3.1*)

sack NOUN sack was another word for wine ❑ *My man-monster hath drowned his tongue in sack.* (*The Tempest 3.2*)

sad ADJ in this context sad means serious, grave ❑ *comes me the Prince and Claudio… in sad conference* (*Much Ado About Nothing 1.3*)

sampler NOUN a piece of embroidery, which often showed the family tree ❑ *Both on one sampler, sitting on one cushion* (*A Midsummer Night's Dream 3.2*)

saucy ADJ saucy means rude ❑ *I heard you were saucy at my gates* (*Twelfth Night 1.5*)

schooling NOUN schooling means advice ❑ *I have some private schooling for you both.* (*A Midsummer Night's Dream 1.1*)

seething ADJ seething in this case means boiling – we now use seething when we are very angry ❑ *Lovers and madmen have such seething brains* (*A Midsummer Night's Dream 5.1*)

semblative ADJ semblative means resembling or looking like ❑ *And all is semblative a woman's part.* (*Twelfth Night 1.4*)

several ADJ several here means separate or different ❑ *twenty several messengers* (*Anthony and Cleopatra 1.5*)

shrew NOUN An annoying person or someone who makes you cross ❑ *Bless you, fair shrew.* (*Twelfth Night 1.3*)

shroud VERB to shroud is to hide or shelter ❑ *I will here, shroud till the dregs of the storm be past* (*The Tempest 2.2*)

sickleman NOUN a sickleman was someone who used a sickle to harvest crops ❑ *You sunburnt sicklemen, of August weary* (*The Tempest 4.1*)

soft ADV soft here means wait a moment or stop ❑ *But, soft, what nymphs are these* (*A Midsummer Night's Dream 4.1*)

something ADV something here means somewhat or rather ❑ *Be something scanter of your maiden presence* (*Hamlet 1.3*)

sooth NOUN truly ❑ *Yes, sooth; and so do you* (*A Midsummer Night's Dream 3.2*)

spleen NOUN spleen means fury or anger ❑ *That, in a spleen, unfolds both heaven and earth* (*A Midsummer Night's Dream 1.1*)

sport NOUN sport means recreation or entertainment ❑ *I see our wars/ Will turn unto a peaceful comic sport* (*Henry VI part I 2.2*)

strain NOUN a strain is a tune or a musical phrase ❑ *and so die/ That strain again! it had a dying fall* (*Twelfth Night 1.1*)

suffer VERB in this context suffer means perish or die ❑ *but an islander that hath lately suffered by a thunderbolt.* (*The Tempest 2.2*)

suit NOUN a suit is a petition, request or proposal (marriage) ❑ *Because she will admit no kind of suit* (*Twelfth Night 1.2*)

sup VERB to sup is to have supper ❑ *Go know of Cassio where he supped tonight* (*Othello 5.1*)

surfeit NOUN a surfeit is an amount which is too large ❑ *If music be the food of love, play on;/ Give me excess of it, that, surfeiting,/ The appetite may sicken* (*Twelfth Night 1.1*)

swain NOUN a swain is a suitor or person who wants to marry ❑ *take this transformed scalp/ From off the head of this Athenian swain* (*A Midsummer Night's Dream 4.1*)

thereto ADV thereto meant also ❑ *If she be black, and thereto have a wit* (*Othello 2.1*)

throstle NOUN a throstle was a name for a song-bird ❑ *The throstle with his note so true* (*A Midsummer Night's Dream 3.1*)

tidings NOUN tidings meant news ❑ *that upon certain tidings now arrived, importing the mere perdition of the Turkish fleet* (*Othello 2.2*)

transgress VERB if you transgress you break a moral law or rule of behaviour ❑ *Virtue that transgresses is but patched with sin* (*Twelfth Night 1.5*)

troth, by my PHRASE this phrase means I swear or in truth or on my word ❑ *By my troth, Sir Toby, you must come in earlier o' nights* (*Twelfth Night 1.3*)

trumpery NOUN trumpery means things that look expensive but are worth nothing (often clothing) ❑ *The trumpery in my house, go bring it hither/ For stale catch these thieves* (*The Tempest 4.1*)

twink NOUN In the wink of an eye or no time at all ❑ *Ay, with a twink* (*The Tempest 4.1*)

undone ADJ if something or someone is undone they are ruined, destroyed, brought down ❑ *You have undone a man of fourscore three* (*The Winter's Tale 4.4*)

varlets NOUN varlets were villains or ruffians ❑ *Say again: where didst thou leave these varlets?* (*The Tempest 4.1*)

vaward NOUN the vaward is an old word for the vanguard, front part or earliest ❑ *And since we have the vaward of the day* (*A Midsummer Night's Dream 4.1*)

visage NOUN face ❑ *when Phoebe doth behold/Her silver visage in the watery glass* (*A Midsummer Night's Dream 1.1*)

voice NOUN voice means vote ❑ *He has our voices* (*Coriolanus 2.3*)

waggish ADJ waggish means playful ❑ *As waggish boys in game themselves forswear* (*A Midsummer Night's Dream 1.1*)

wane VERB to wane is to vanish, go down or get slighter. It is most often used to describe a phase of the moon ❑ *but, O, methinks, how slow/This old moon wanes* (*A Midsummer Night's Dream 1.1*)

want VERB to want means to lack or to be without ❑ *a beast that wants discourse of reason/Would have mourned longer* (*Hamlet 1.2*)

warrant VERB to assure, promise, guarantee ❑ *I warrant your grace* (*As You Like It 1.2*)

welkin NOUN welkin is an old word for the sky or the heavens ❑ *The starry welkin cover thou anon/With drooping fog as black as Acheron* (*A Midsummer Night's Dream 3.2*)

wench NOUN wench is an old word for a girl ❑ *Well demanded, wench* (*The Tempest 1.2*)

whence ADV from where ❑ *Whence came you, sir?* (*Twelfth Night 1.5*)

wherefore ADV why ❑ *Wherefore, sweetheart? what's your metaphor?* (*Twelfth Night 1.3*)

wide-chopped ADJ if you were wide-chopped you were big-mouthed ❑ *This wide-chopped rascal* (*The Tempest 1.1*)

wight NOUN wight is an old word for person or human being ❑ *She was a wight, if ever such wight were* (*Othello 2.1*)

wit NOUN wit means intelligence or wisdom ❑ *thou didst conclude hairy men plain dealers, without wit* (*The Comedy of Errors 2.2*)

wits NOUN wits mean mental sharpness ❑ *we that have good wits have much to answer for* (*As You Like It 4.1*)

wont ADJ to wont is to be in the habit of doing something regularly ❑ *When were you wont to use my sister thus?* (*The Comedy of Errors 2.2*)

wooer NOUN a wooer is a suitor, someone who is hoping to marry ❑ *and of a foolish knight that you brought in one night here to be her wooer* (*Twelfth Night 1.3*)

wot VERB wot is an old word which means know or learn ❑ *for well I wot/Thou runnest before me* (*A Midsummer Night's Dream 3.2*)